YOSEMITE
End of the Winter

A Photographic Exploration

Scott Shaw

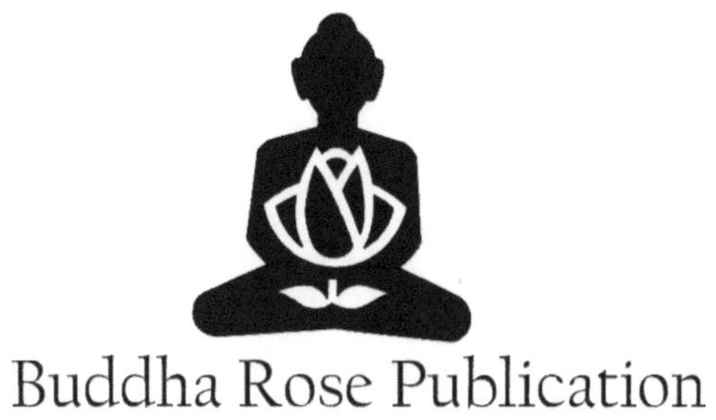

Buddha Rose Publication

Yosemite: End of the Winter

www.scottshaw.com

First Edition 2013

ISBN: 1-877792-70-5
ISBN: 978-1-877792-70-0

Printed in the United States of America

10 9 8 7 6 5 4 3 2 1

YOSEMITE
End of the Winter

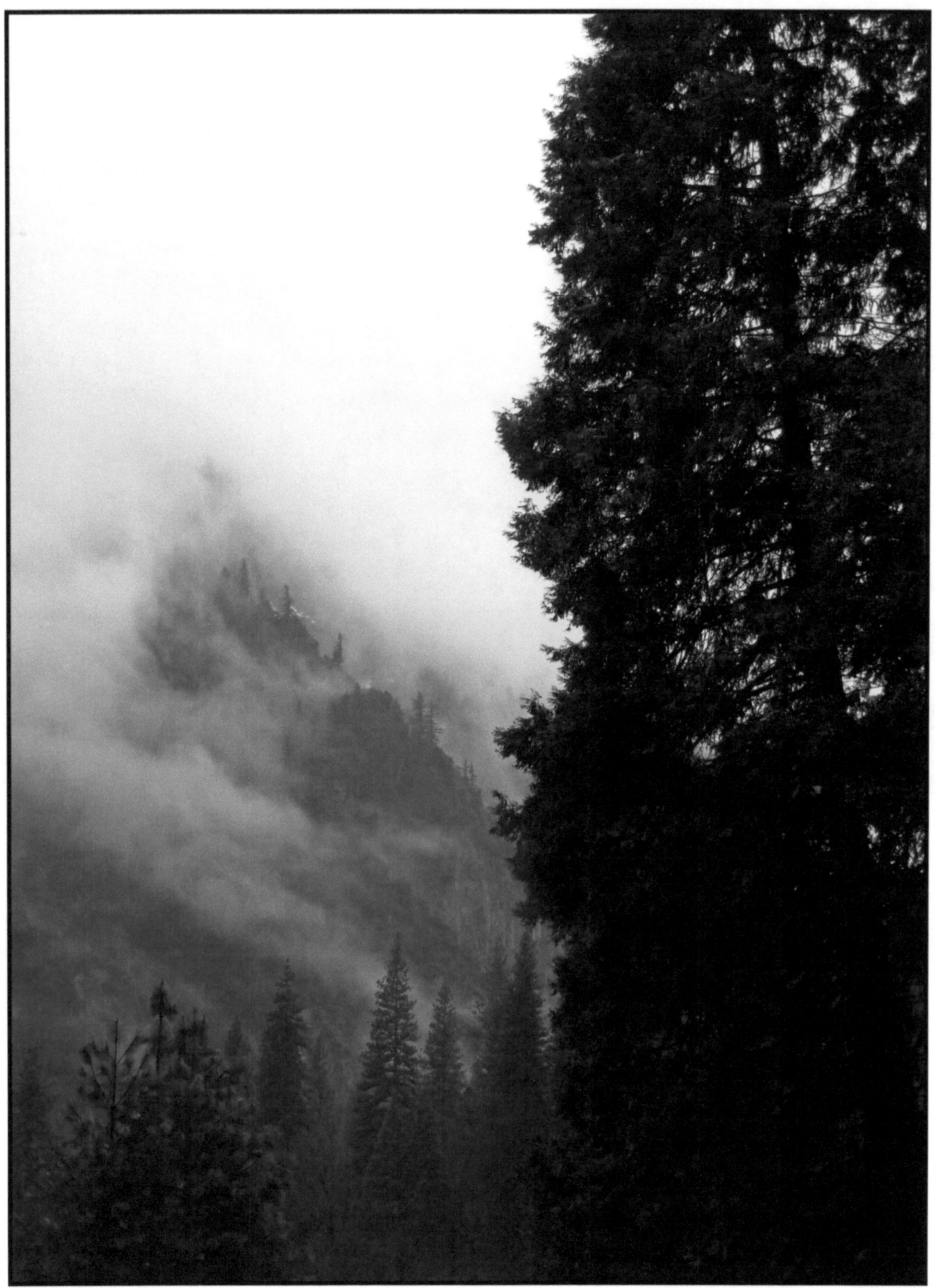

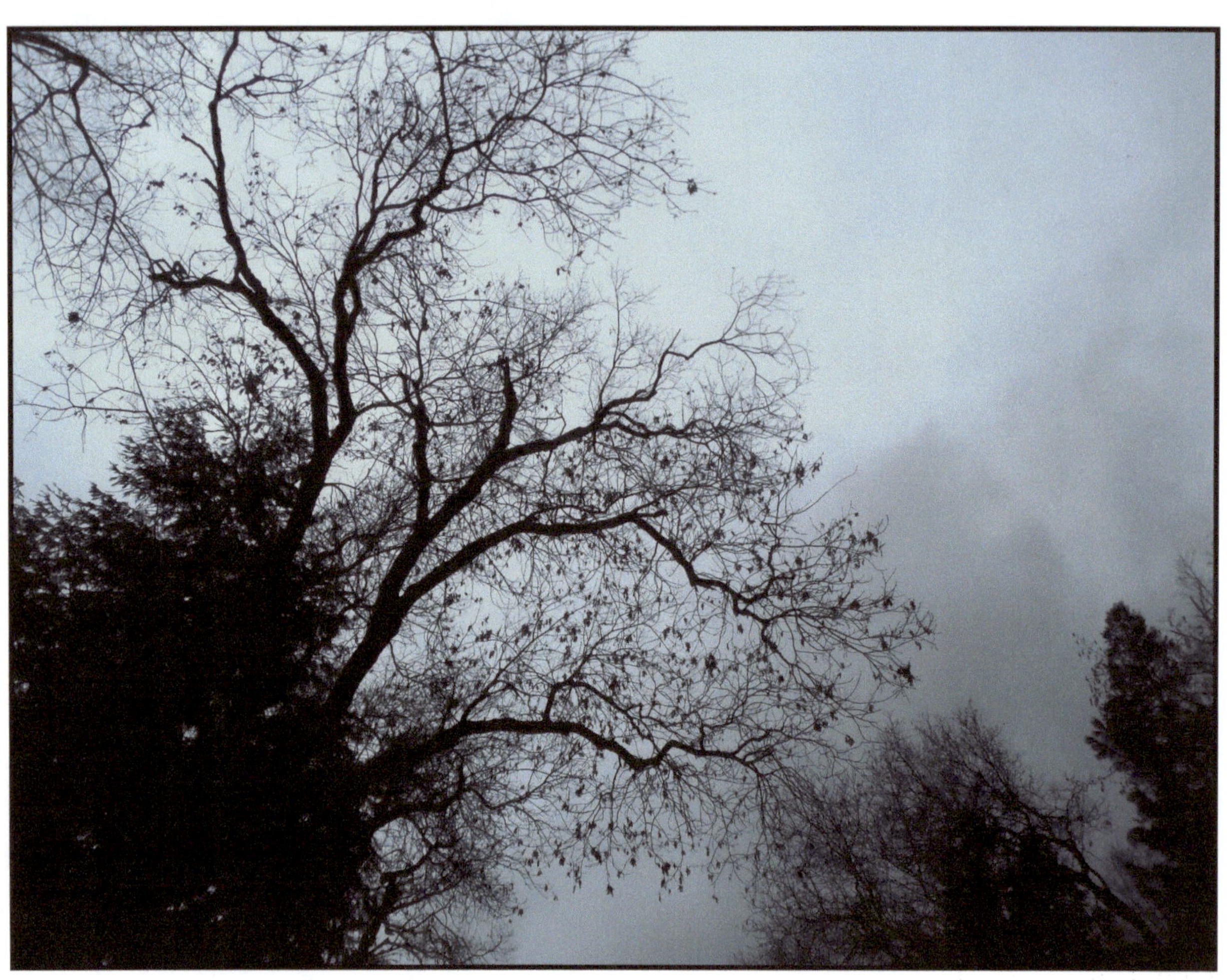

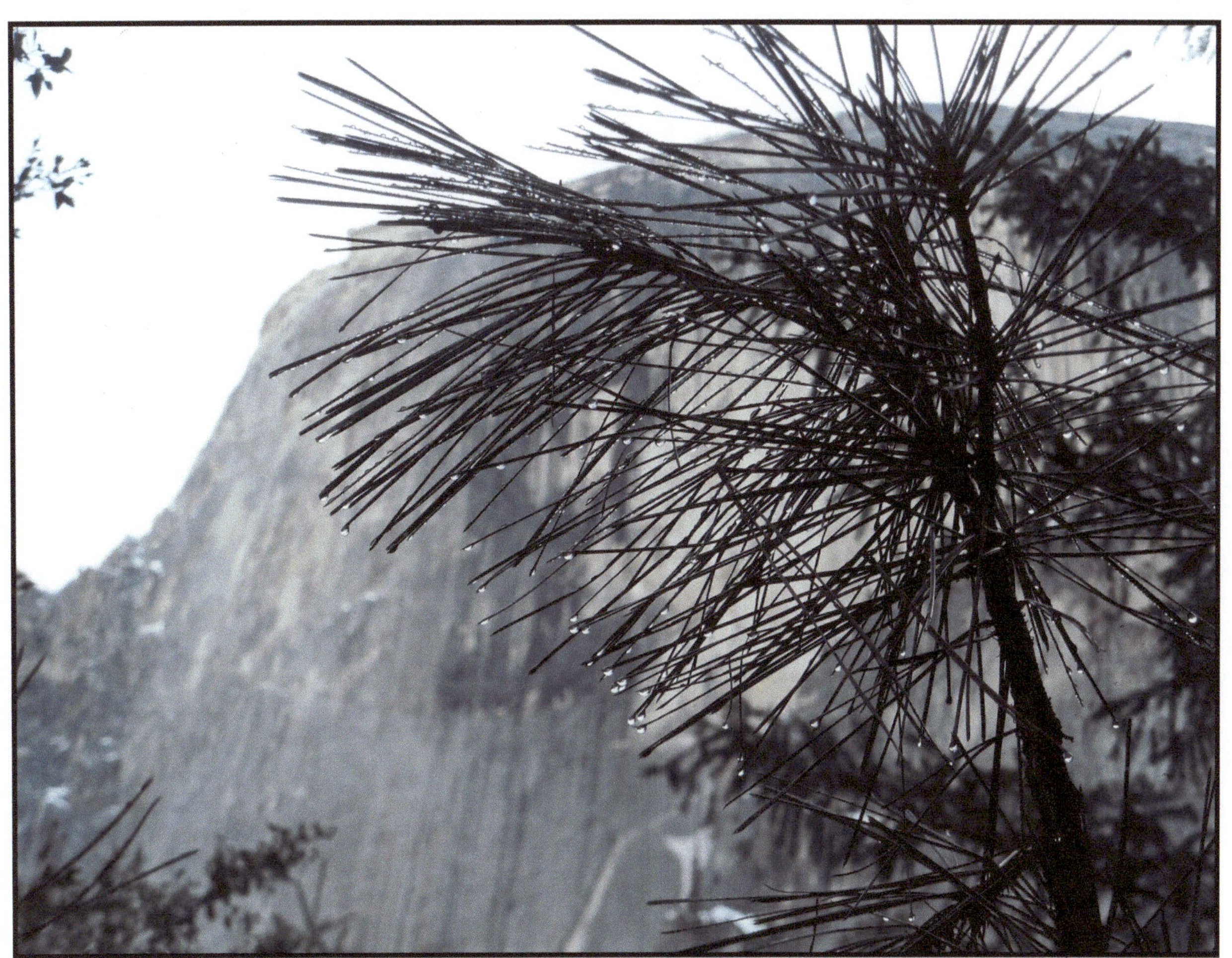

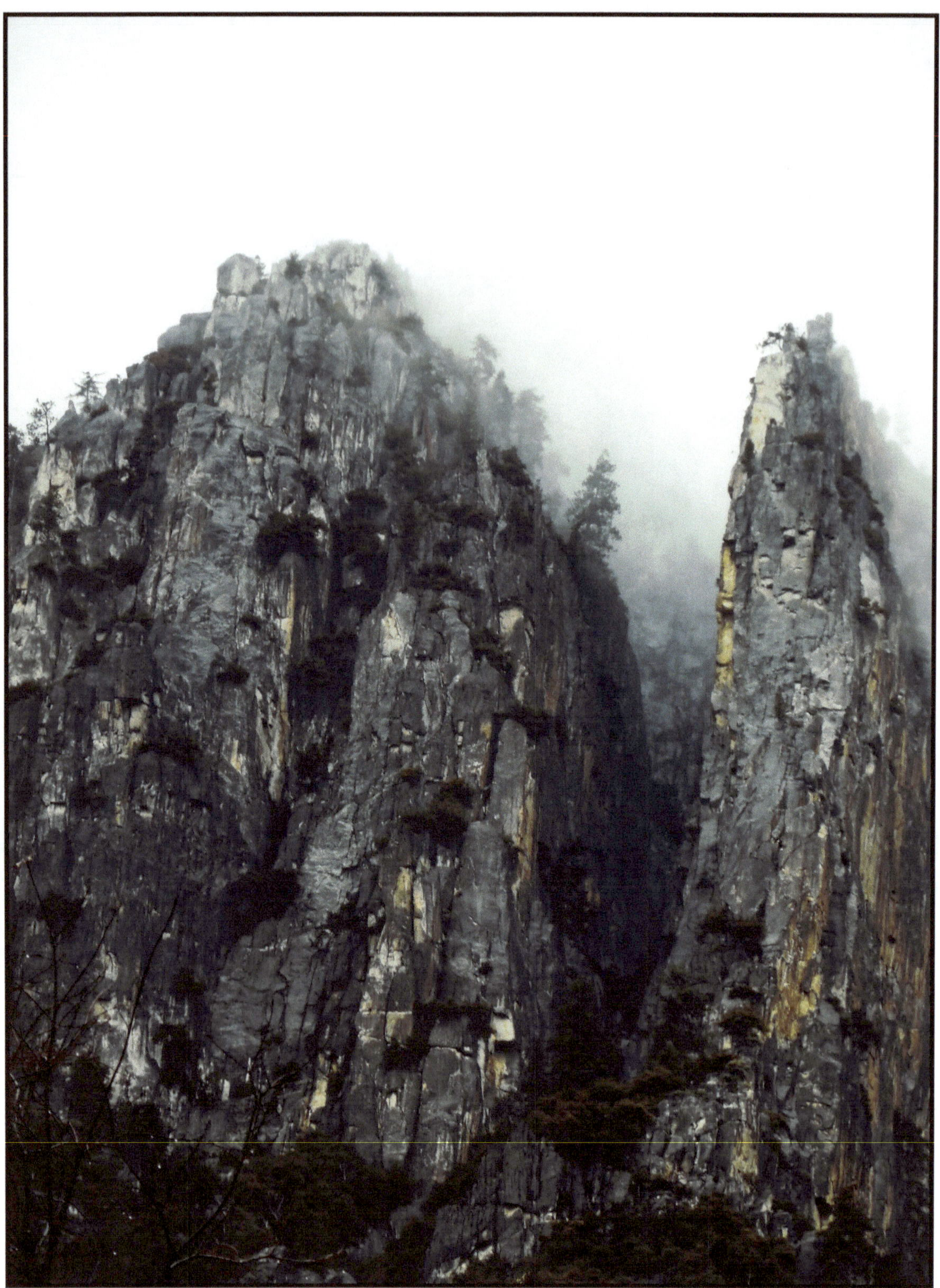

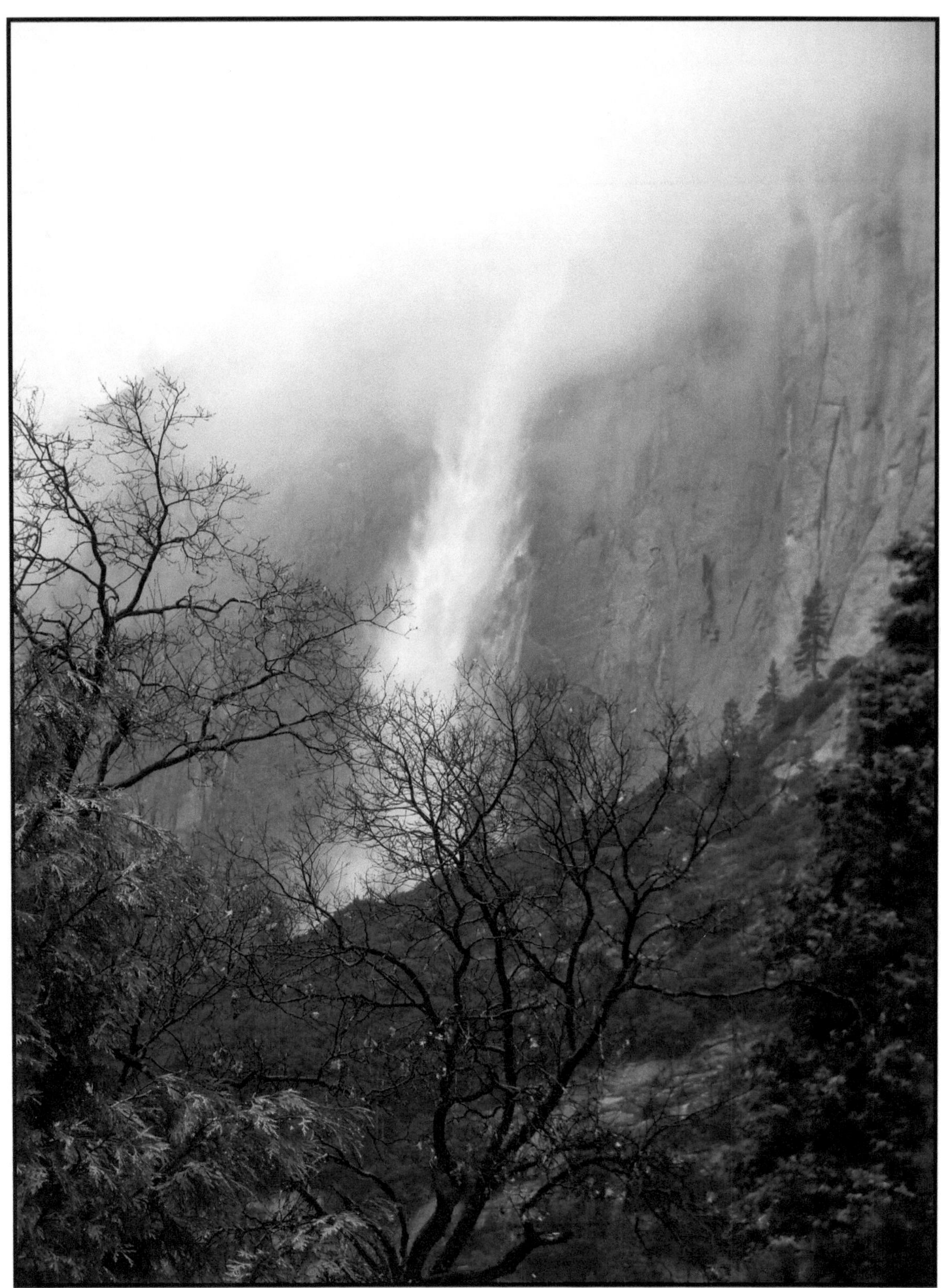

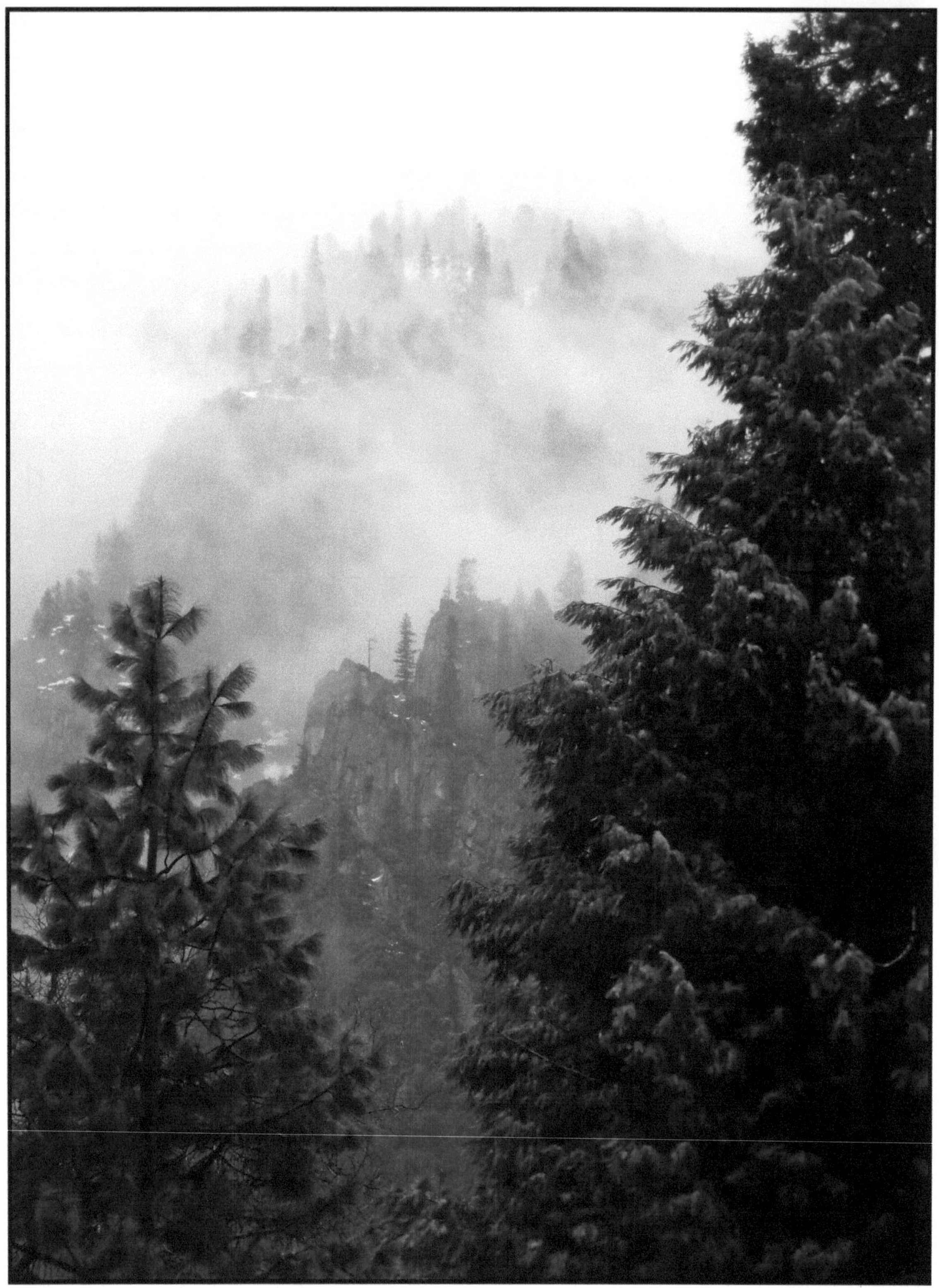

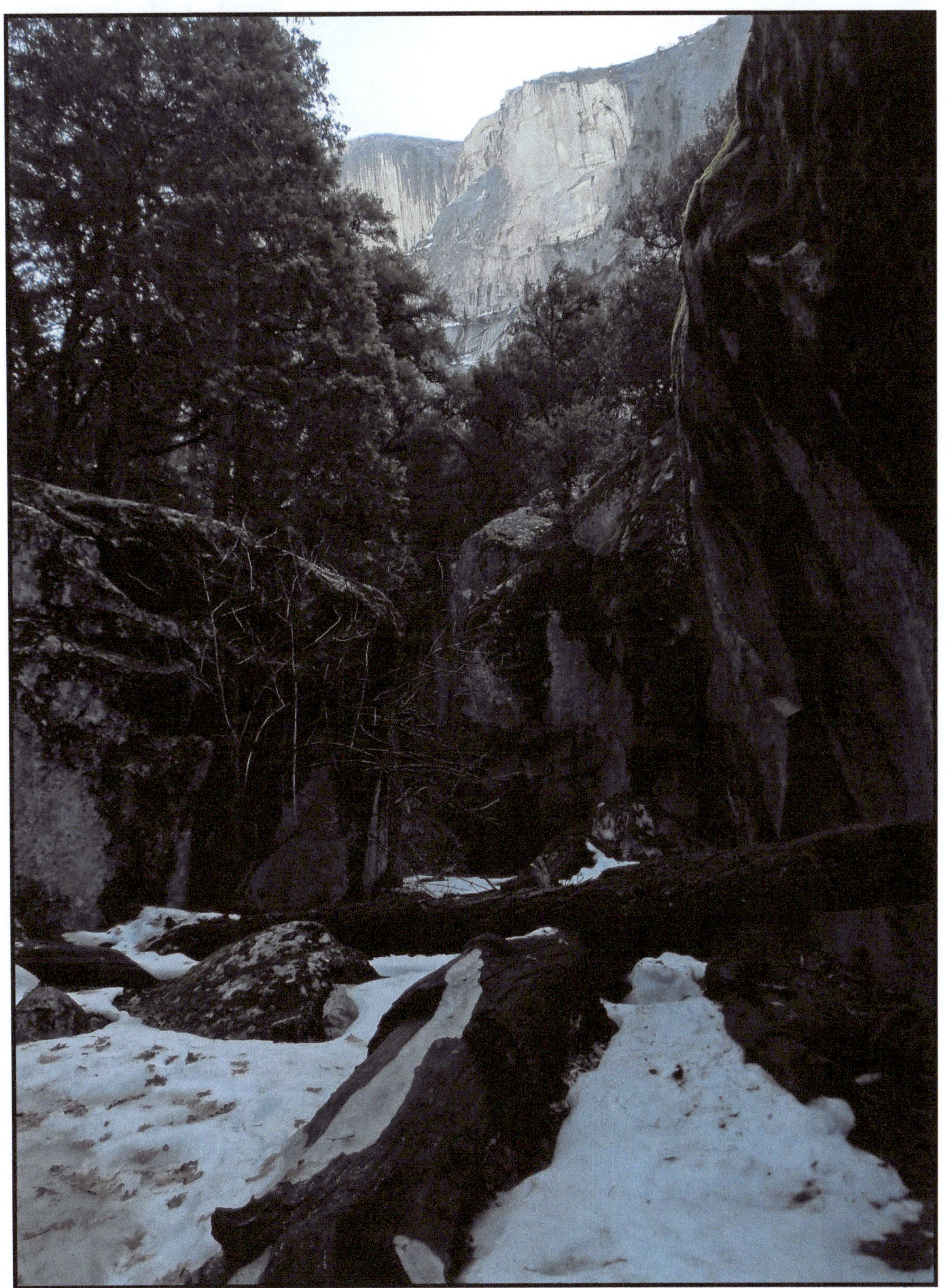

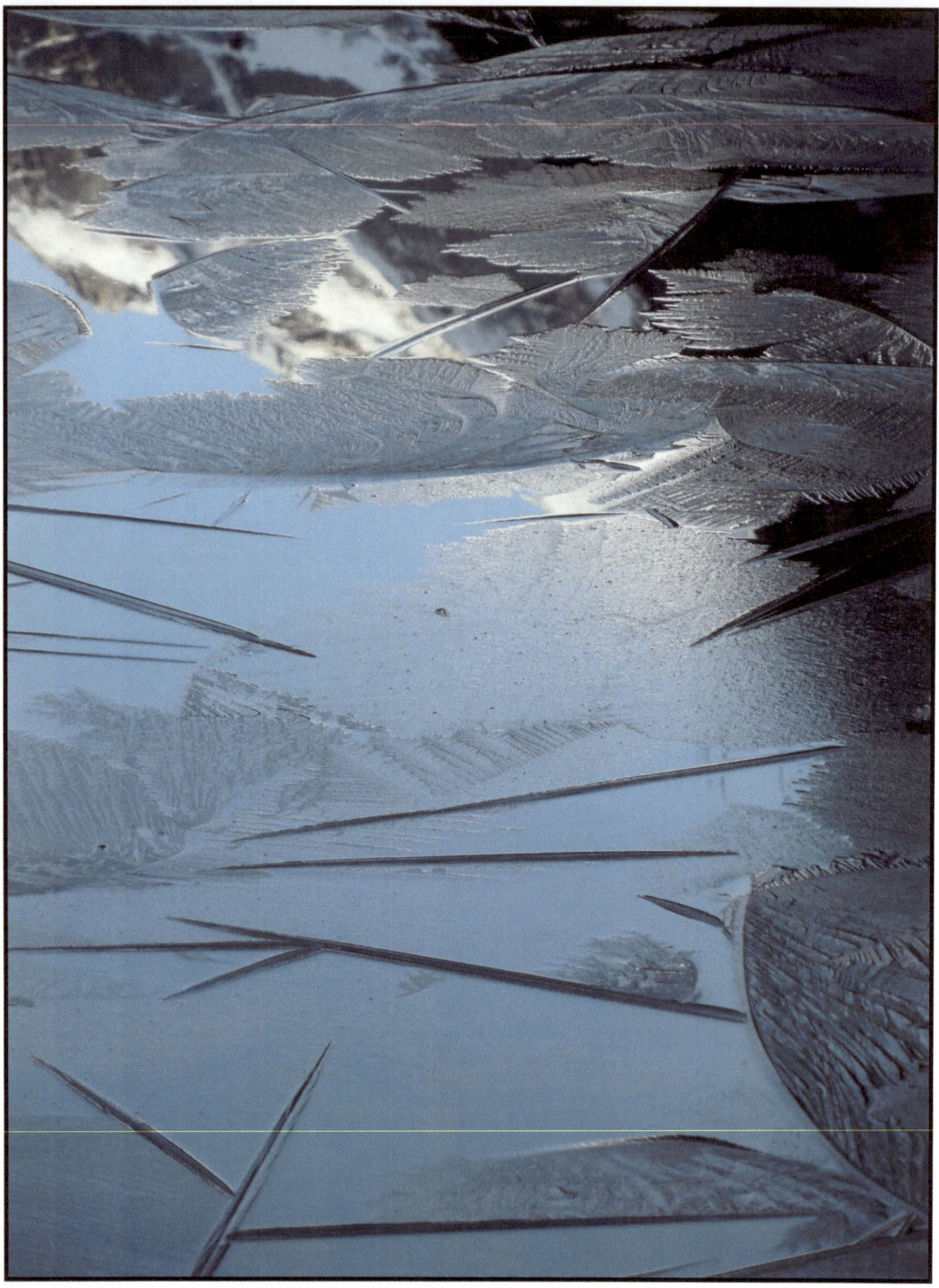

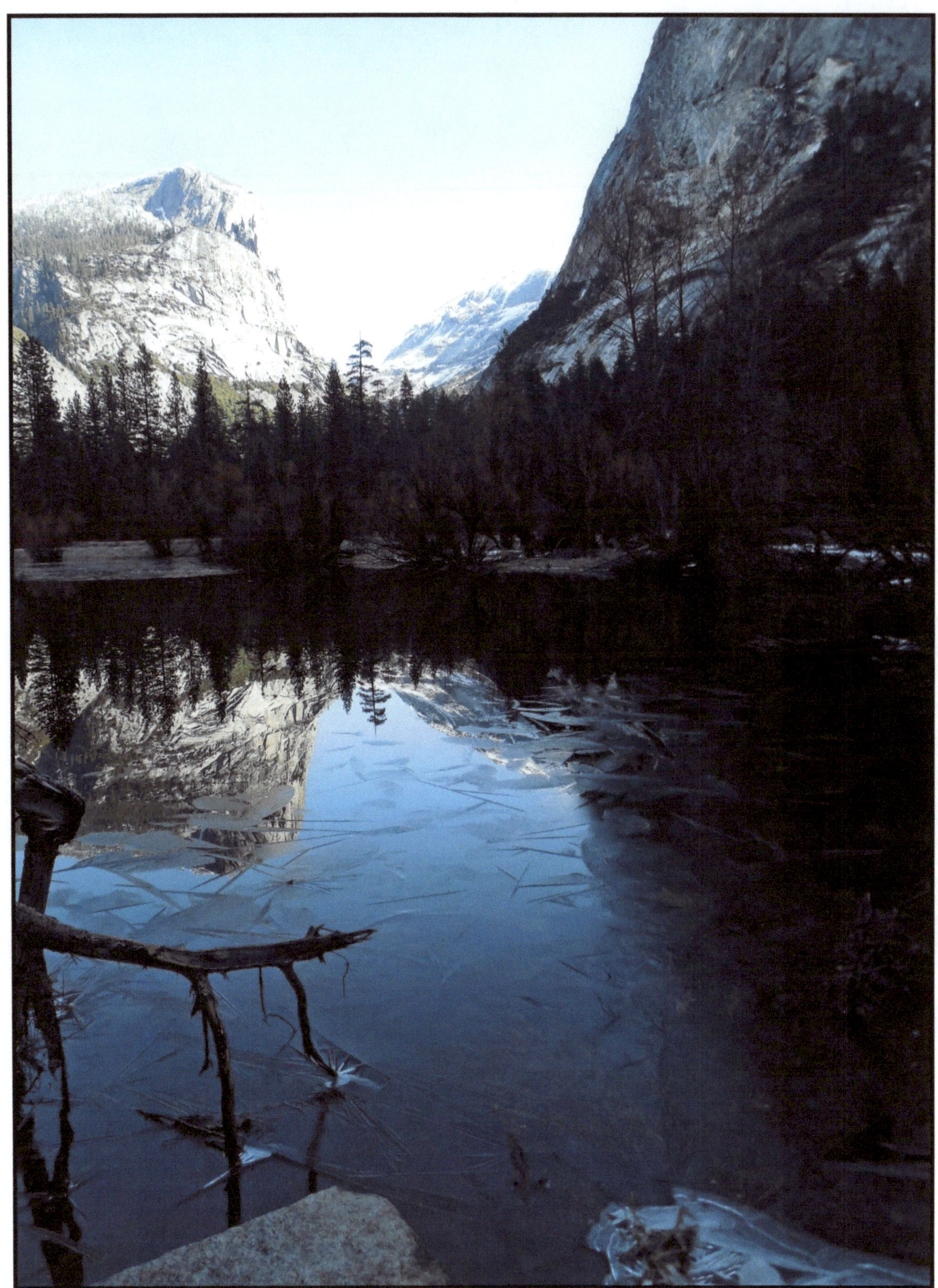

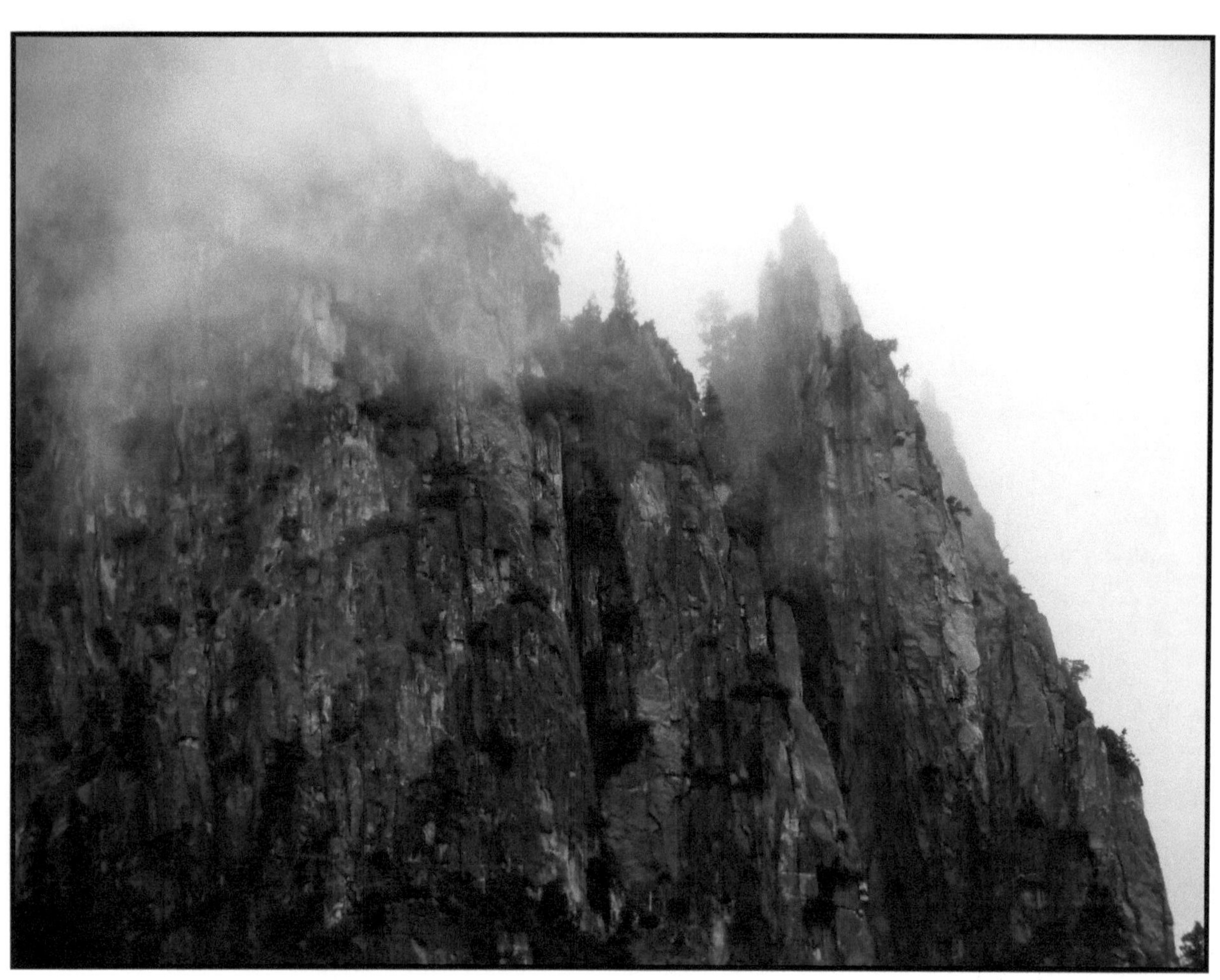

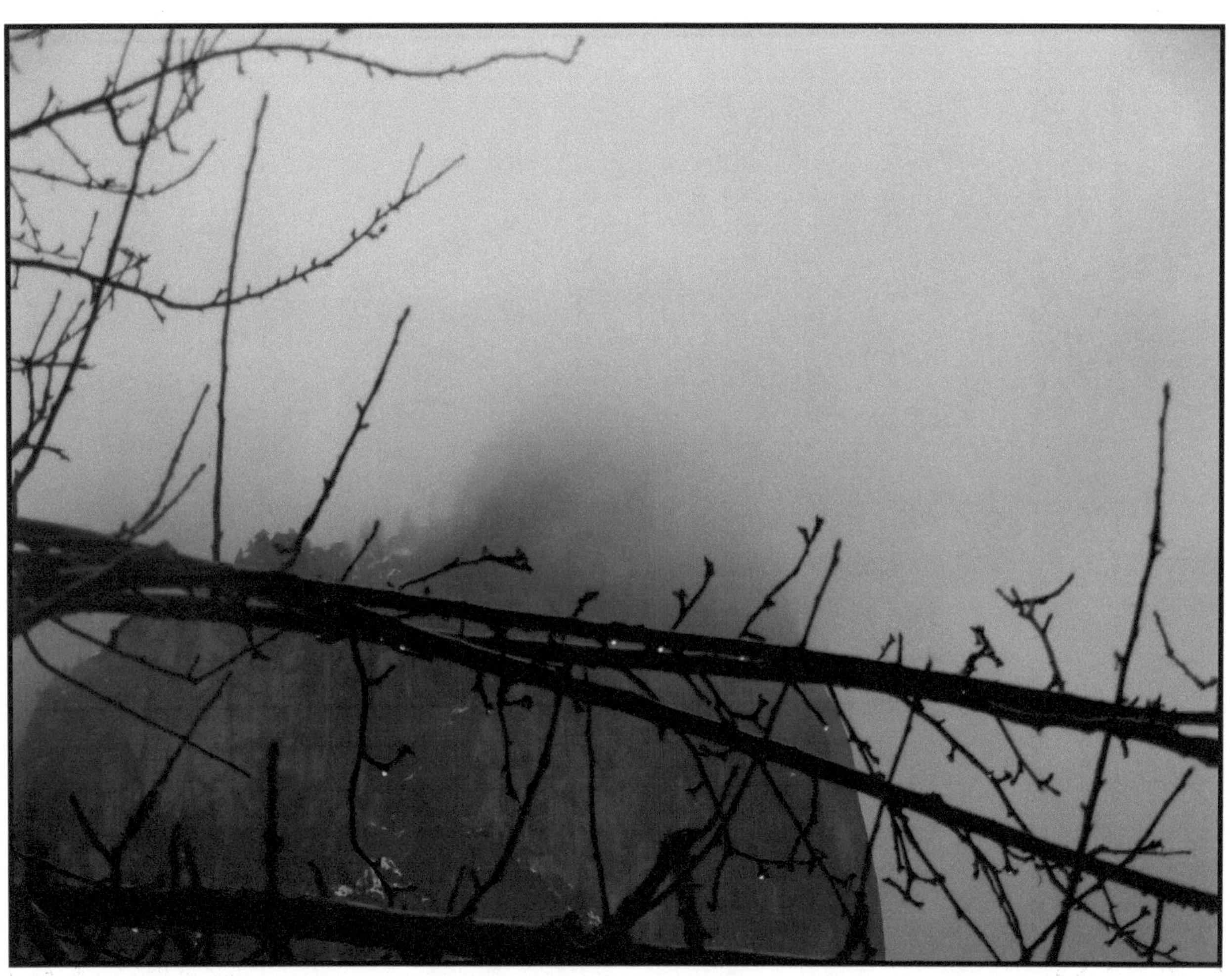

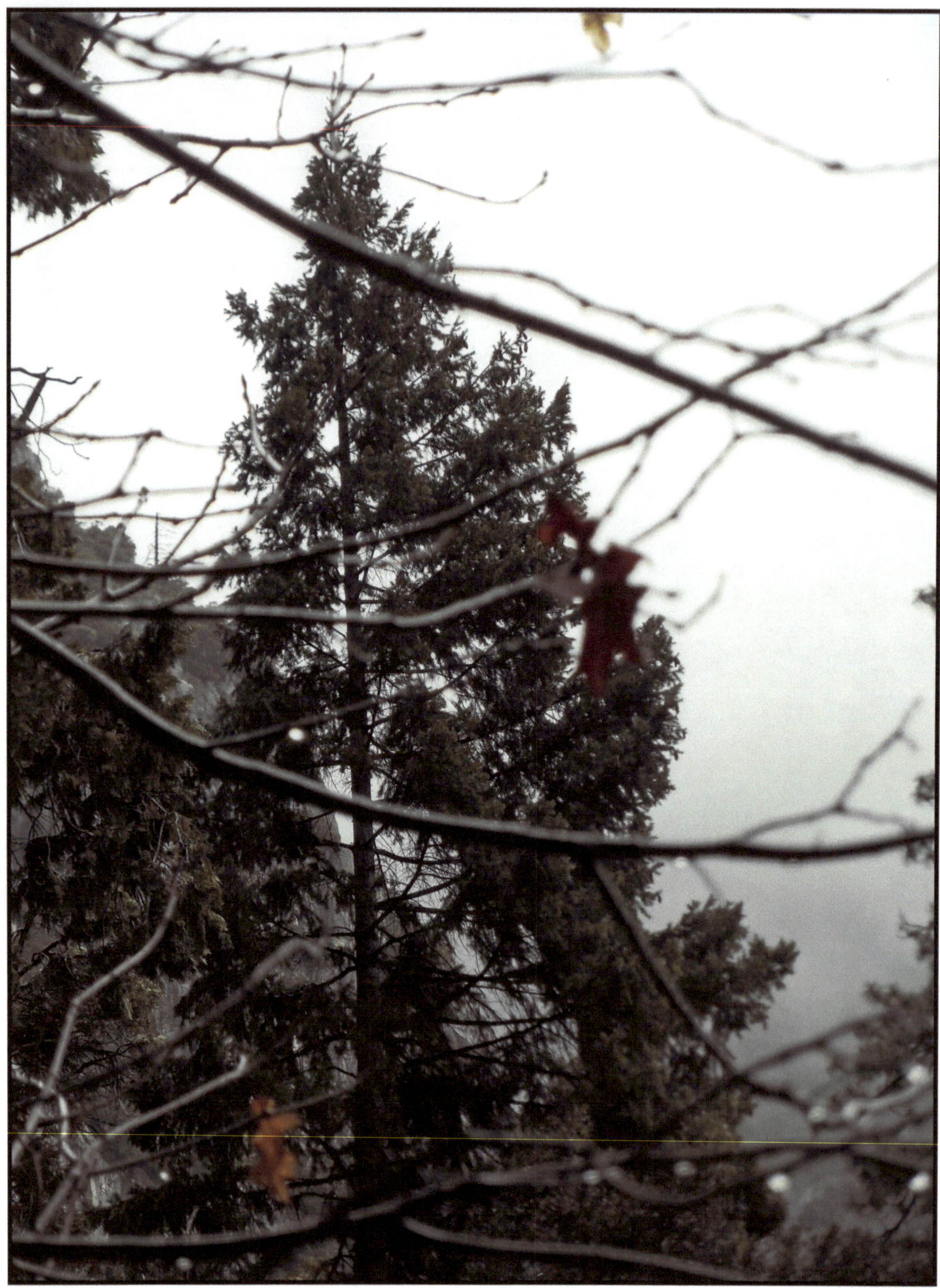

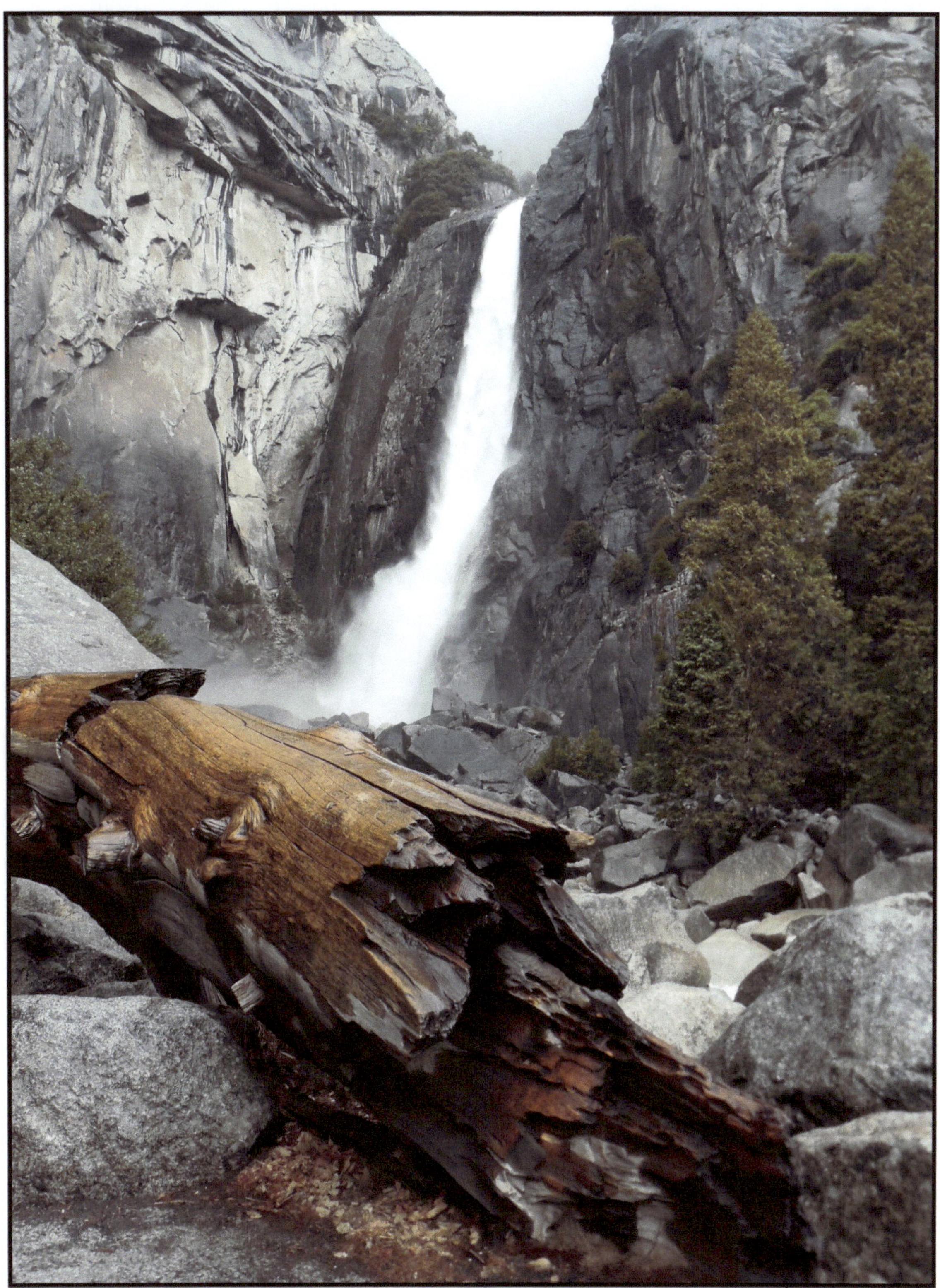

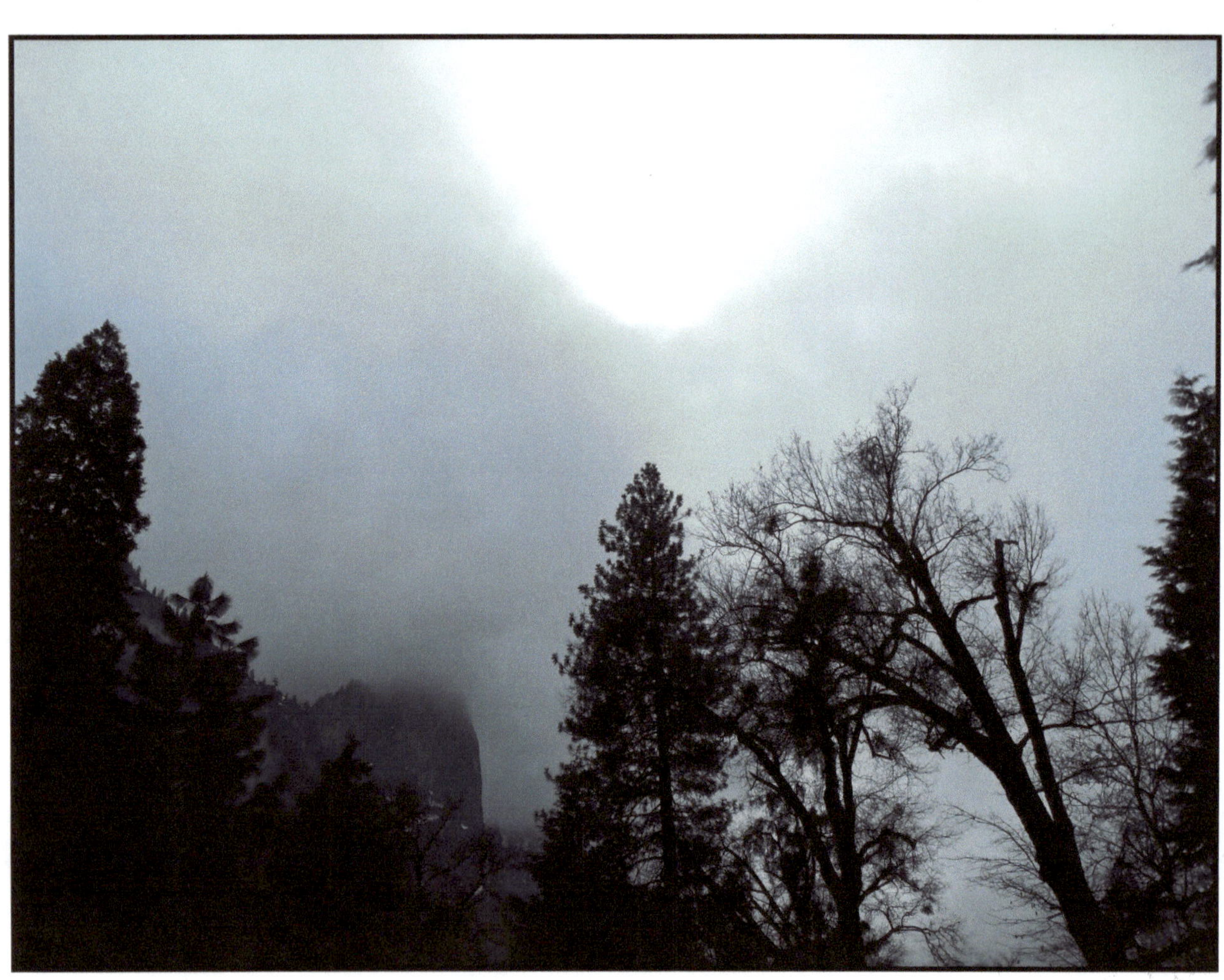

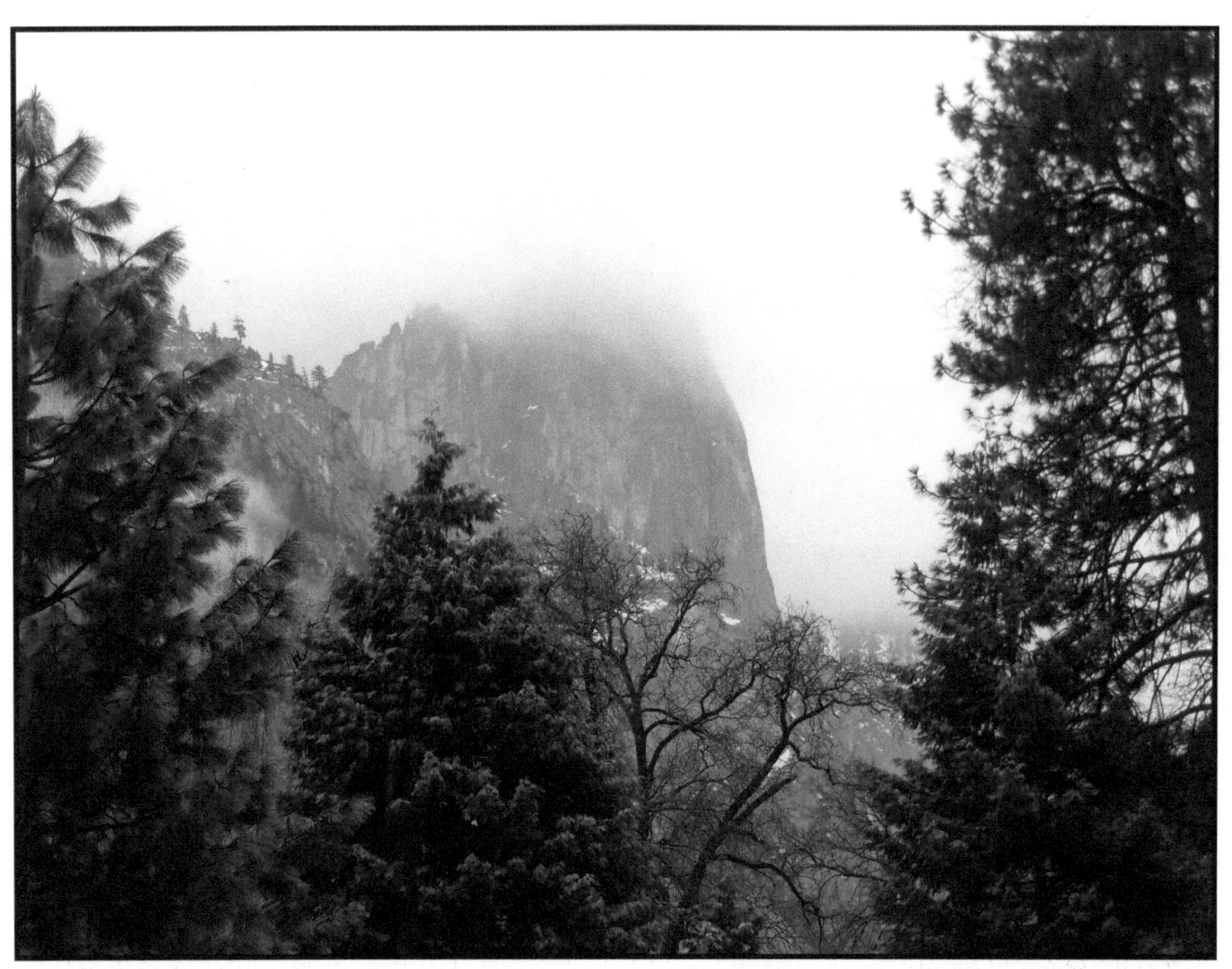

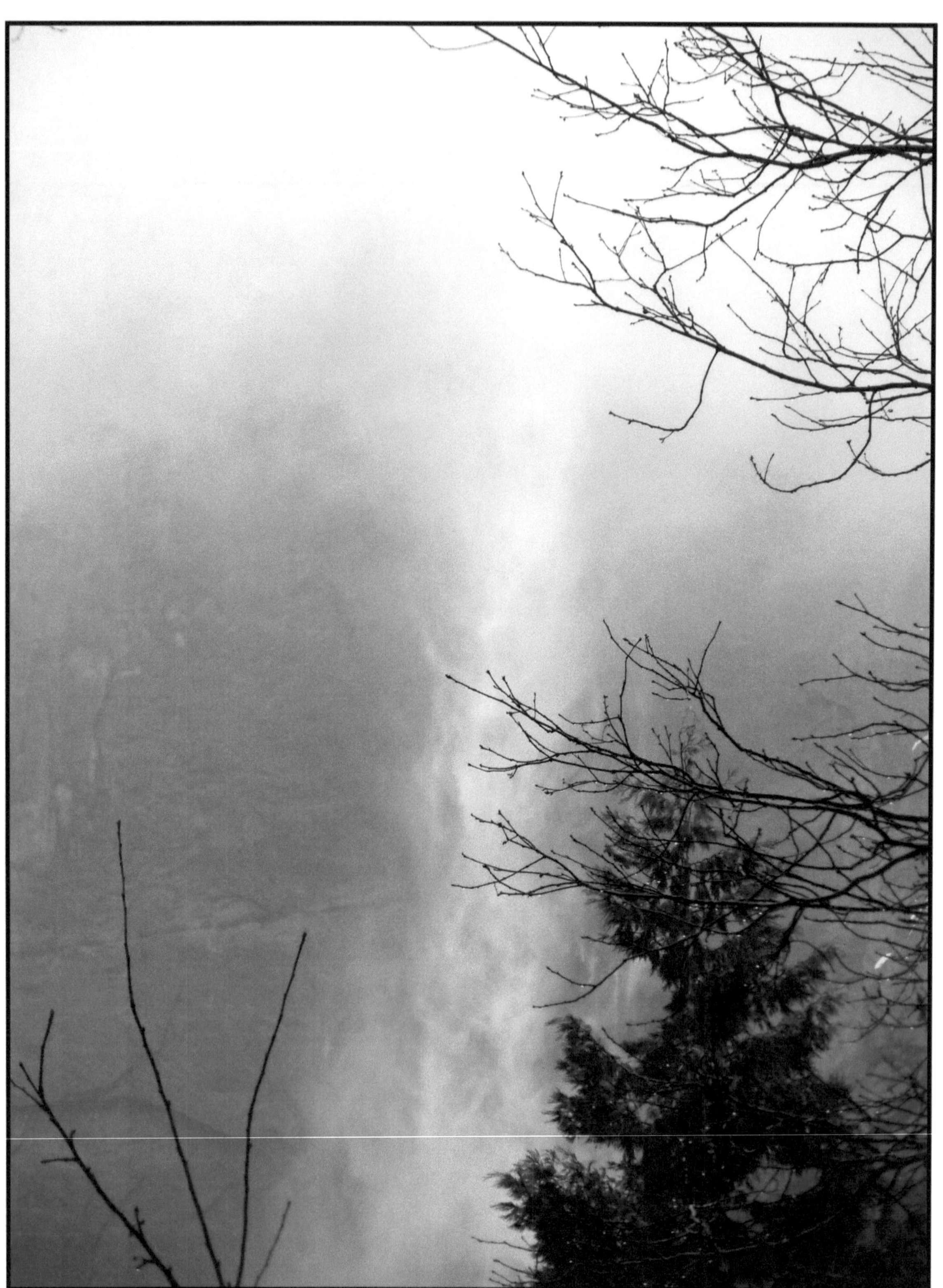

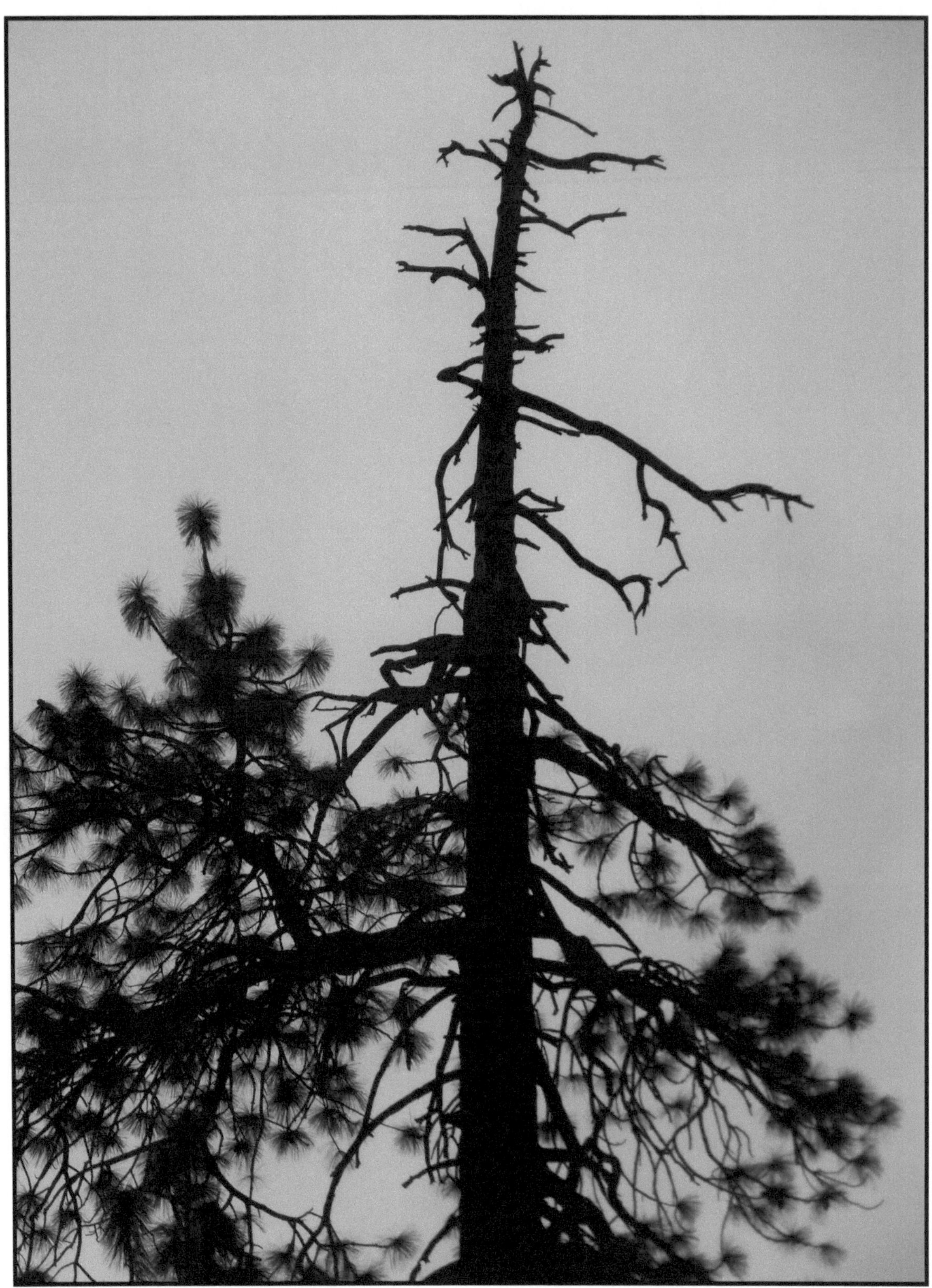

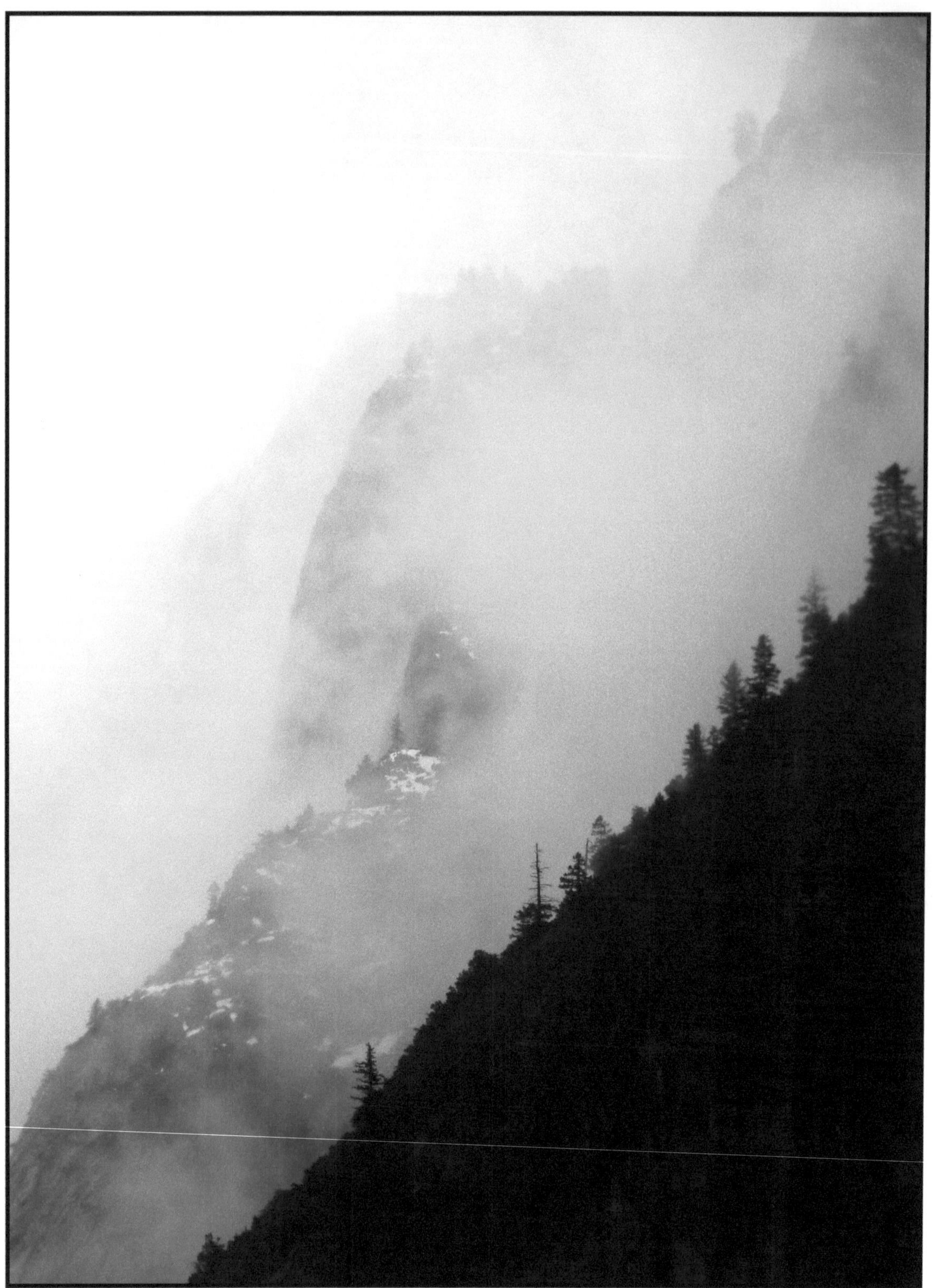

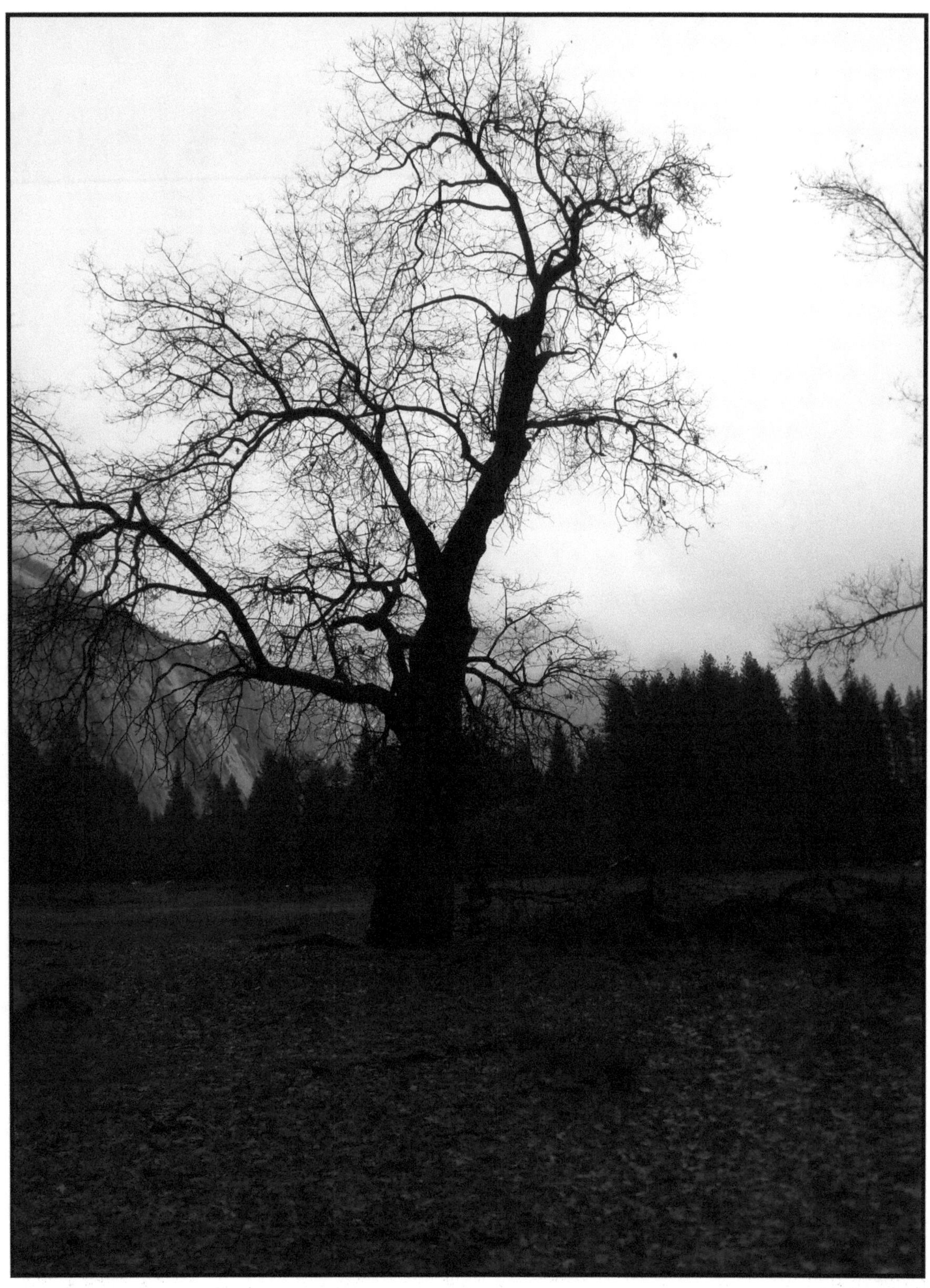

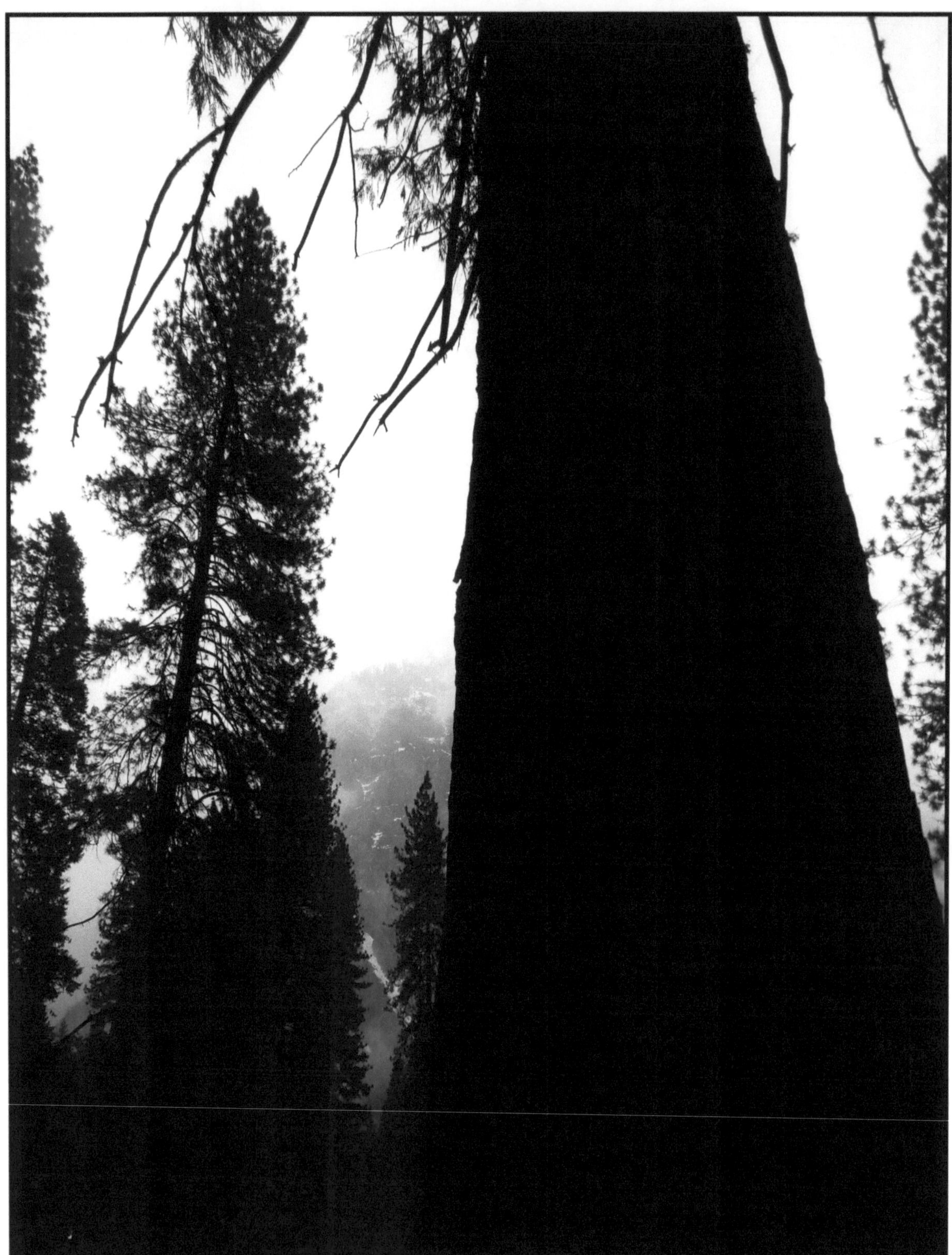

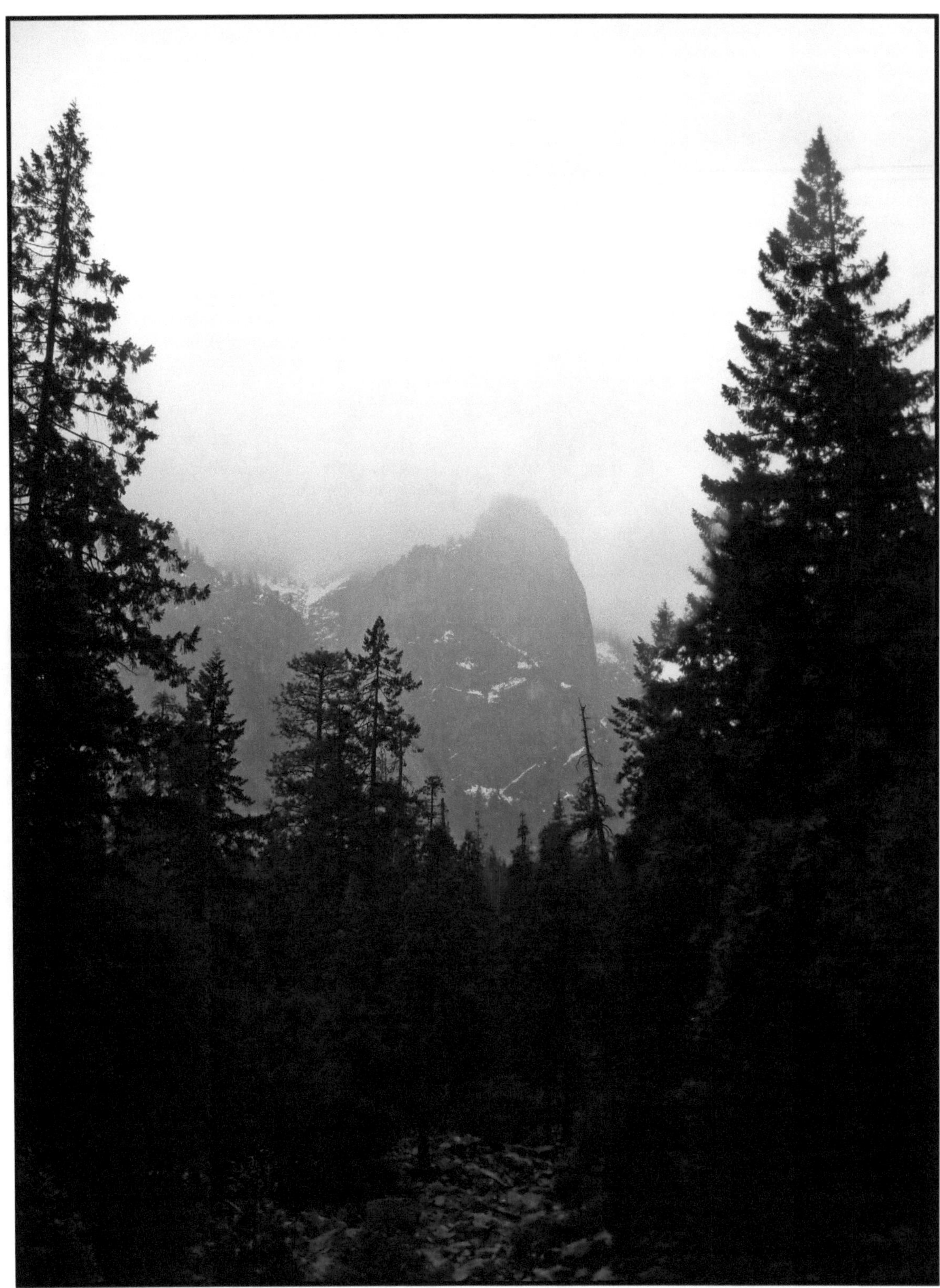

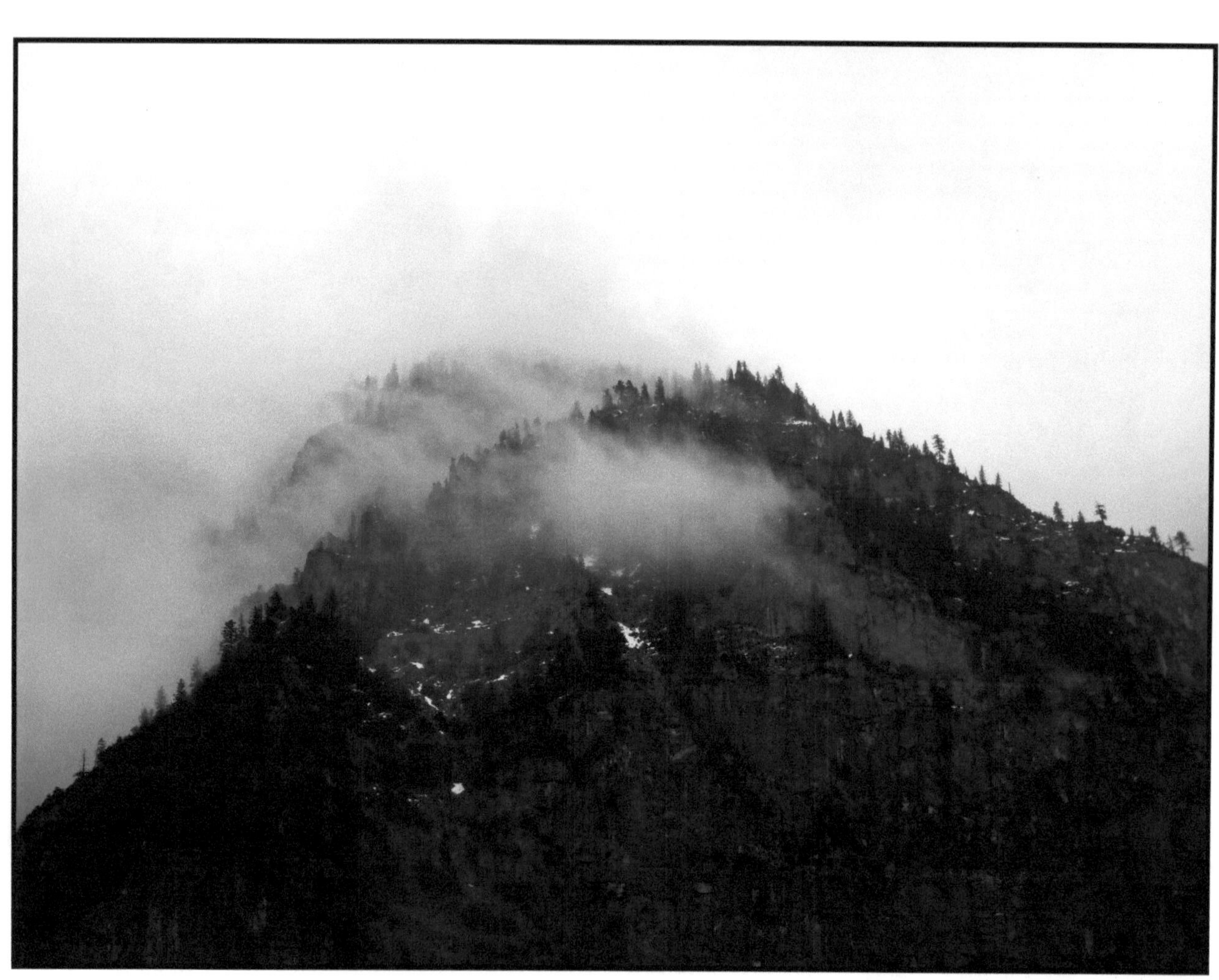

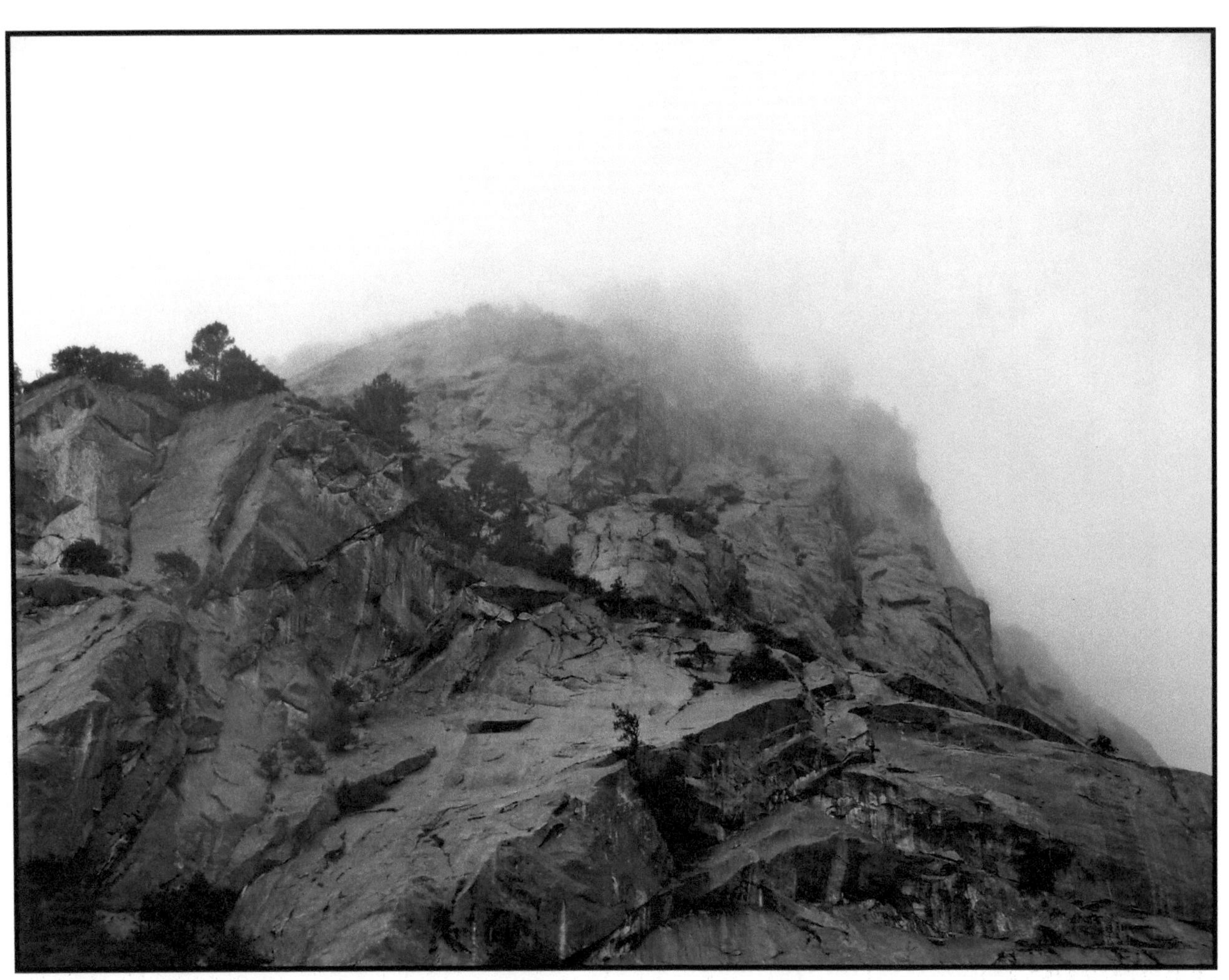

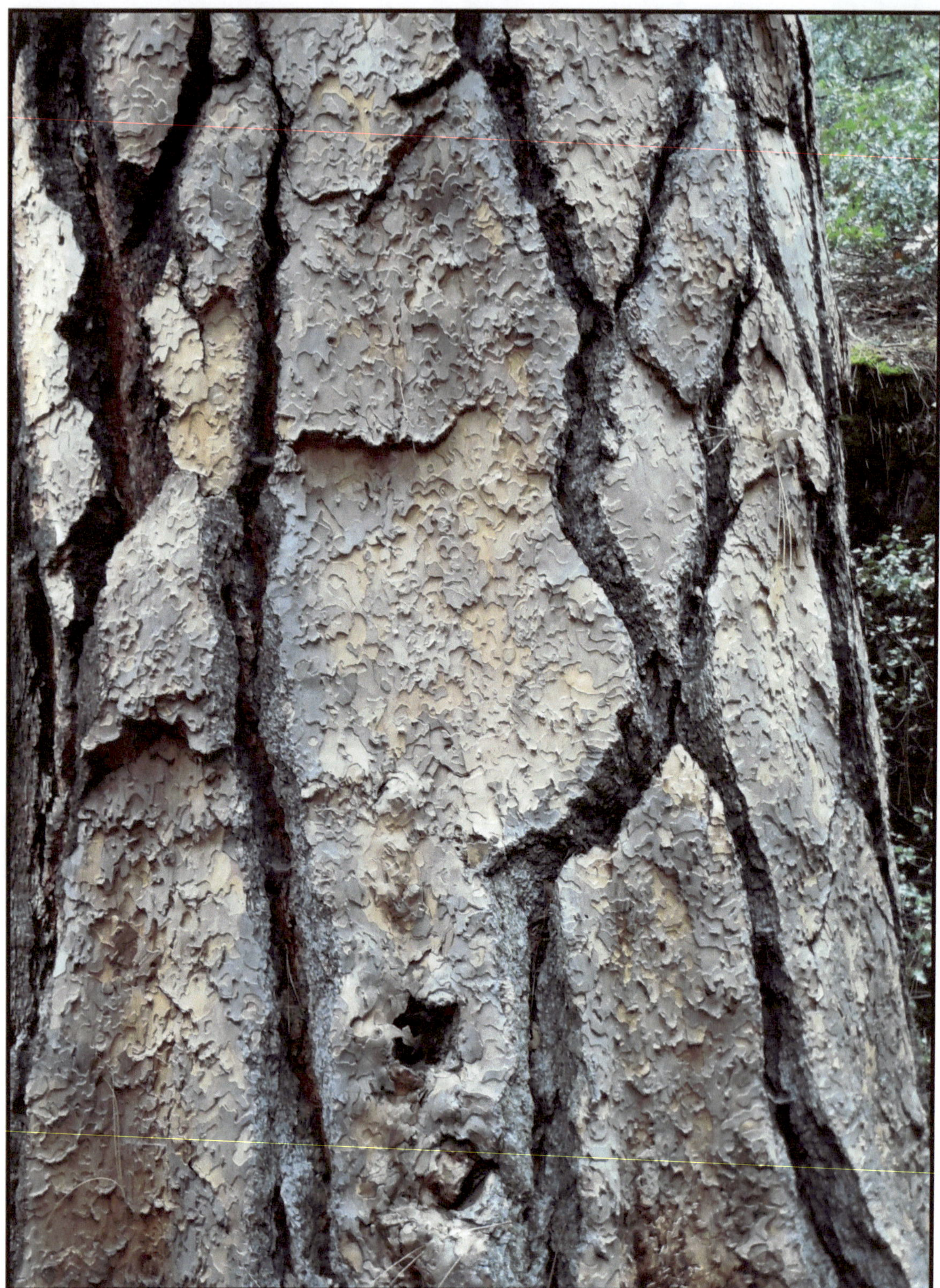

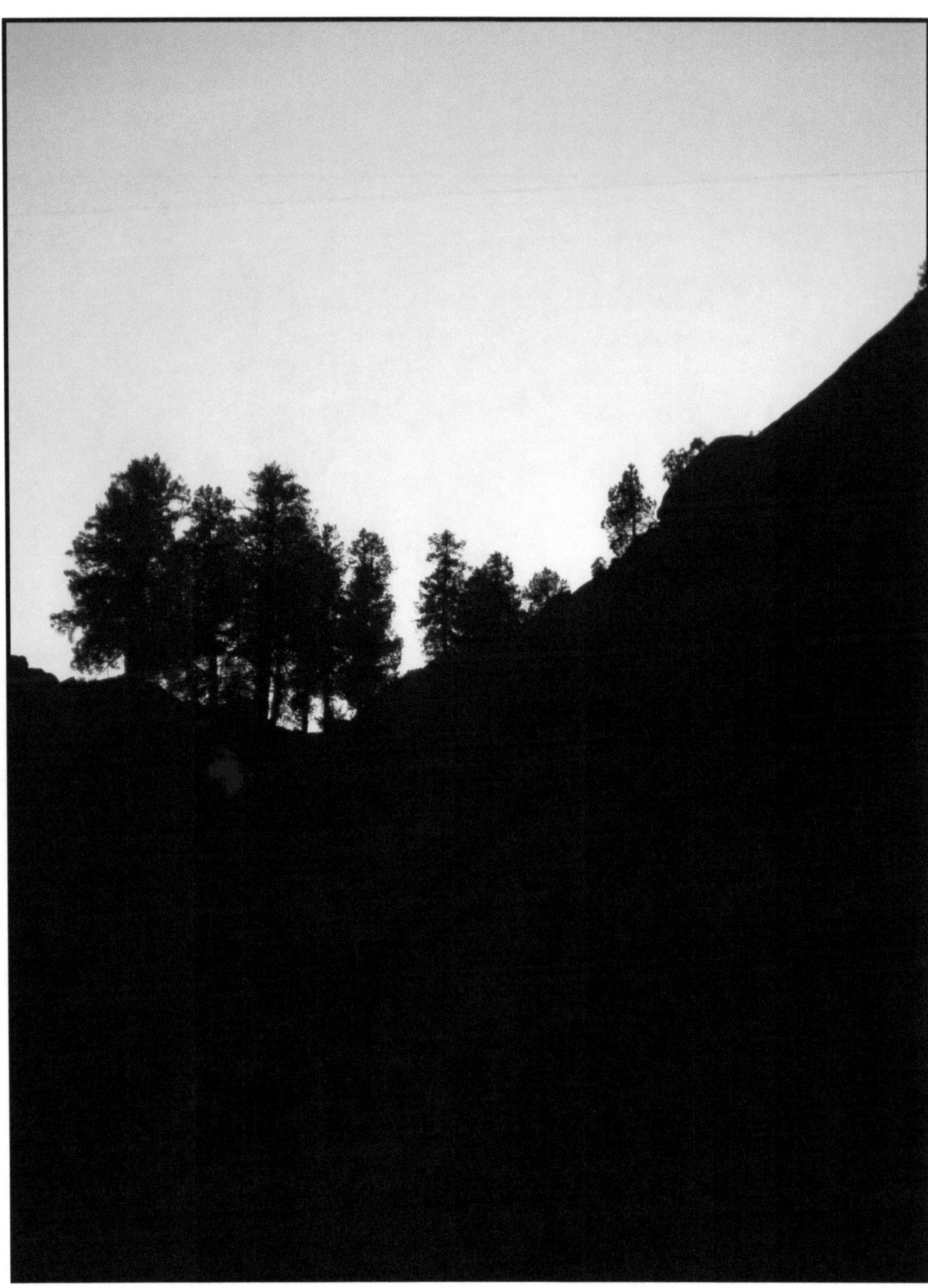

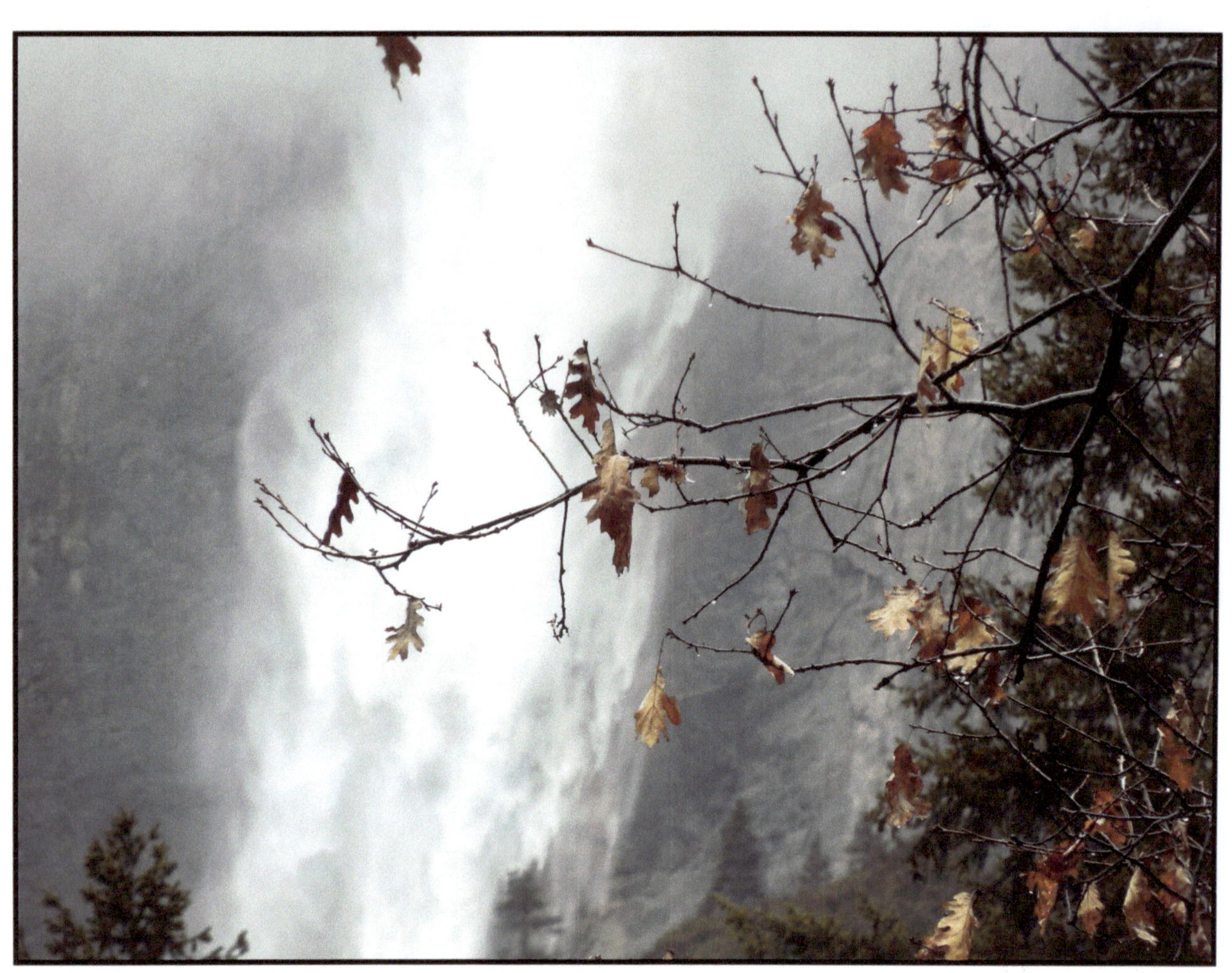

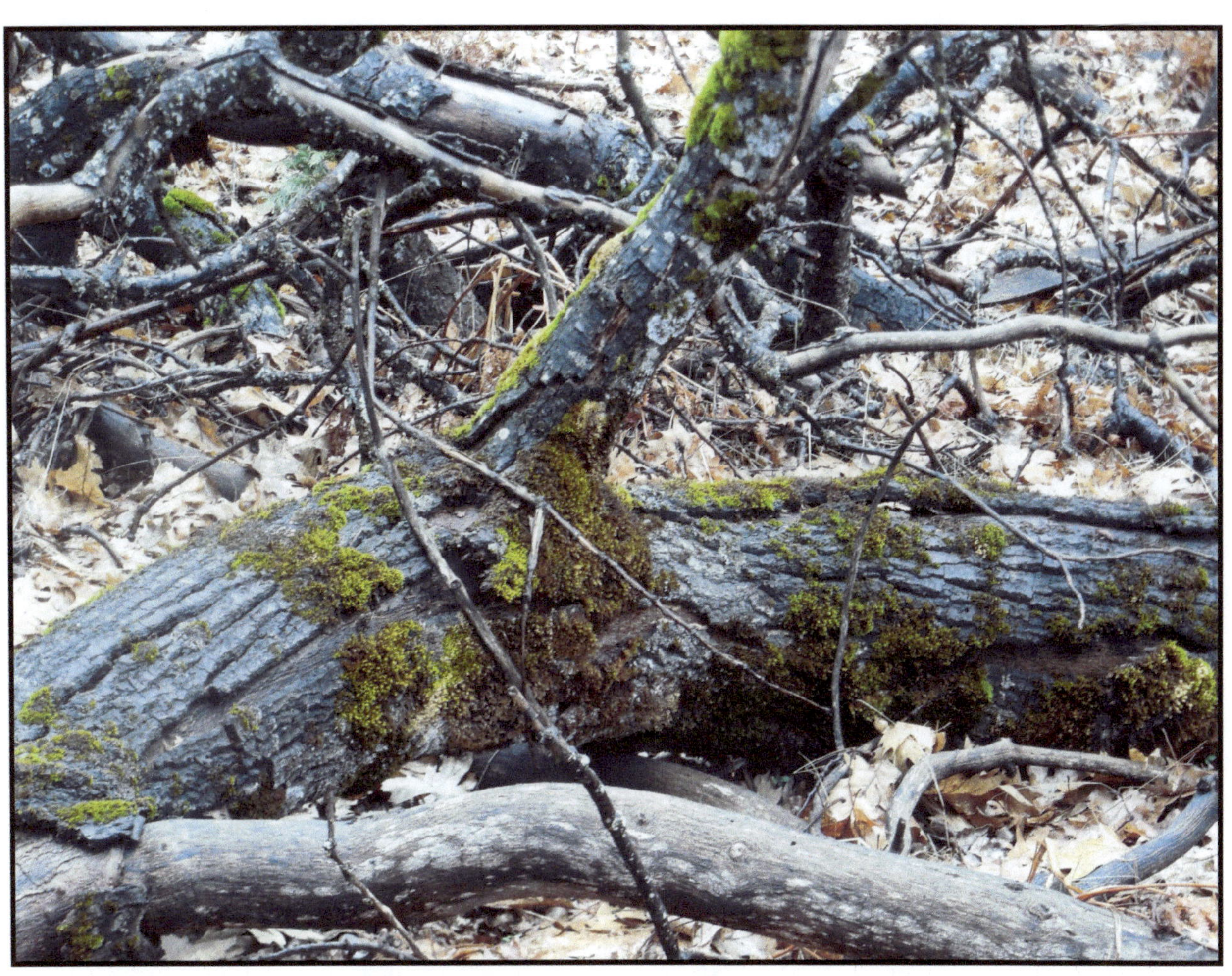

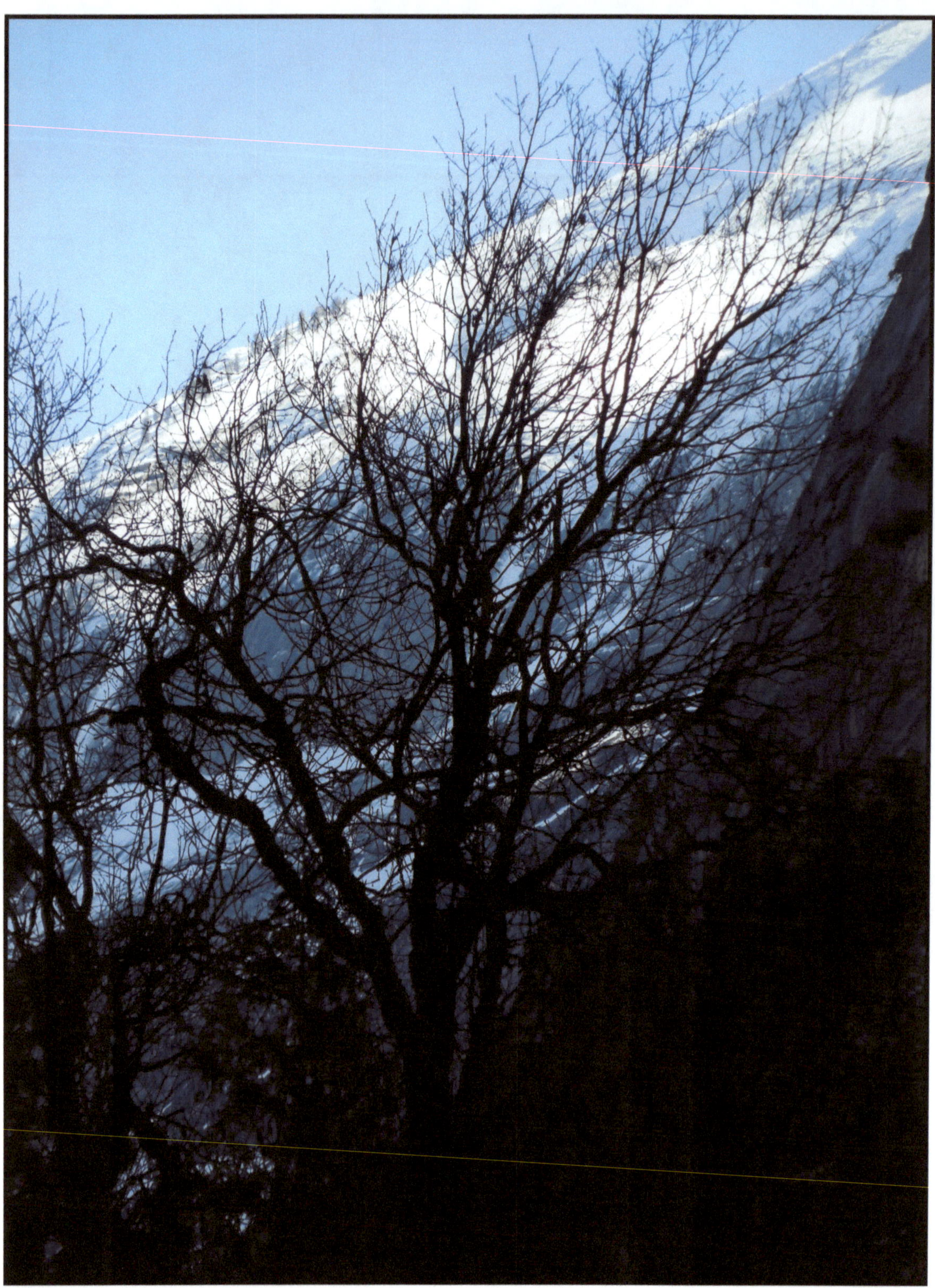

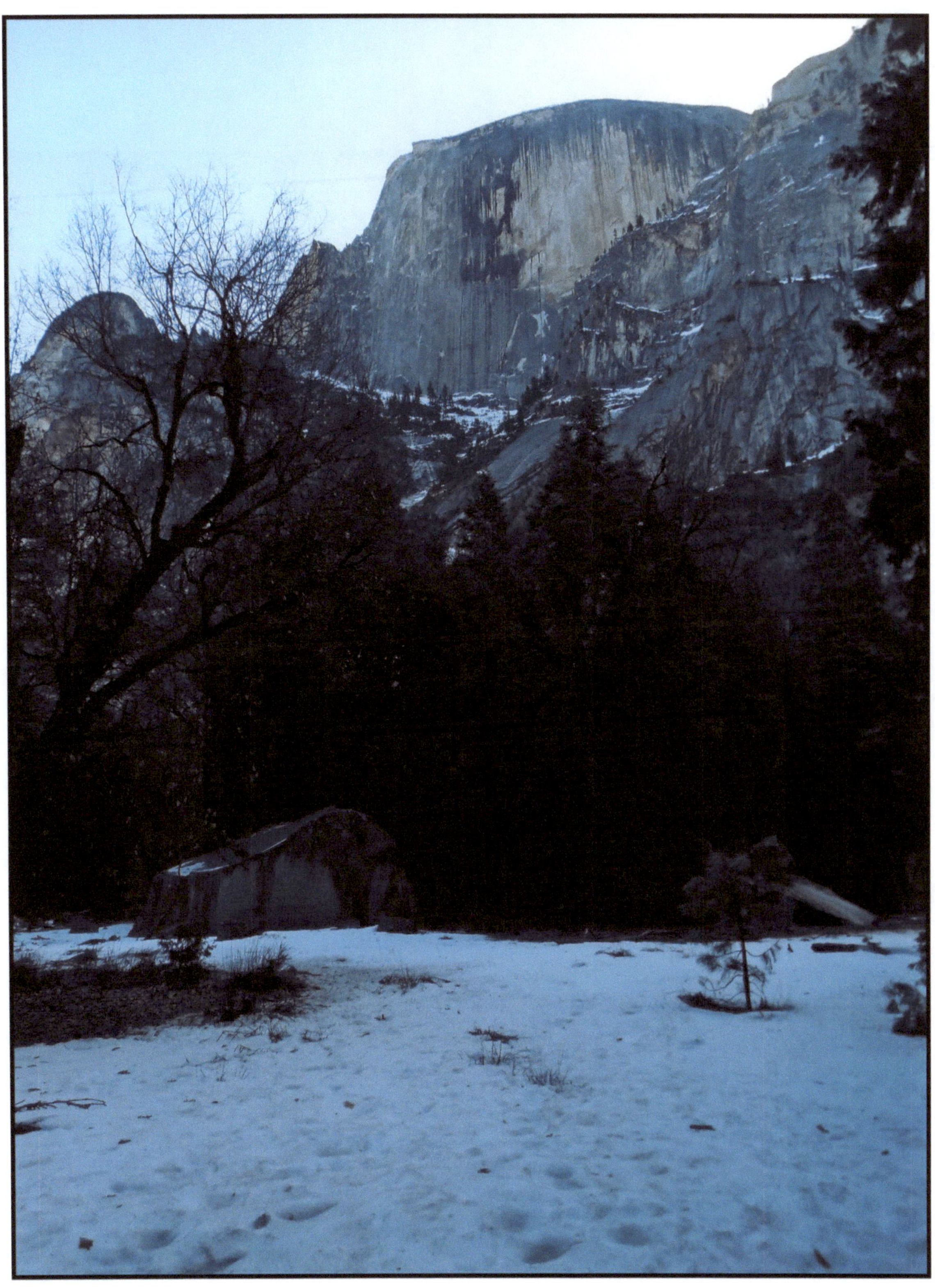

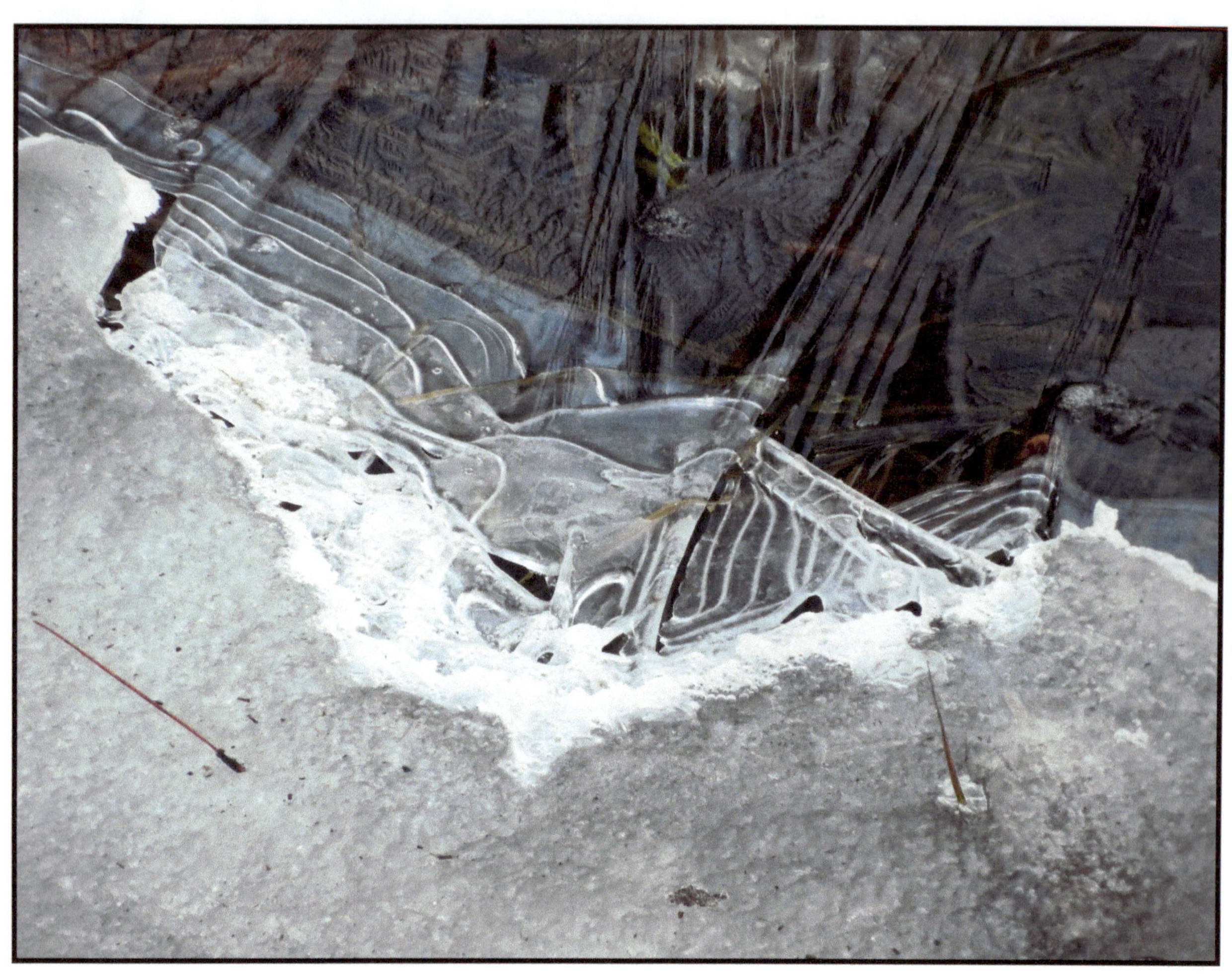

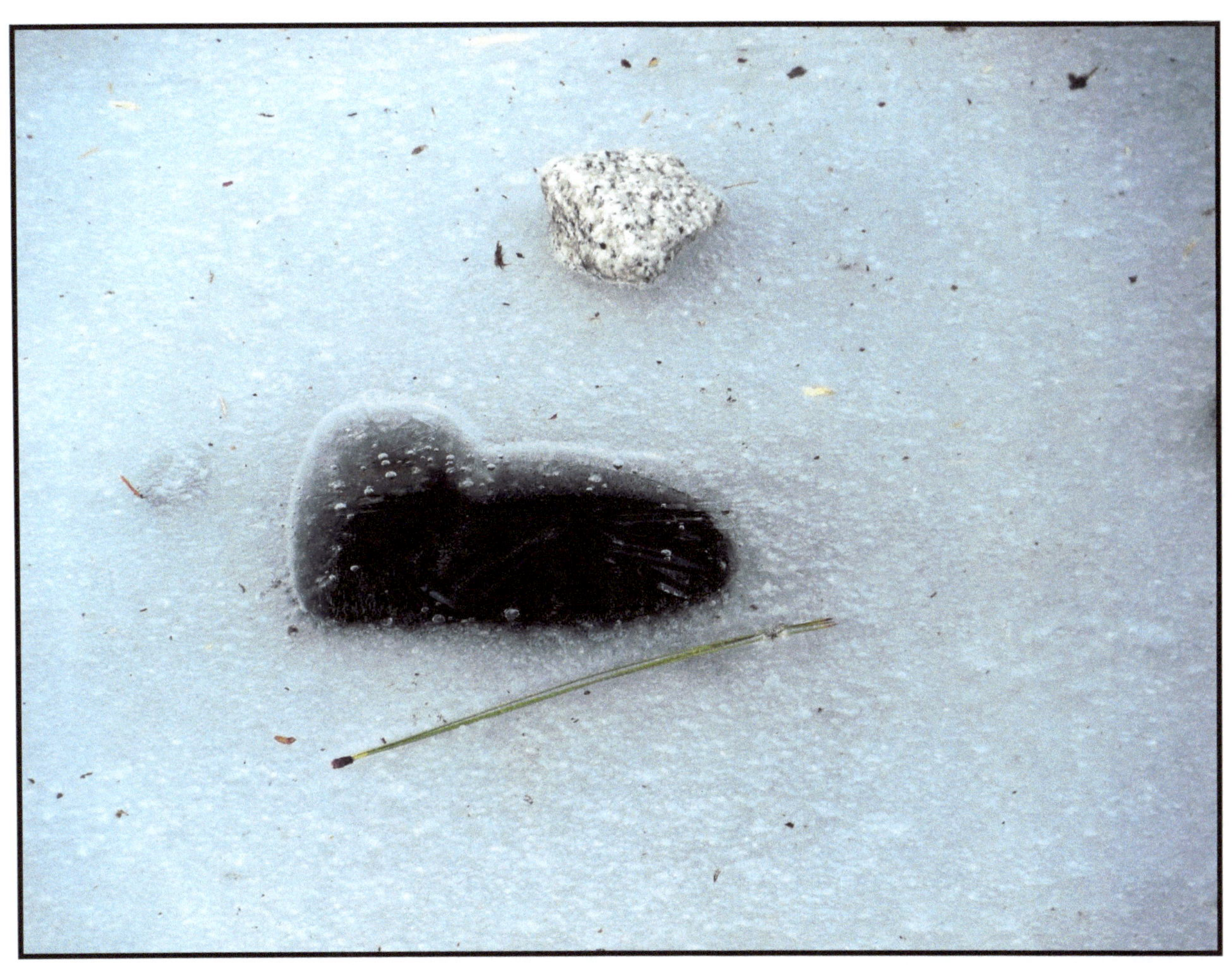

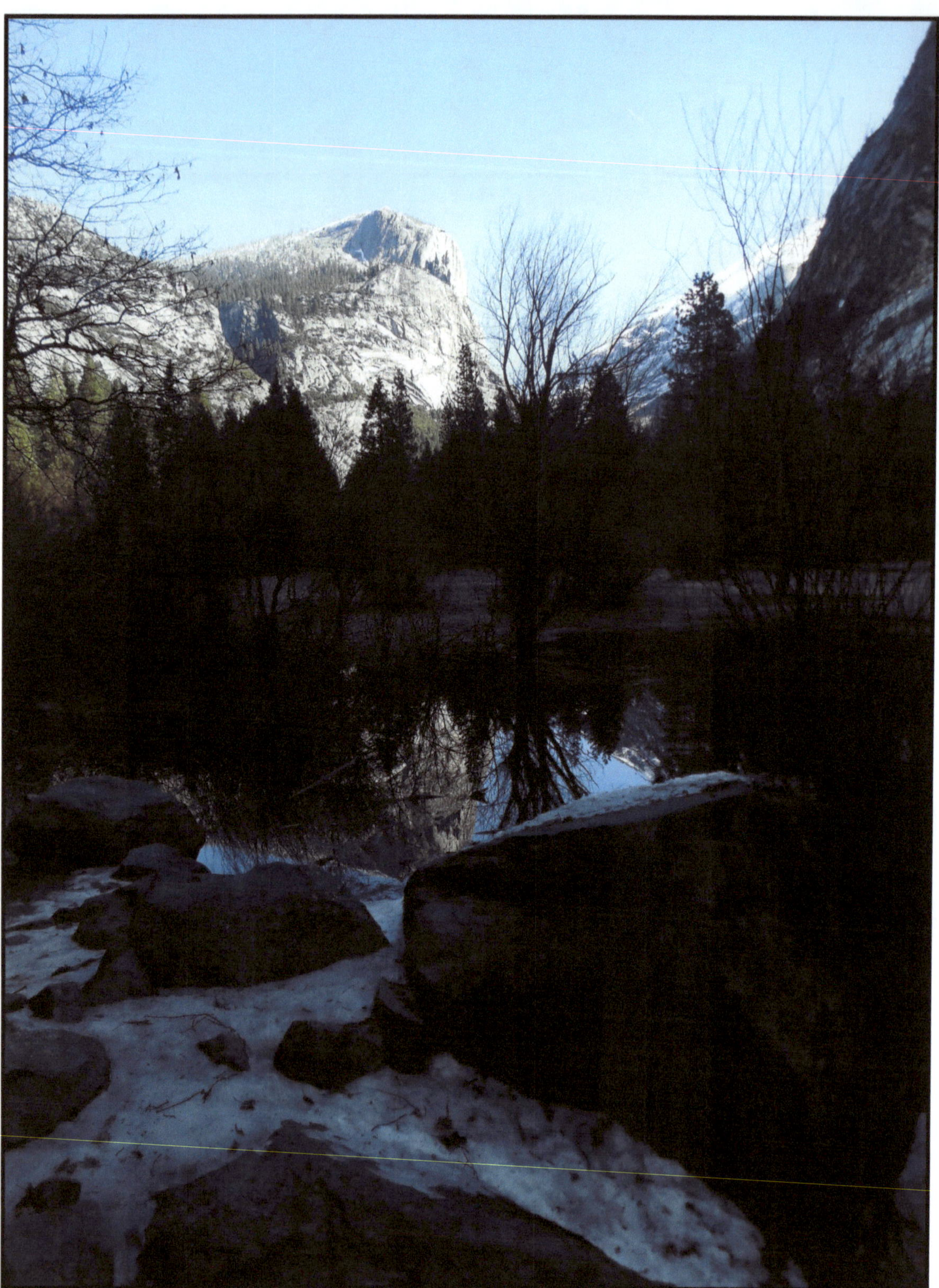

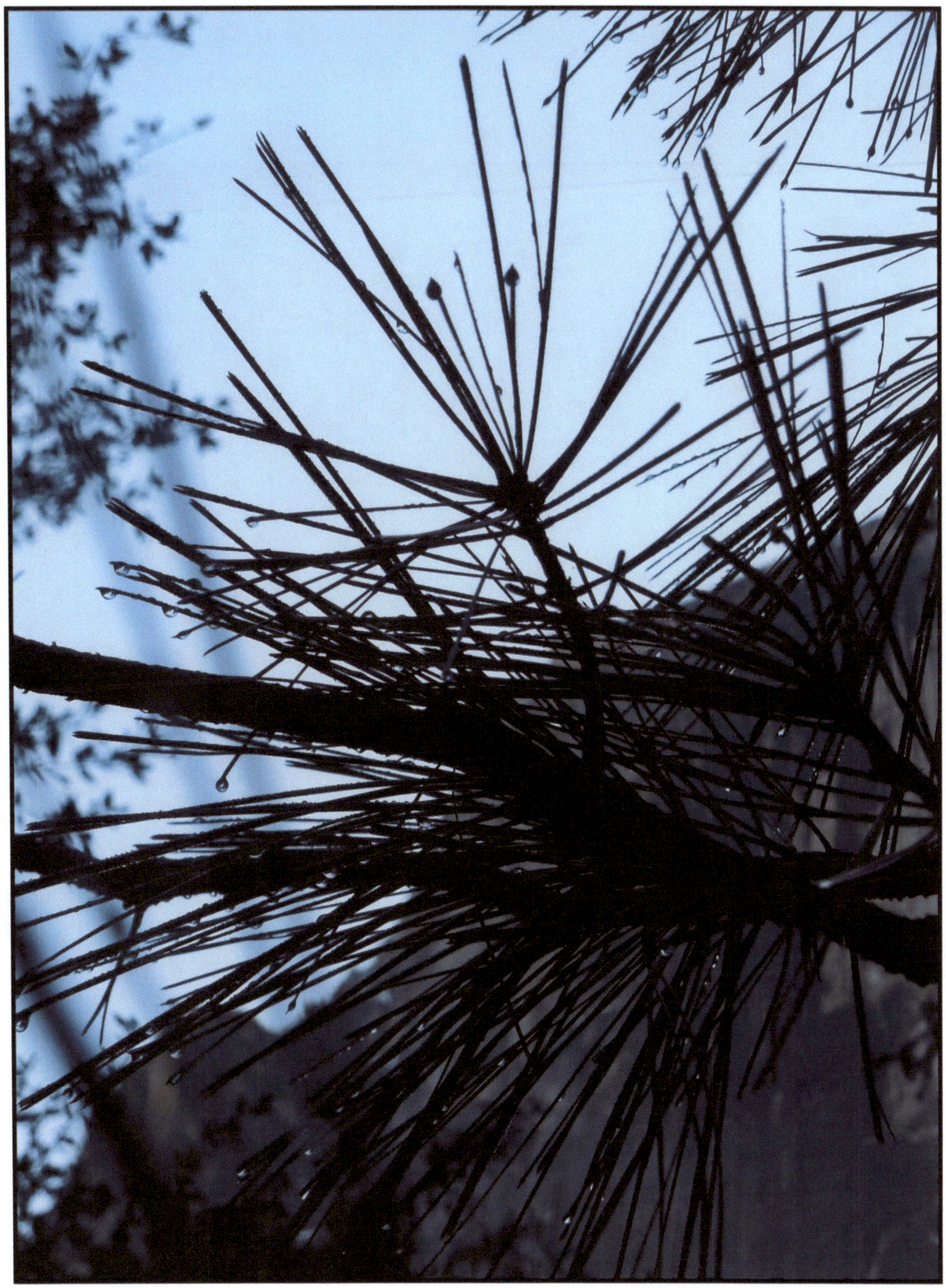

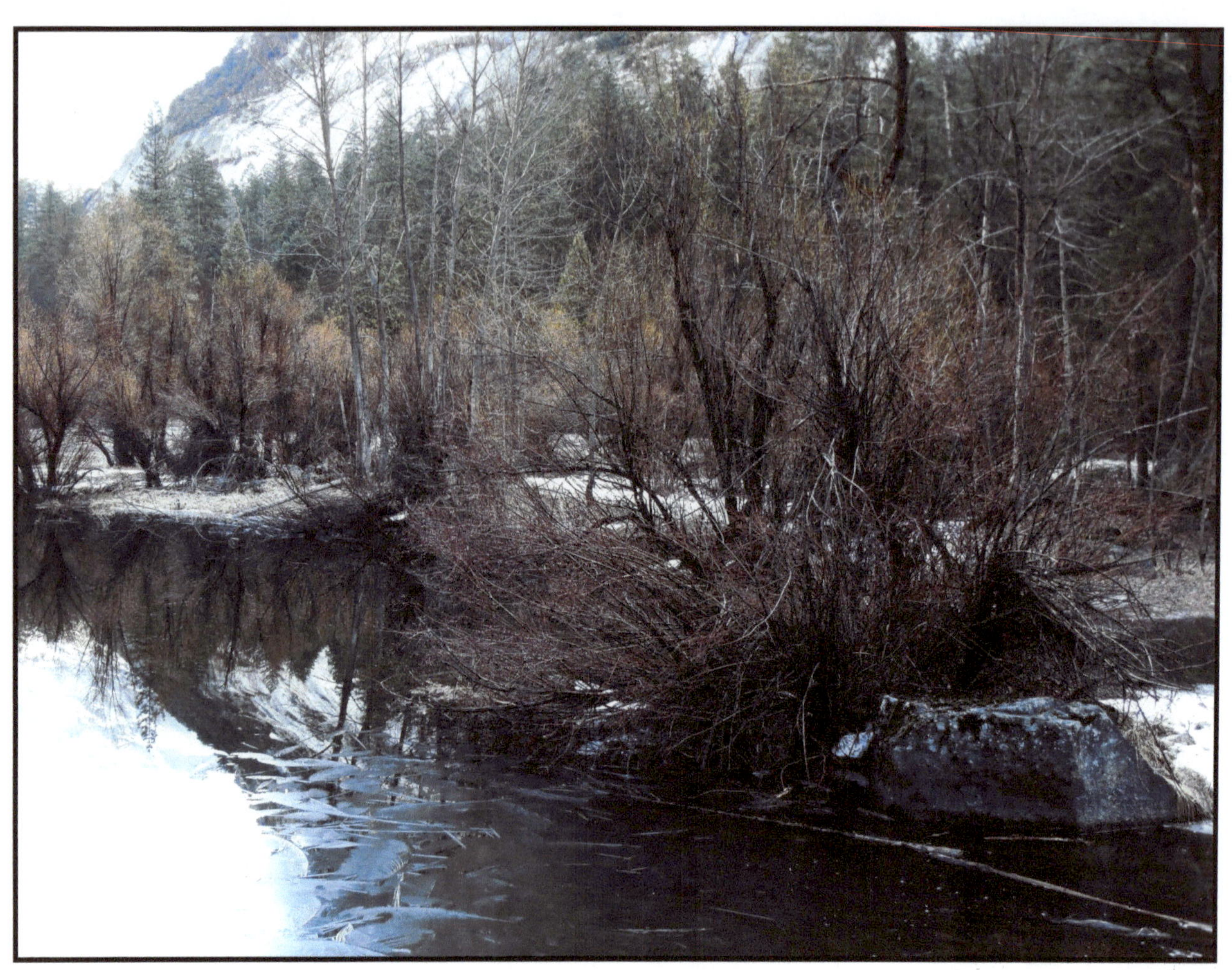

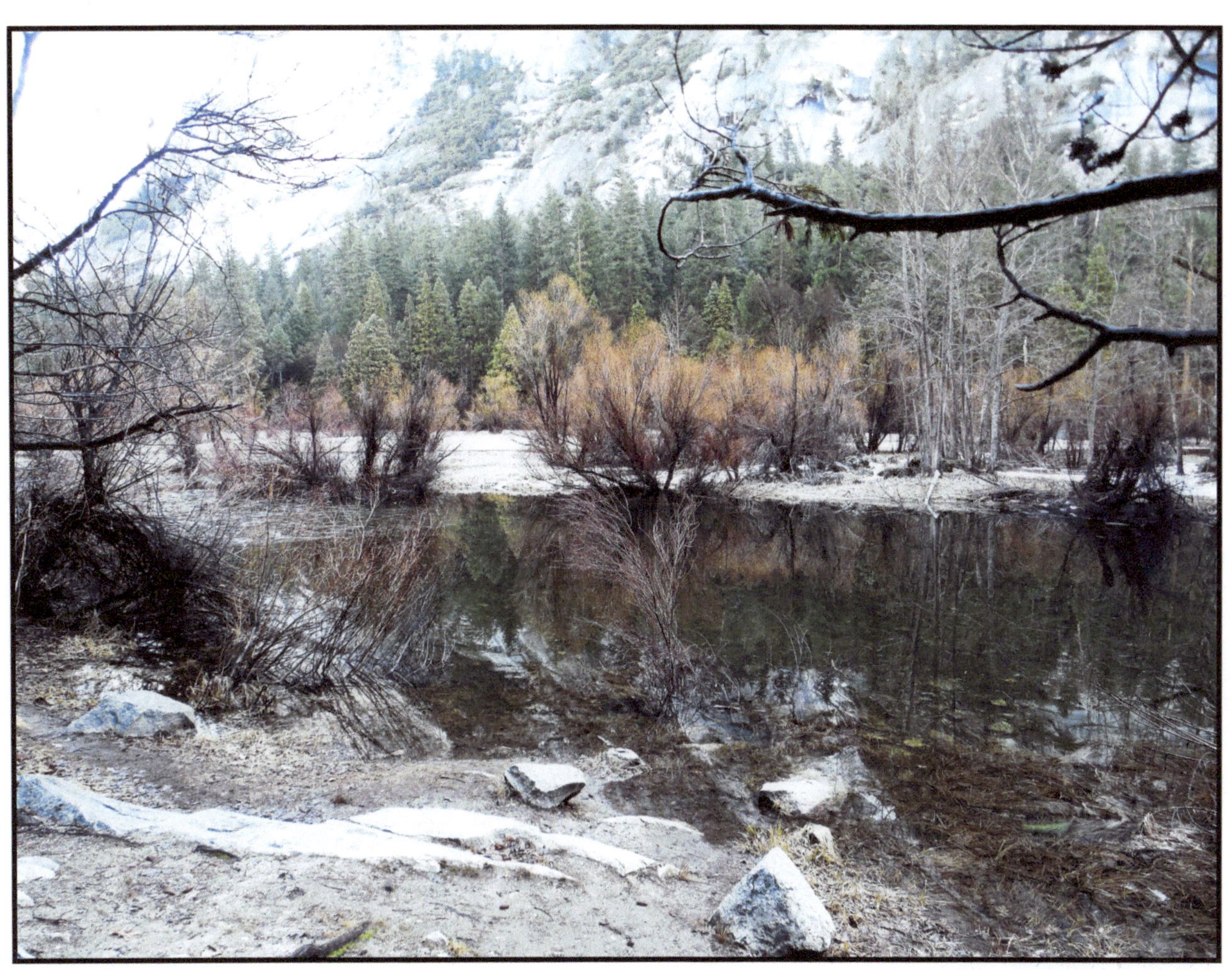

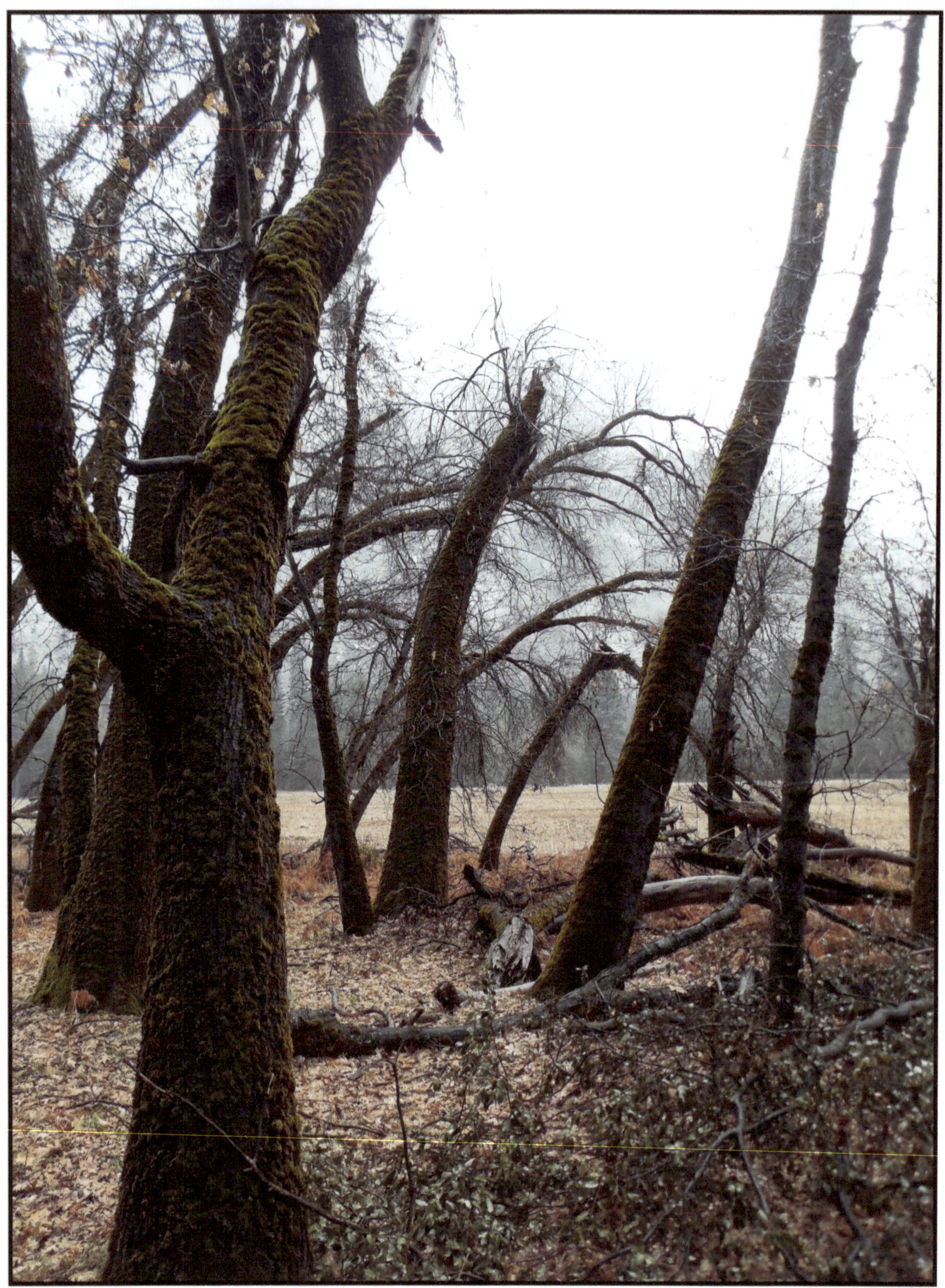

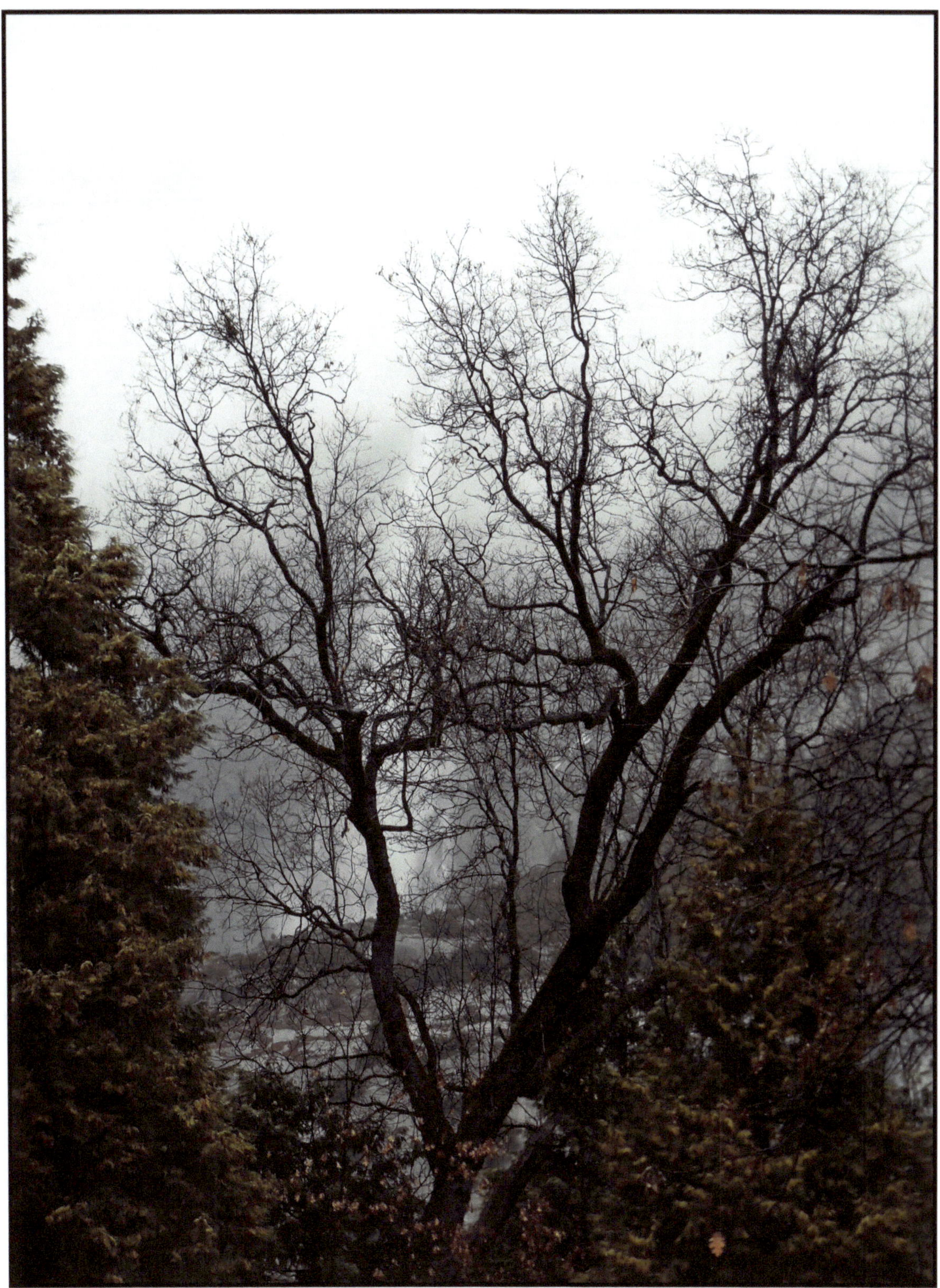

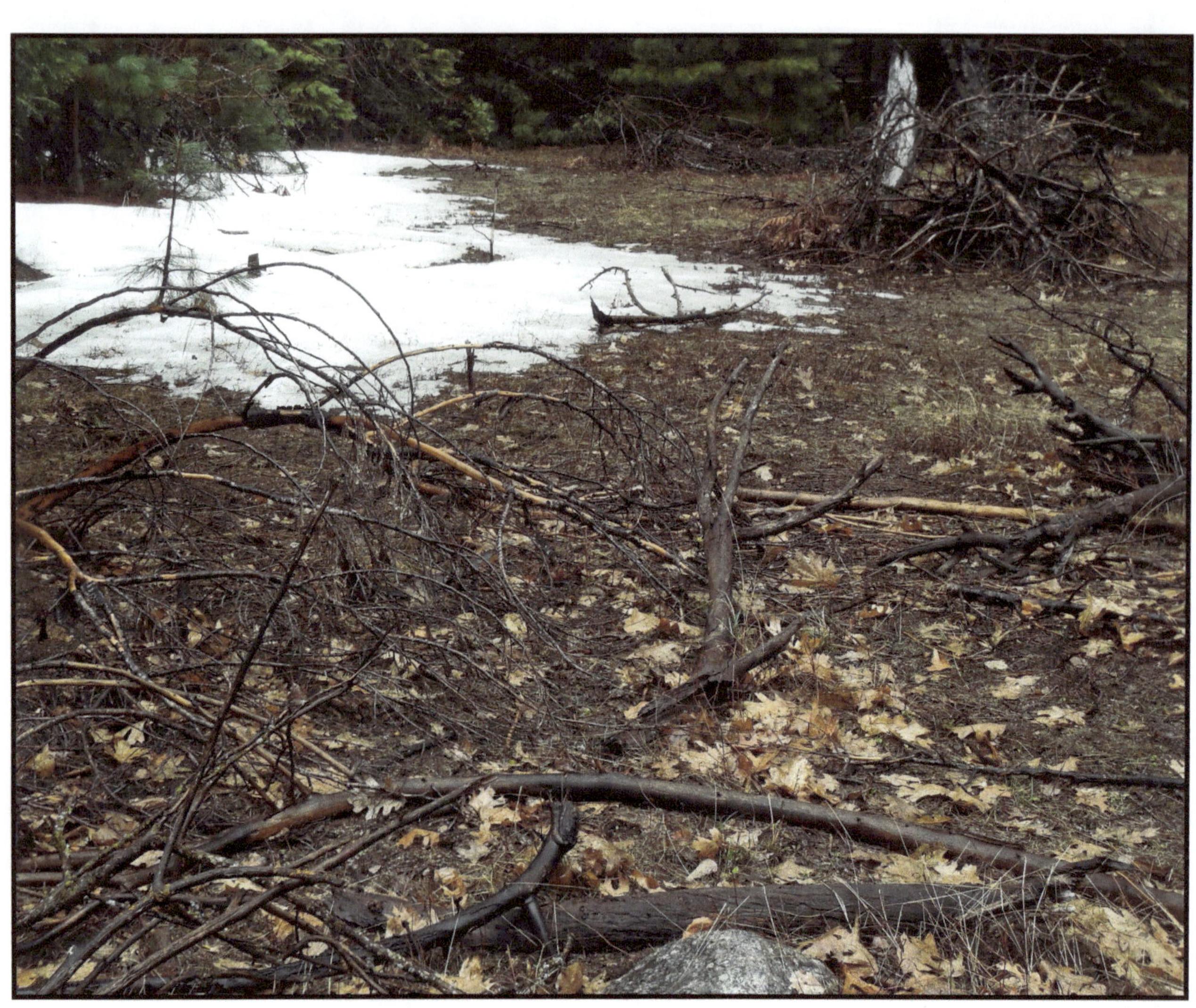

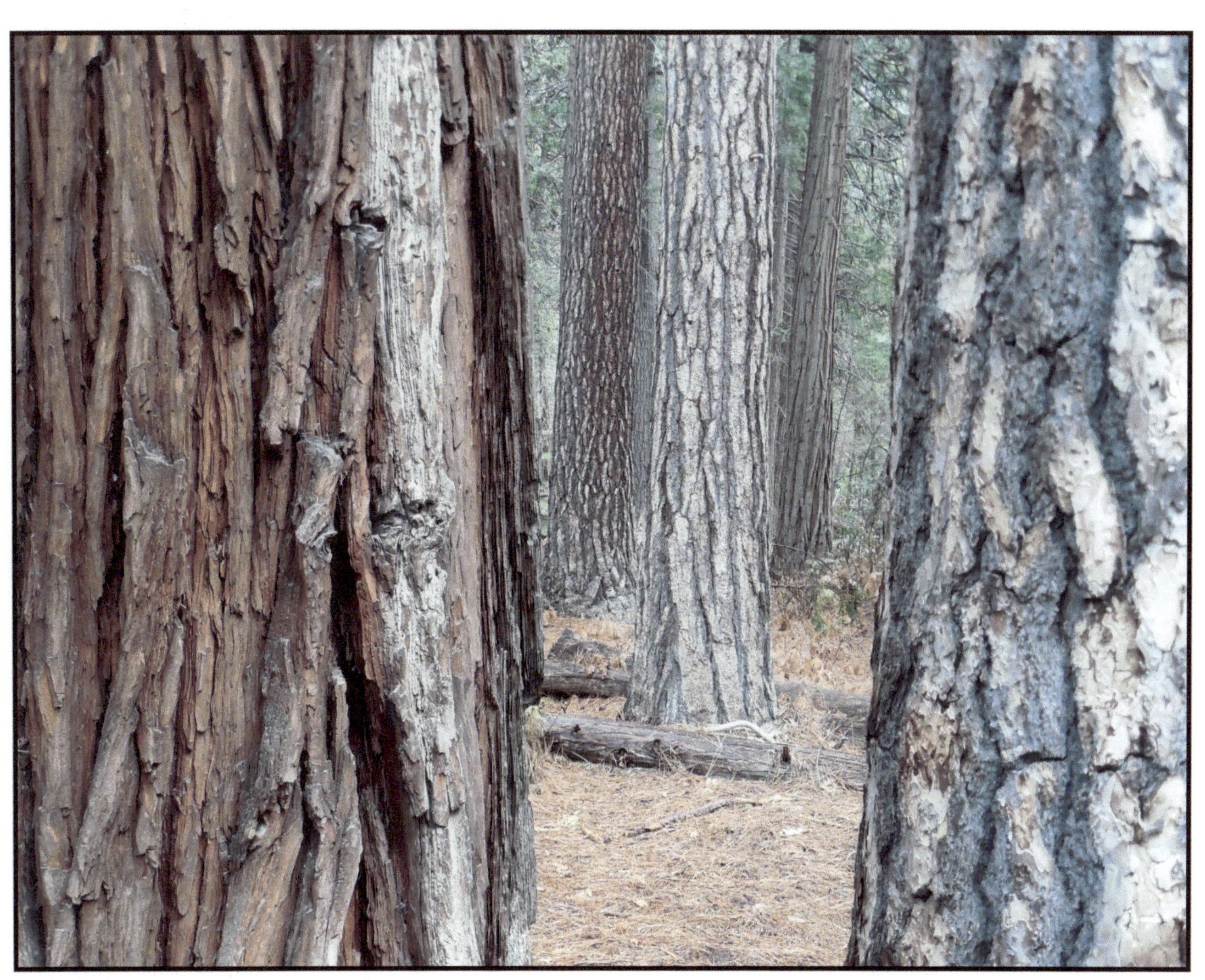

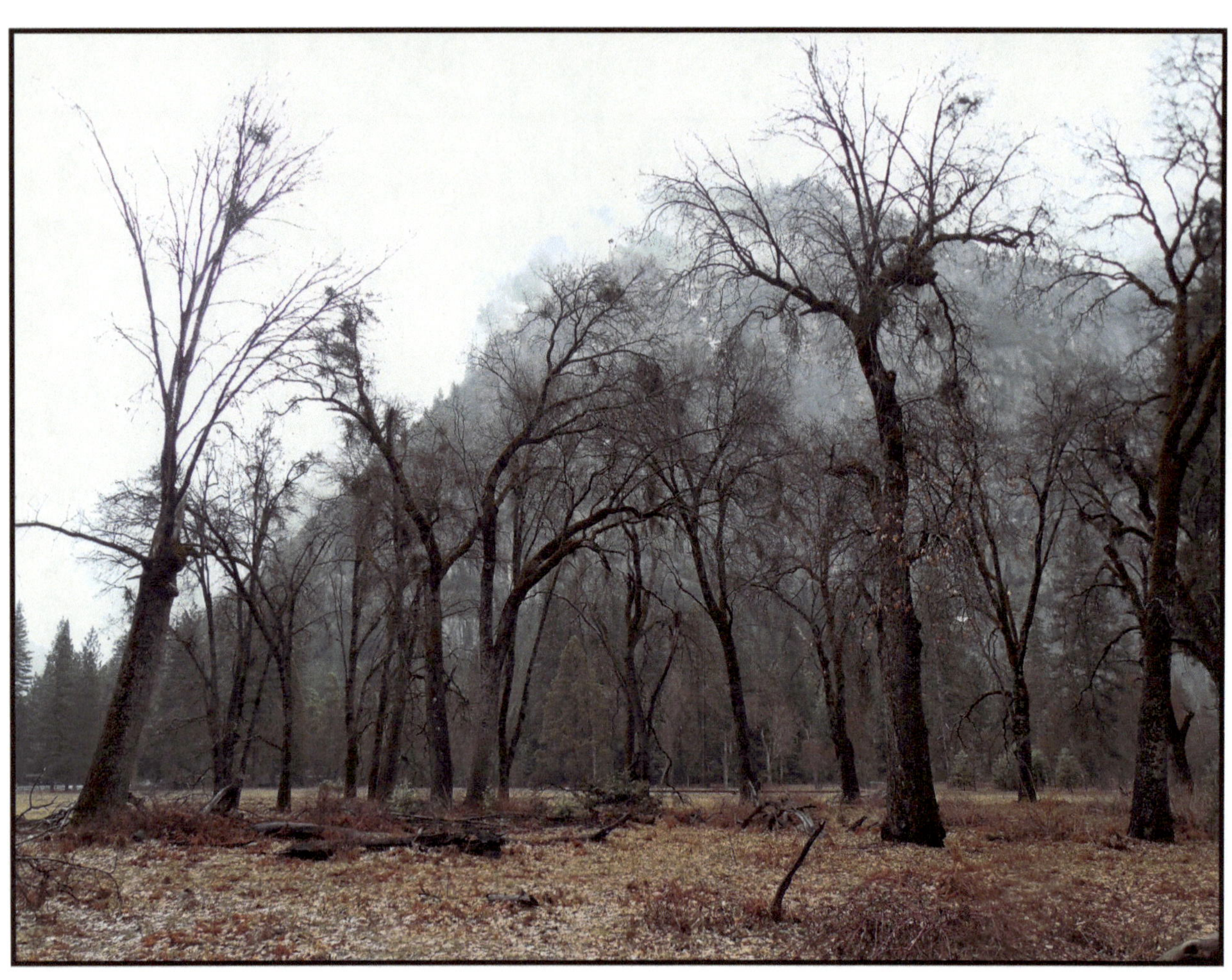

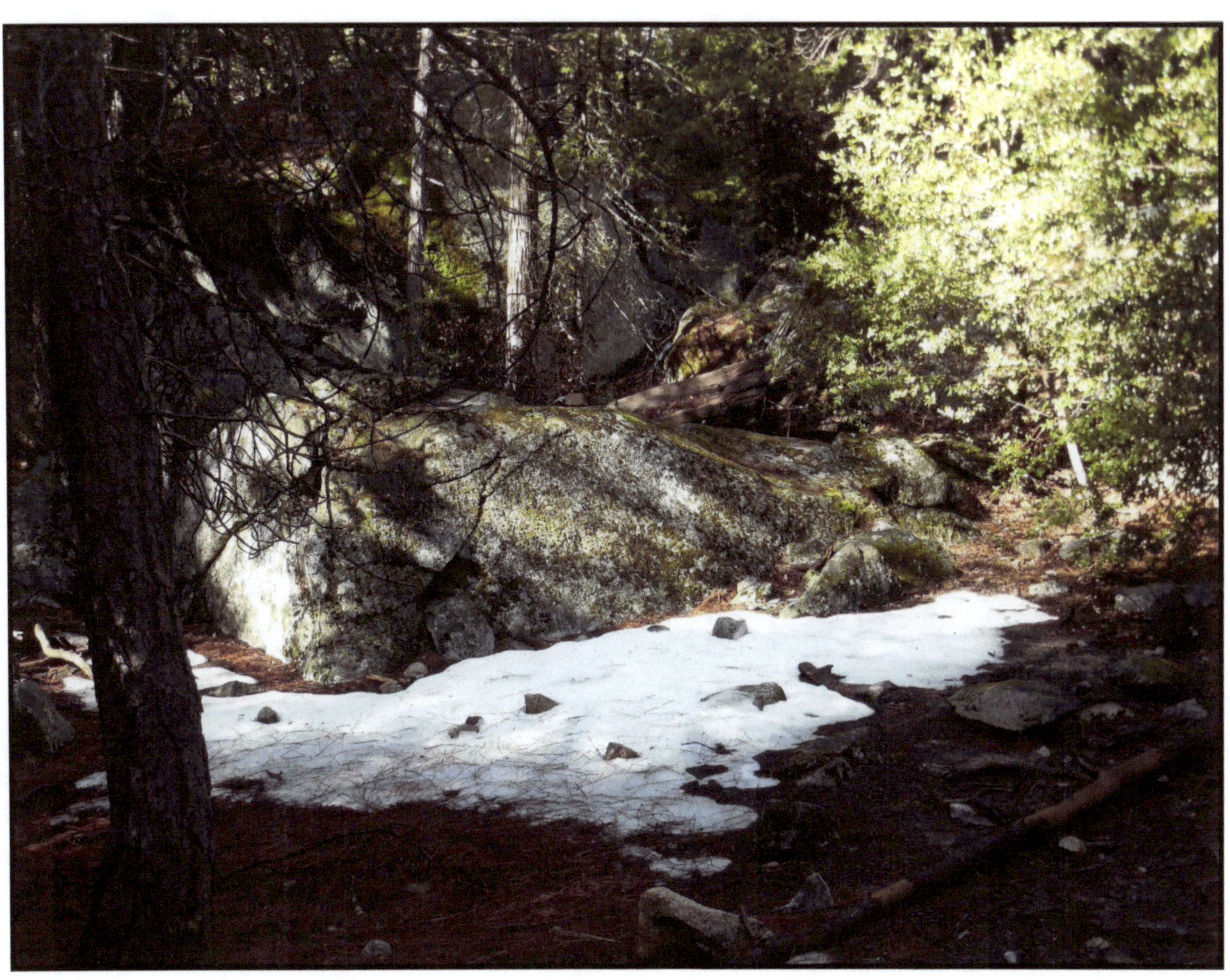

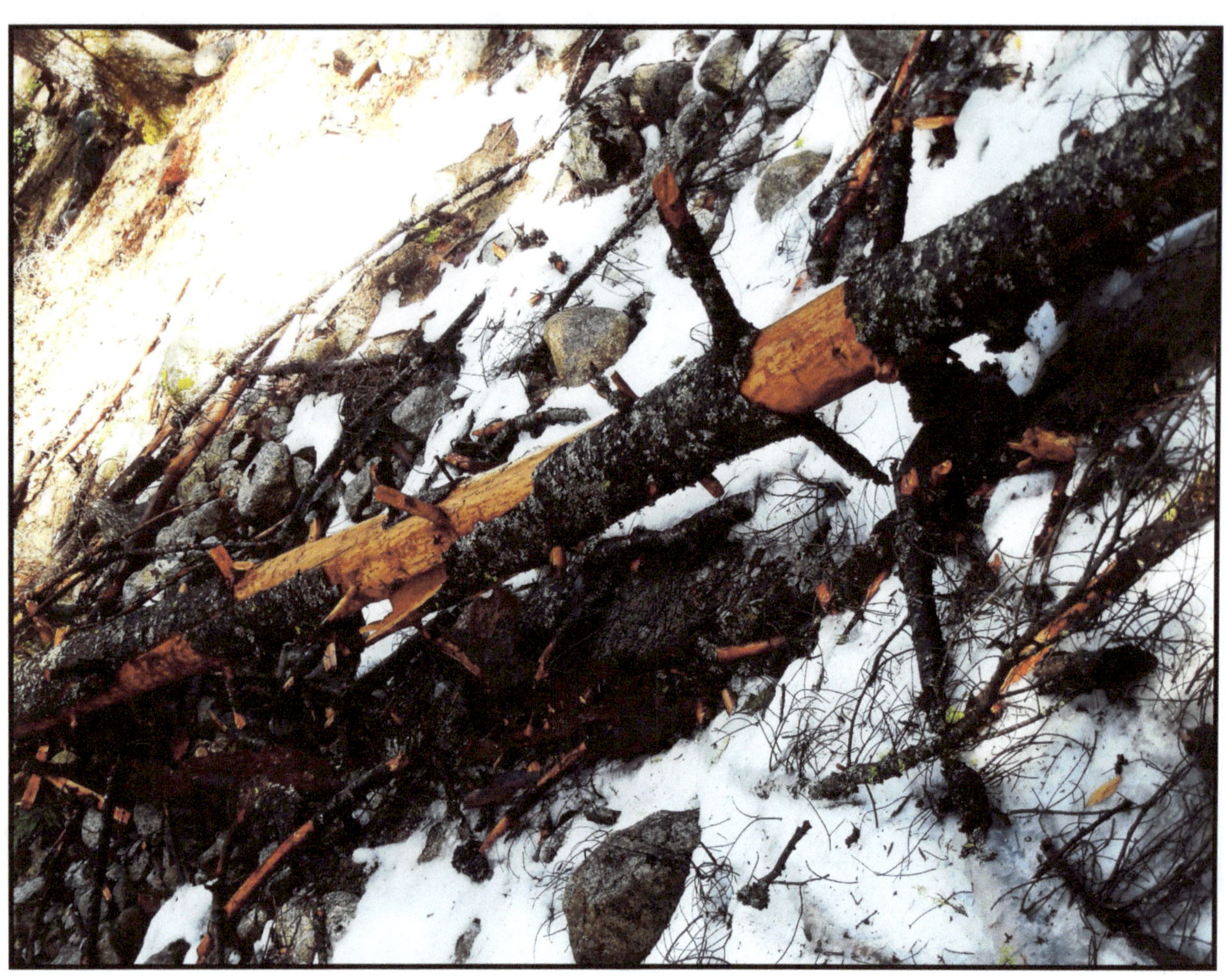

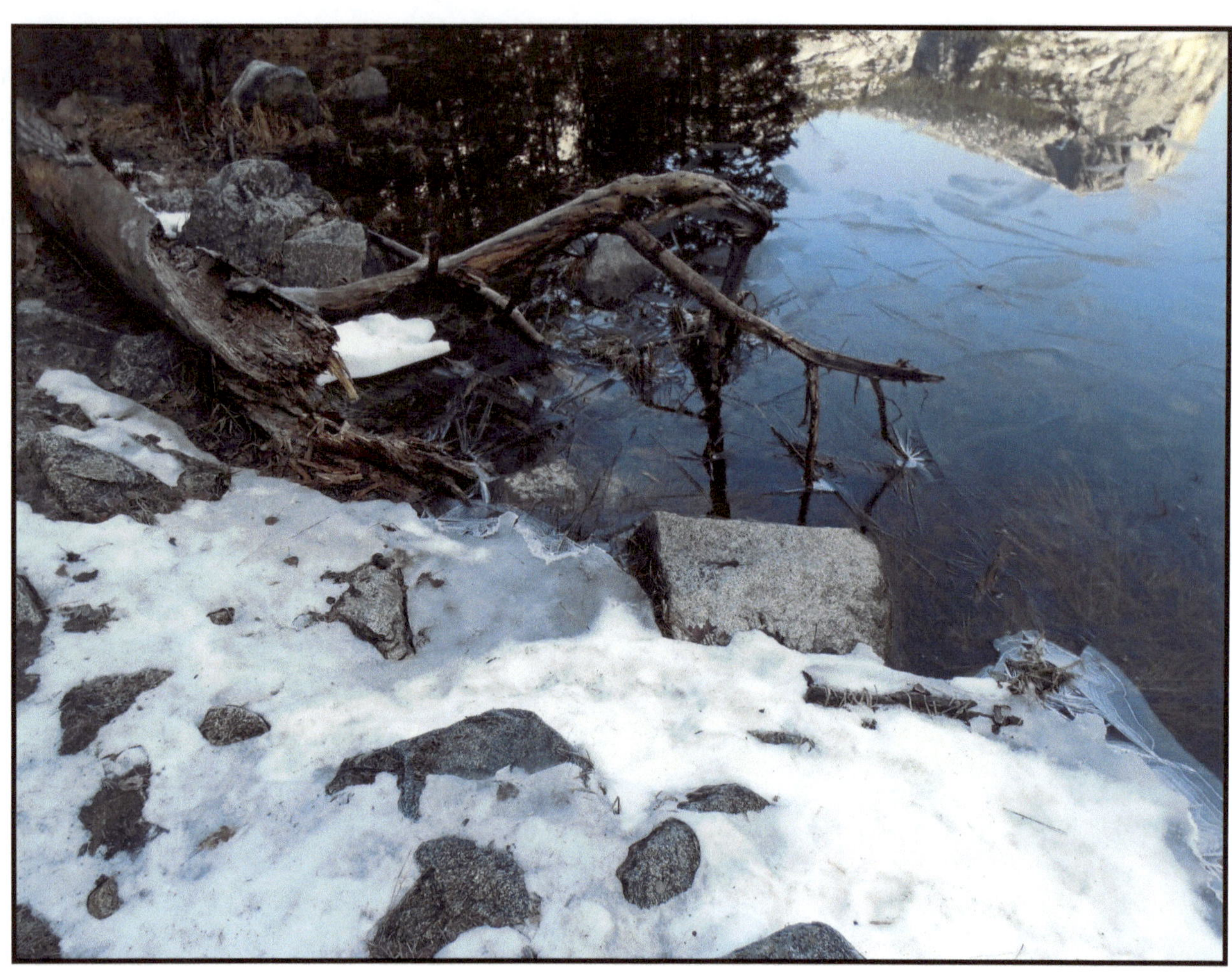

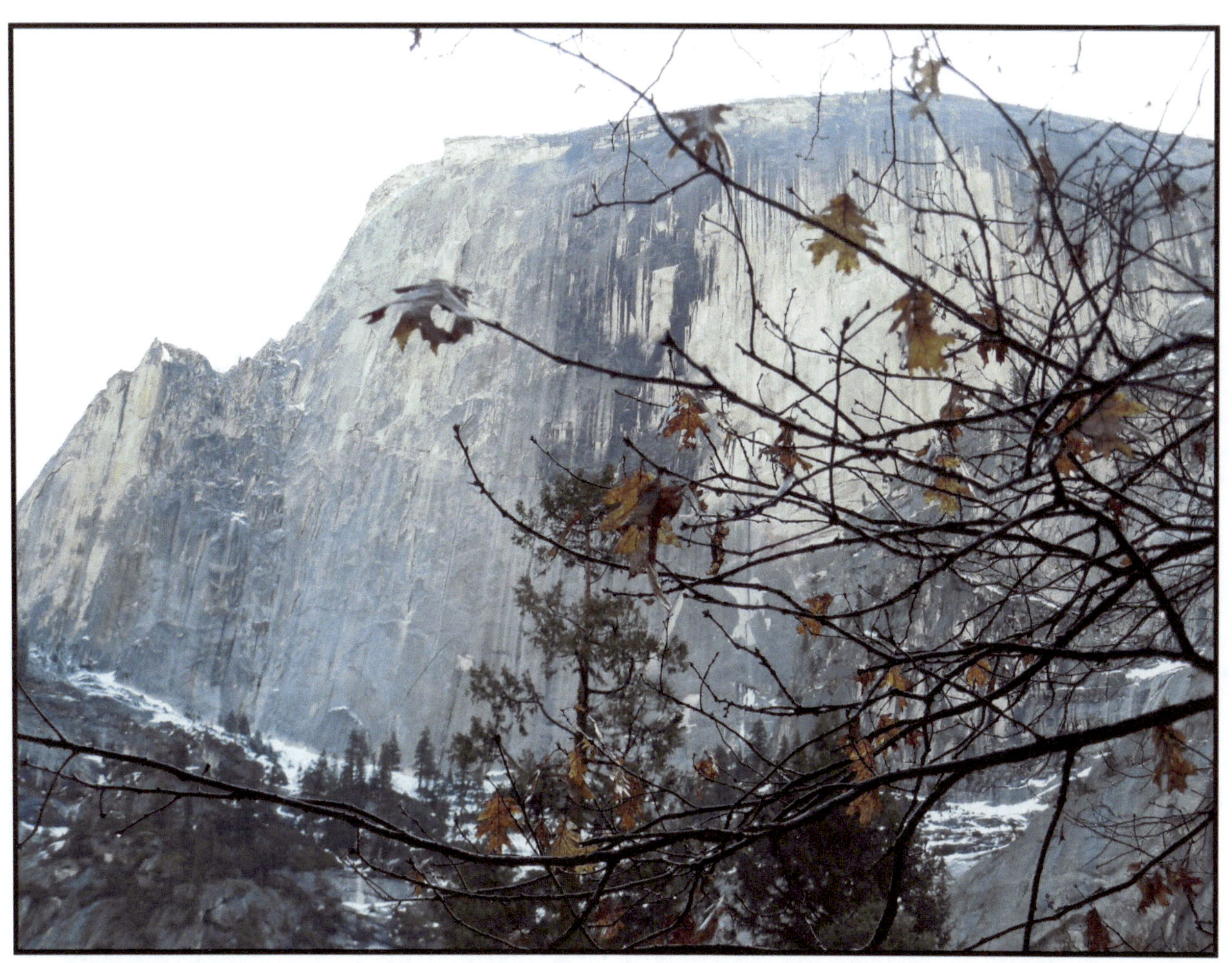

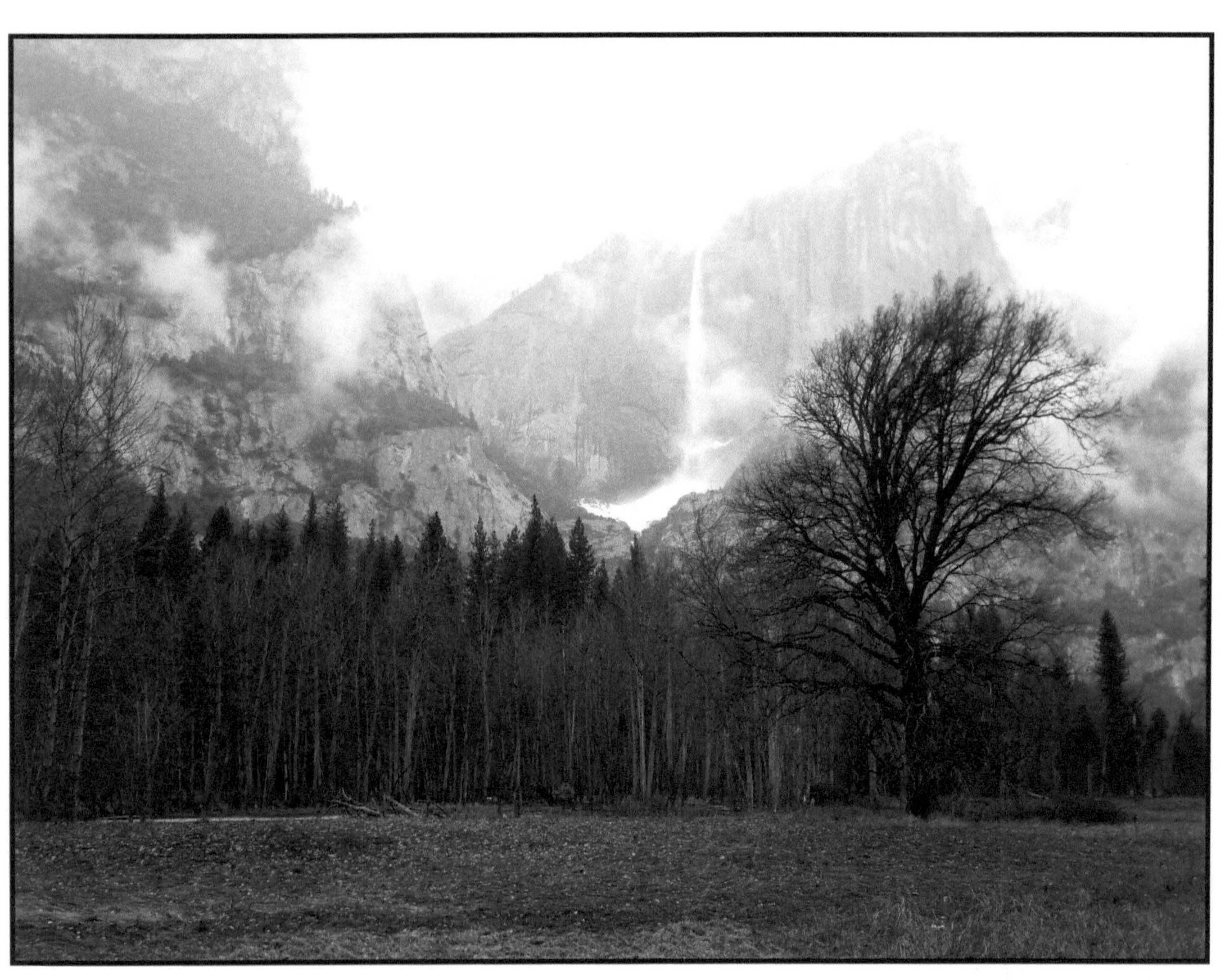

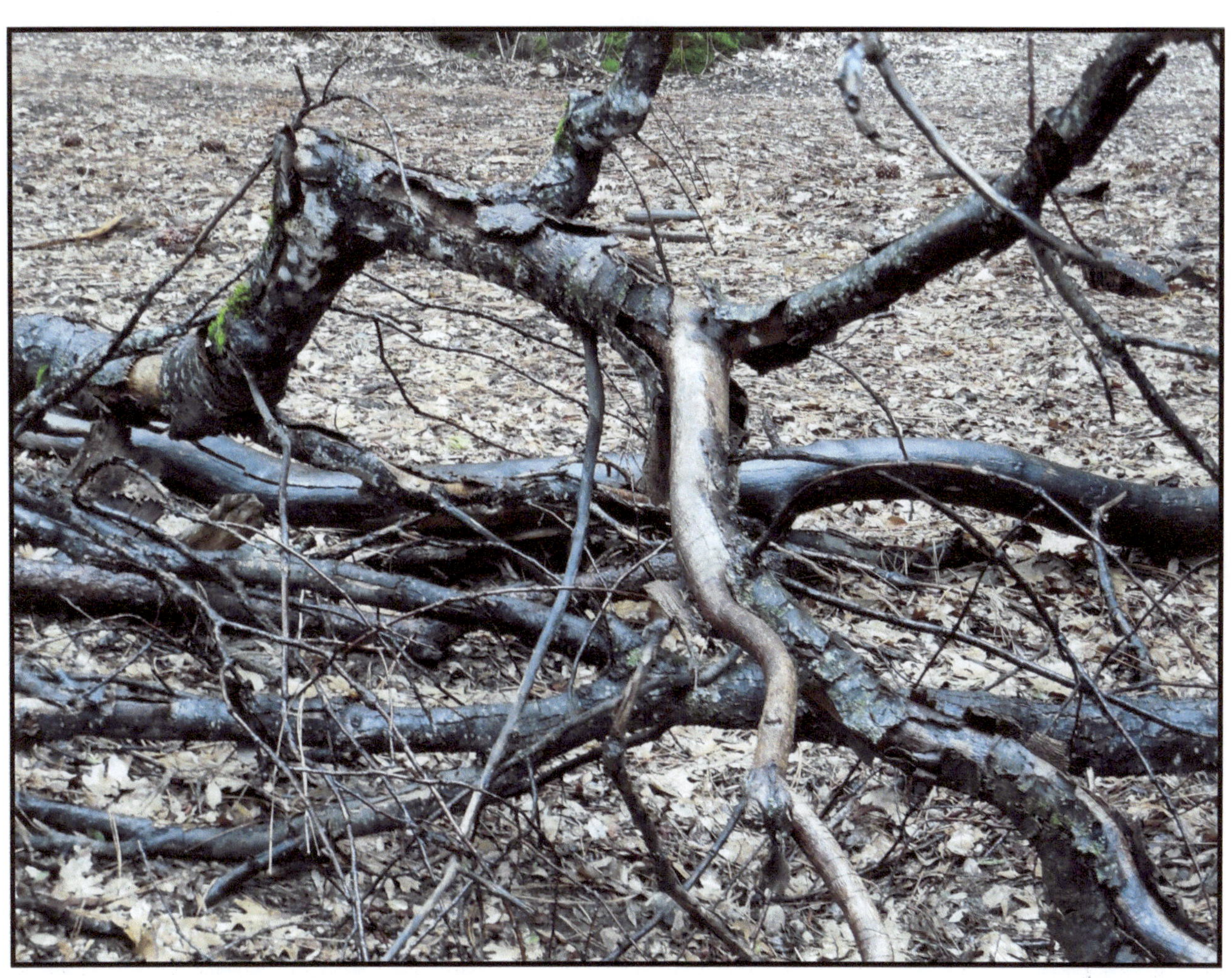

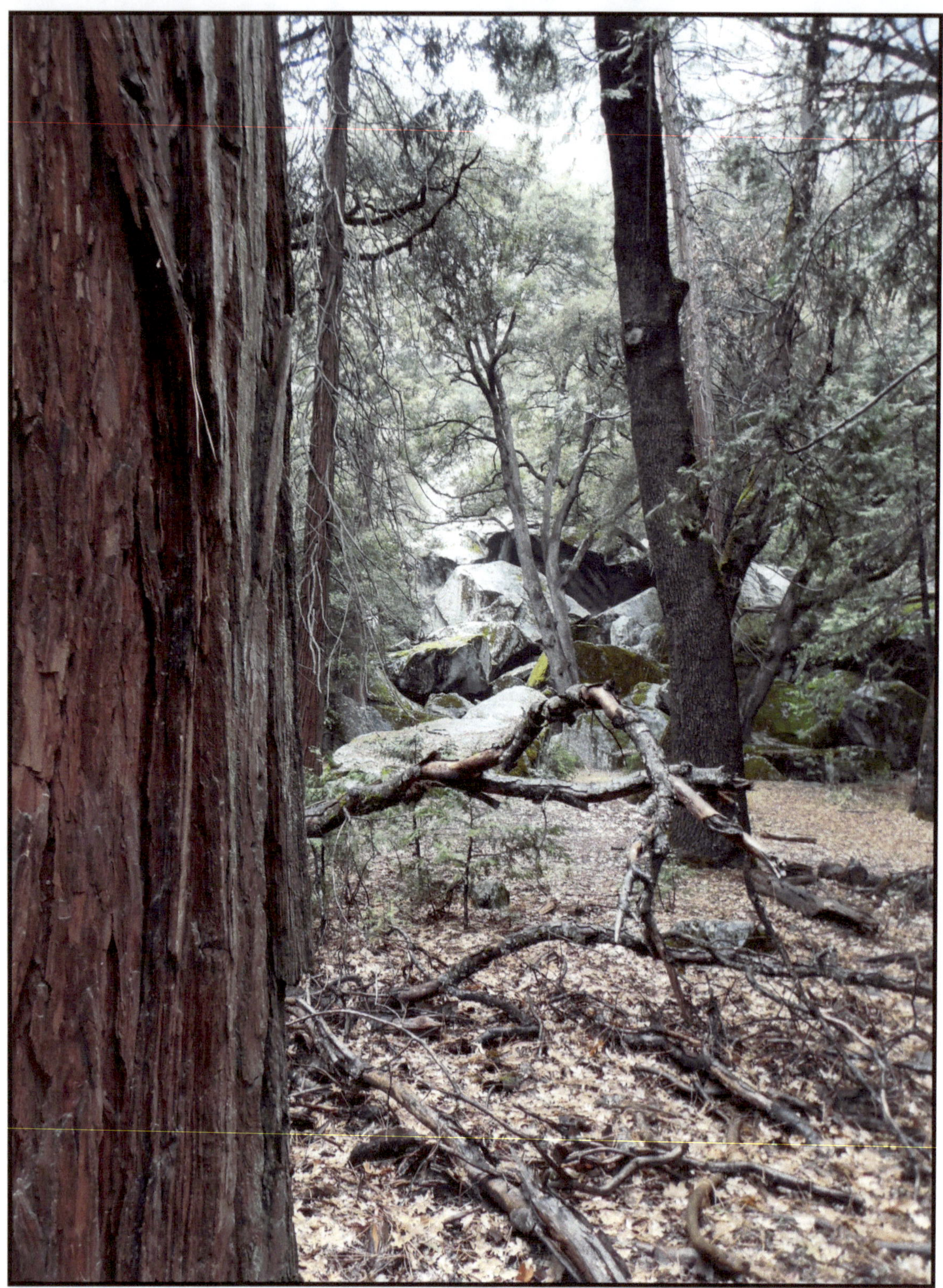

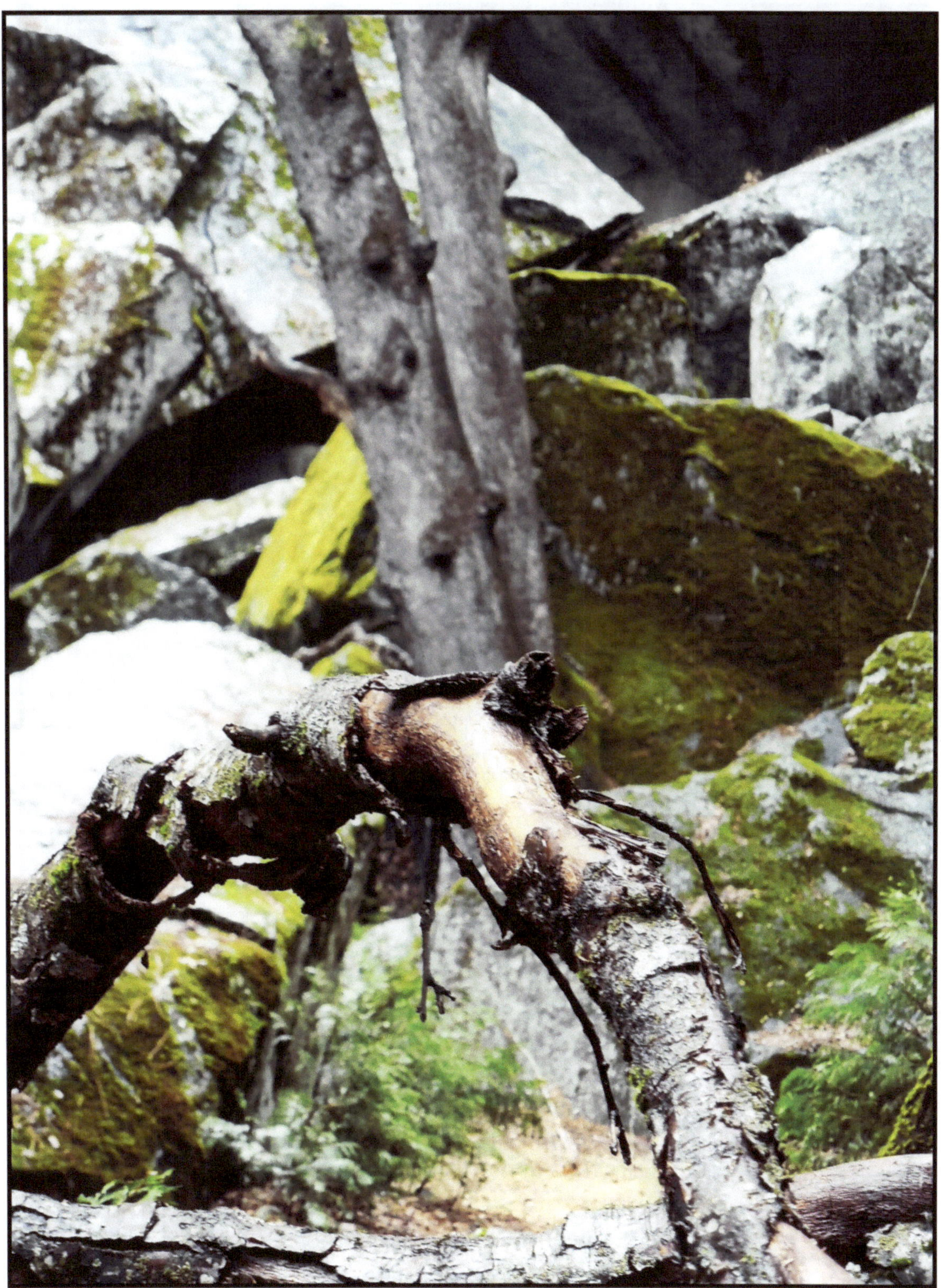

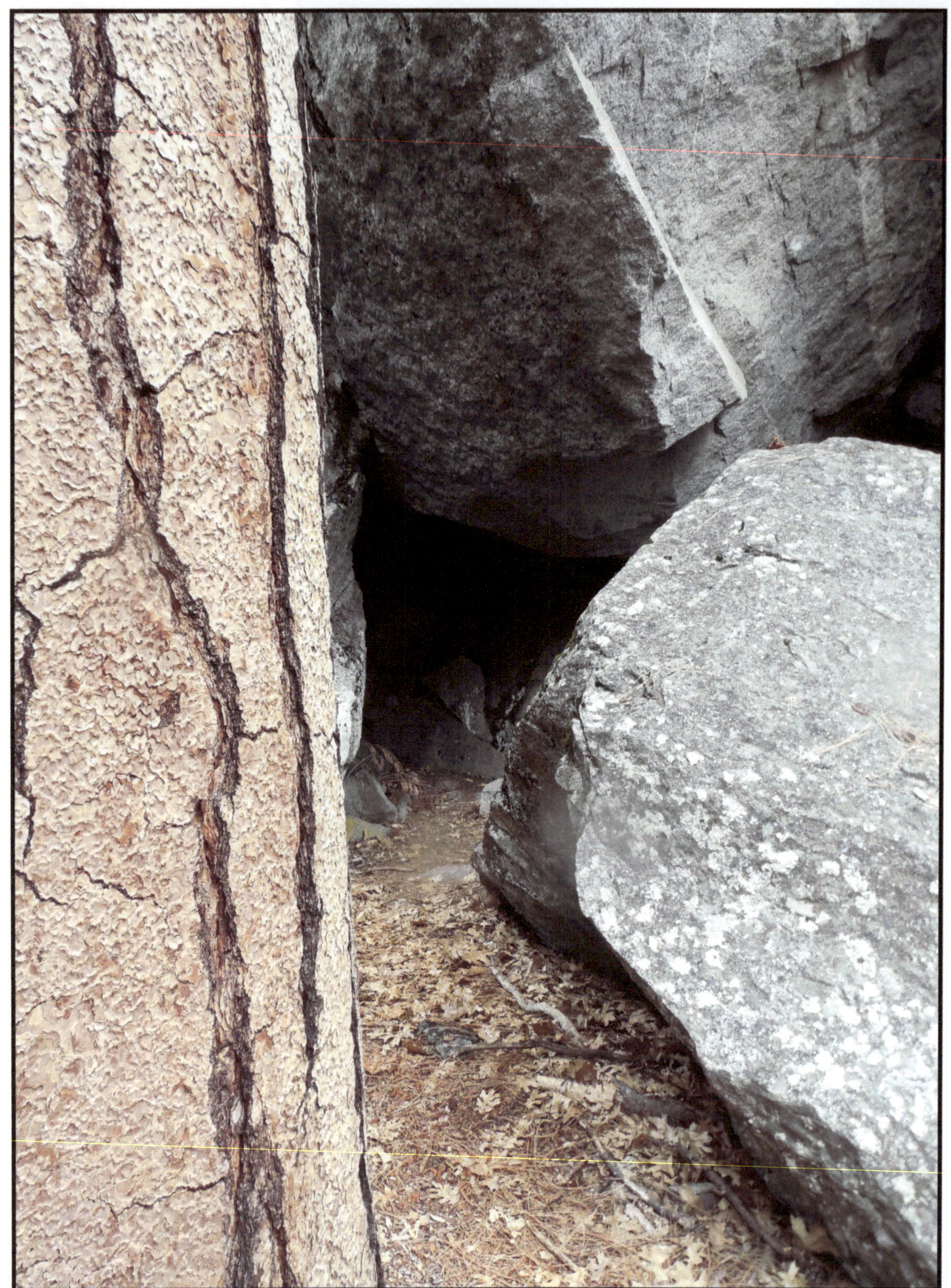

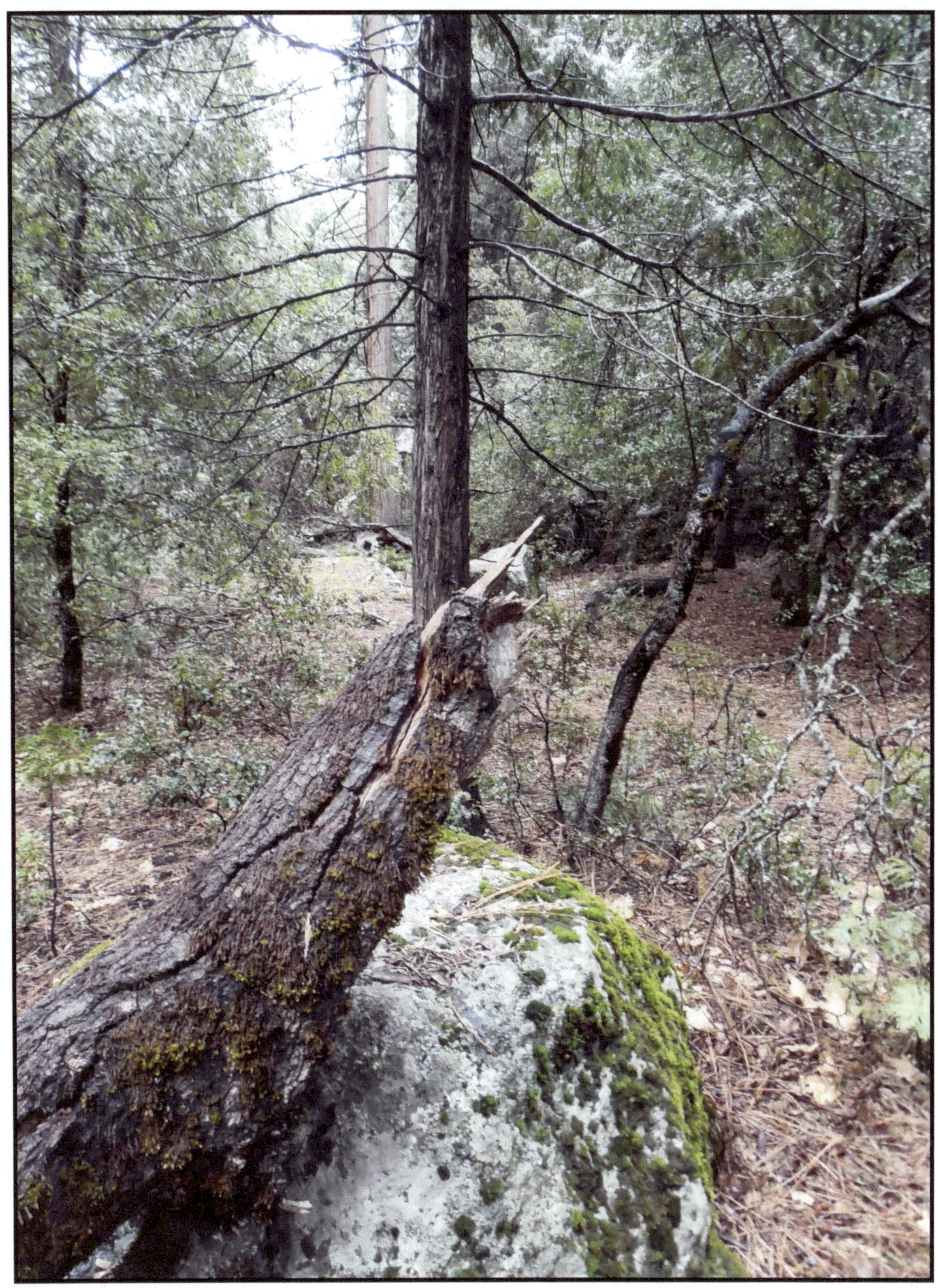

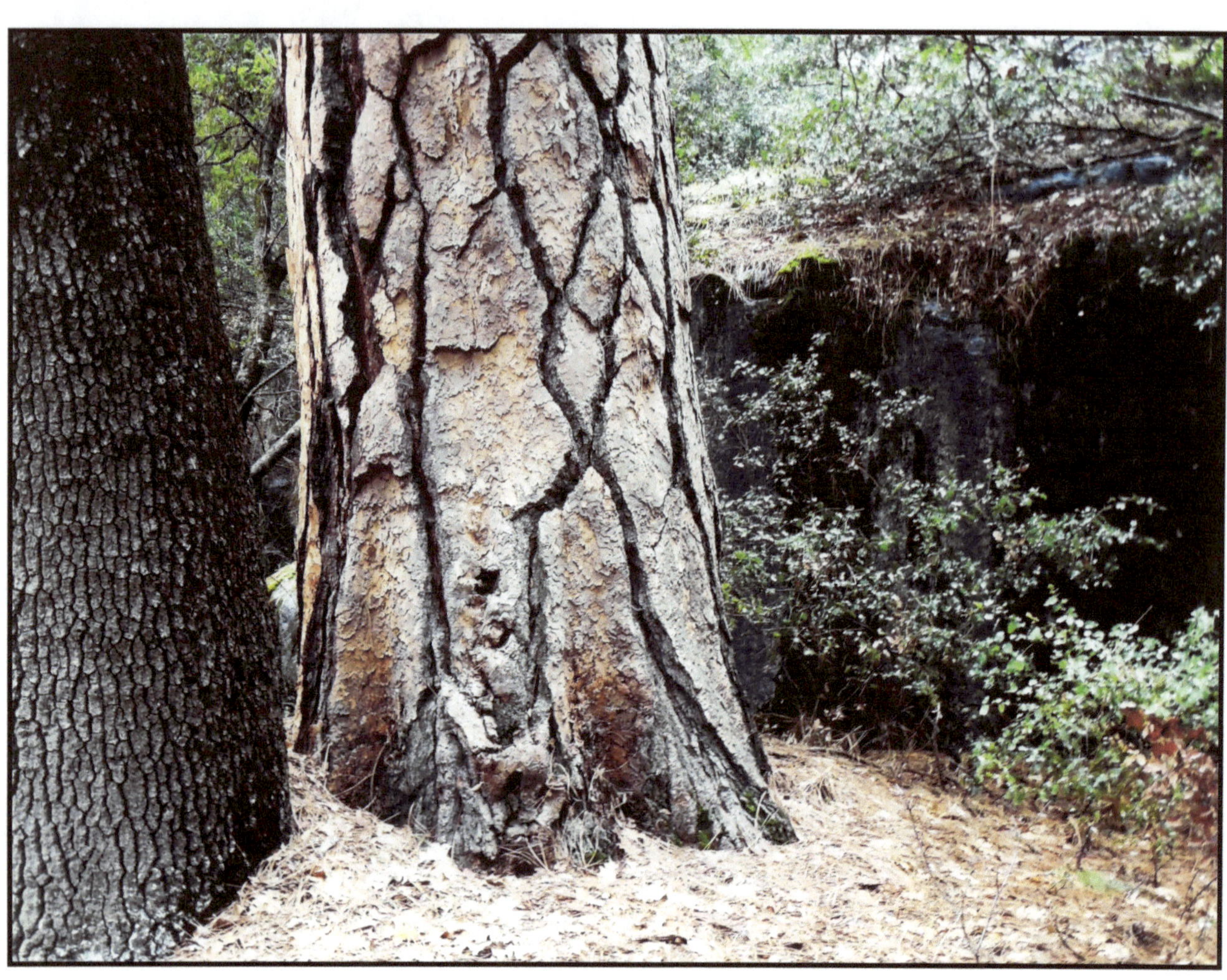

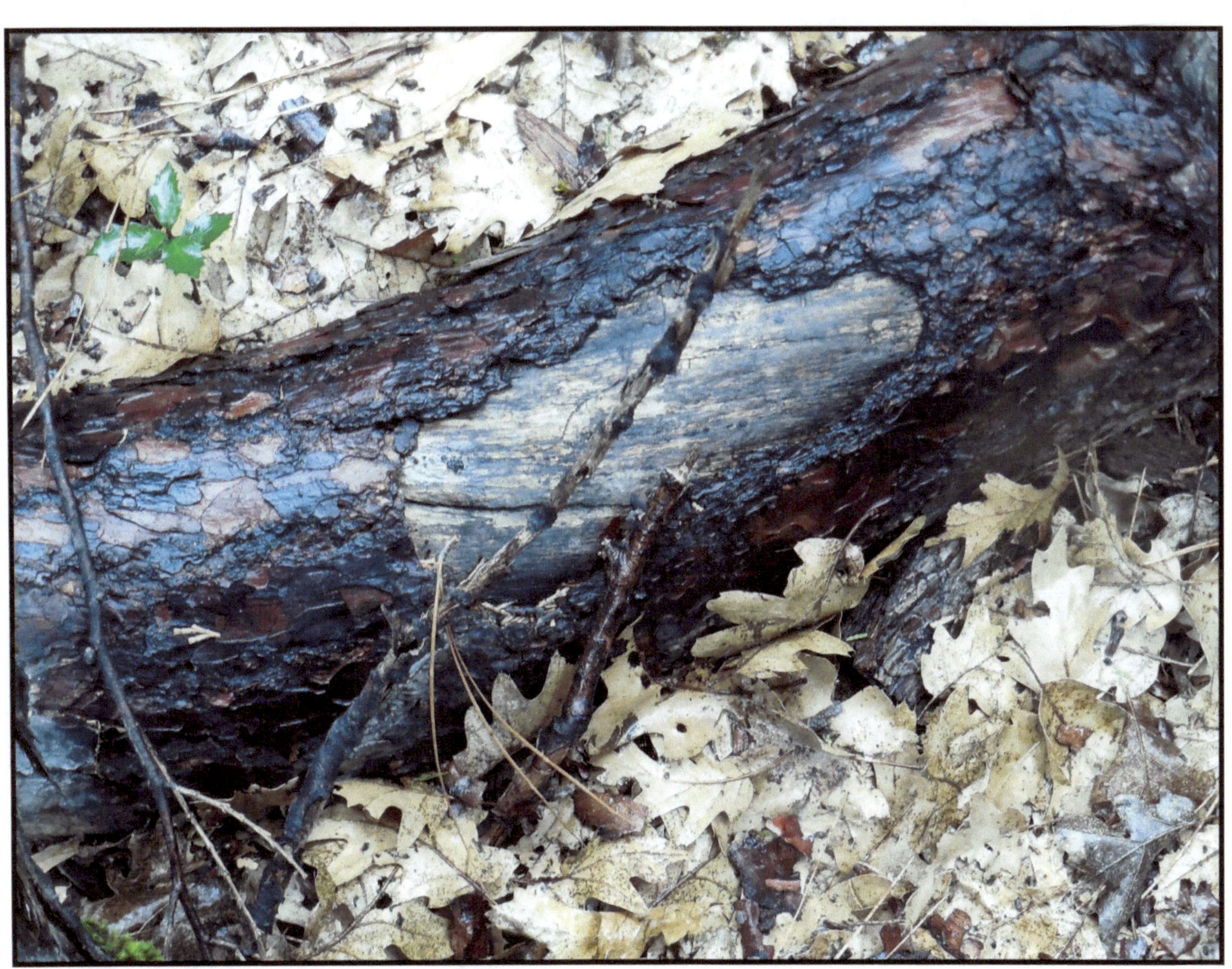

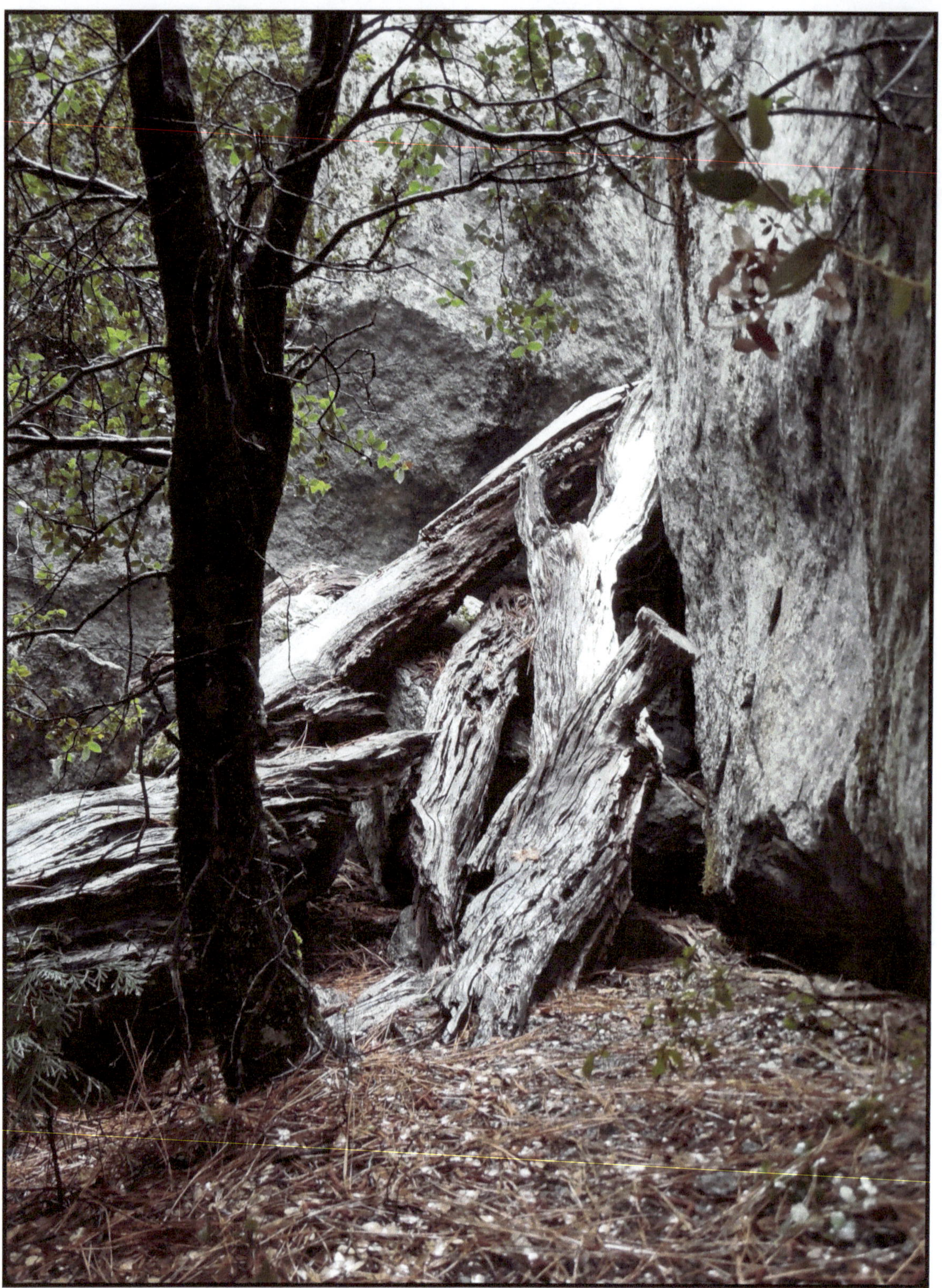

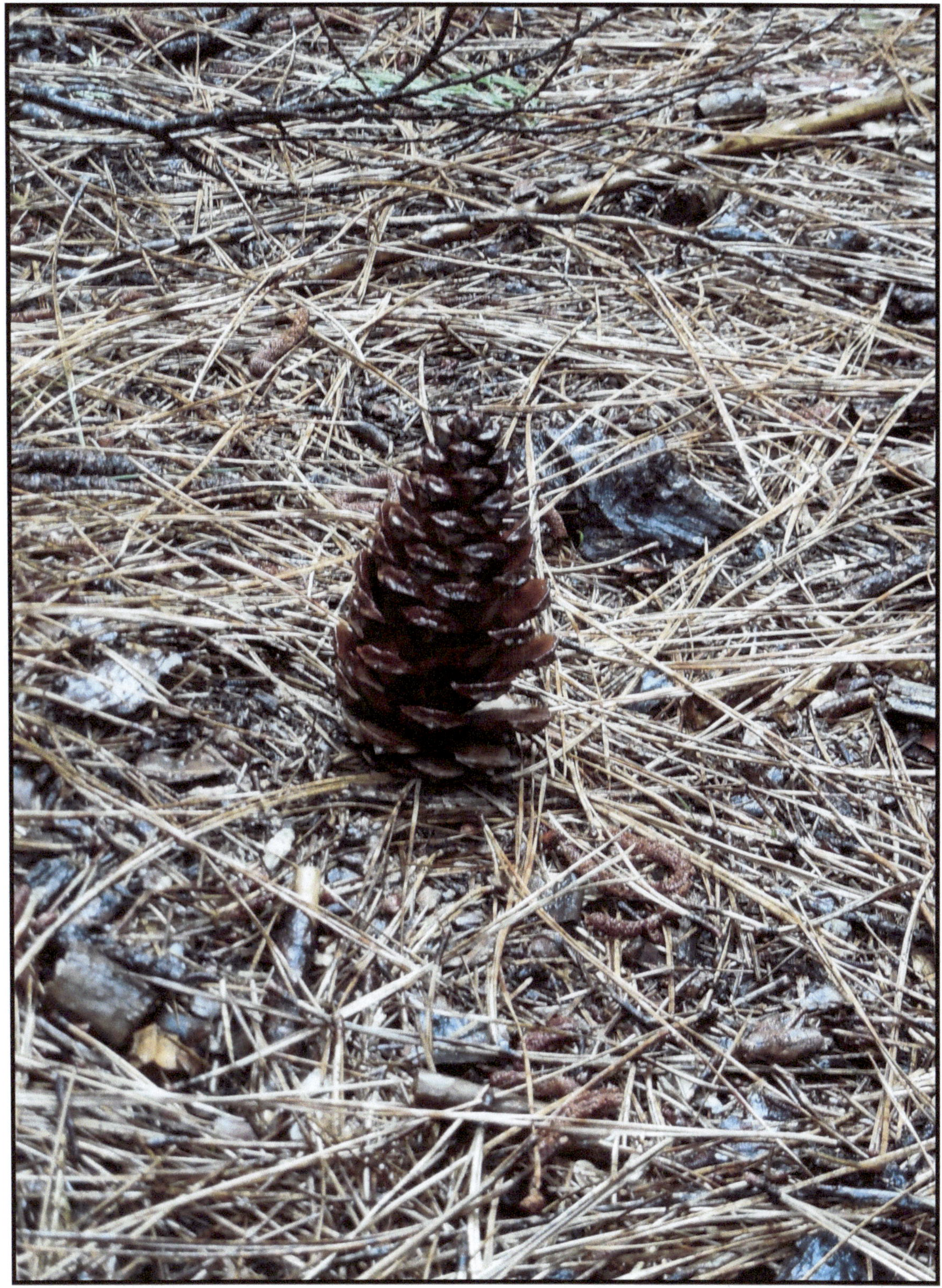

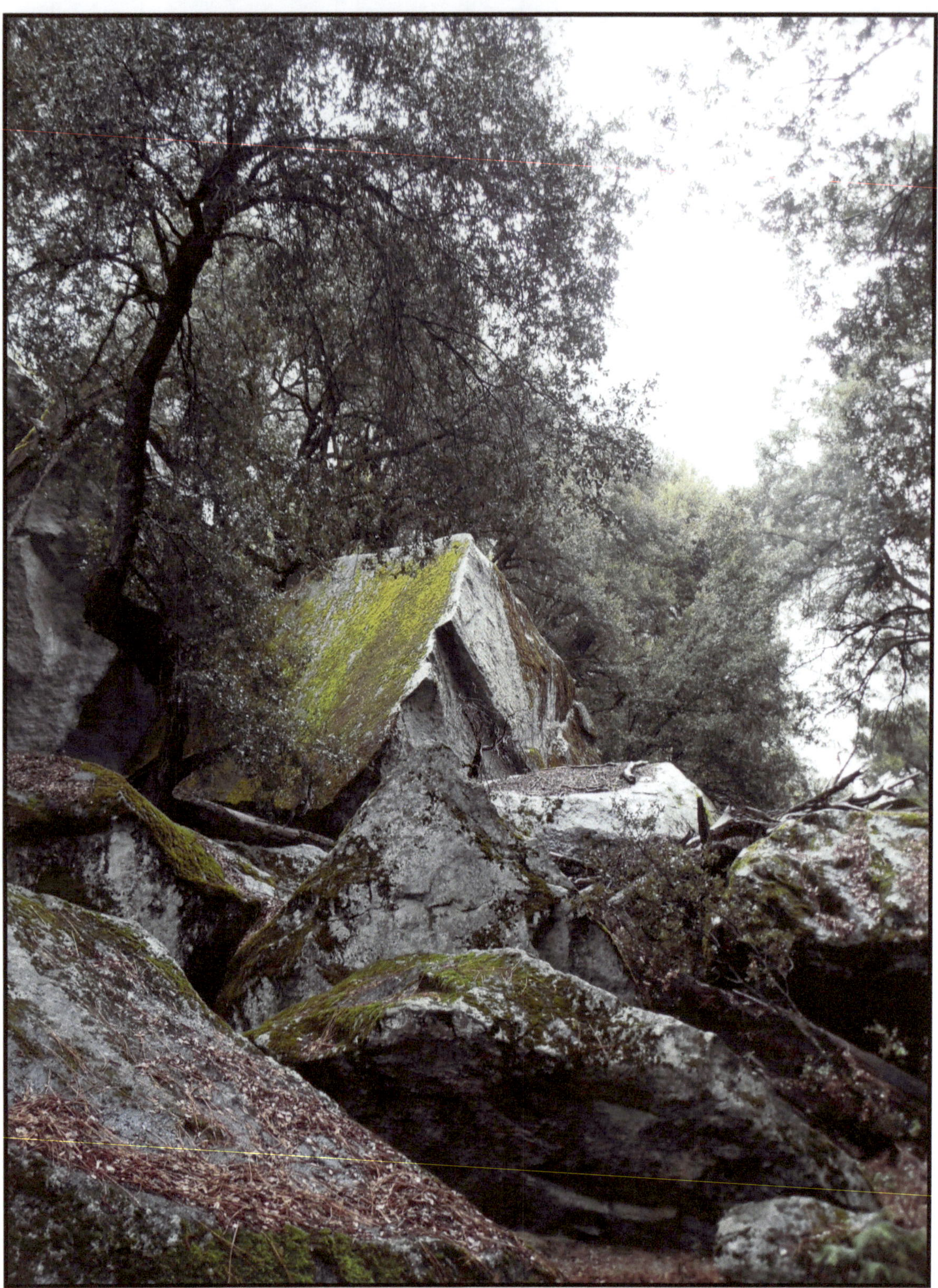

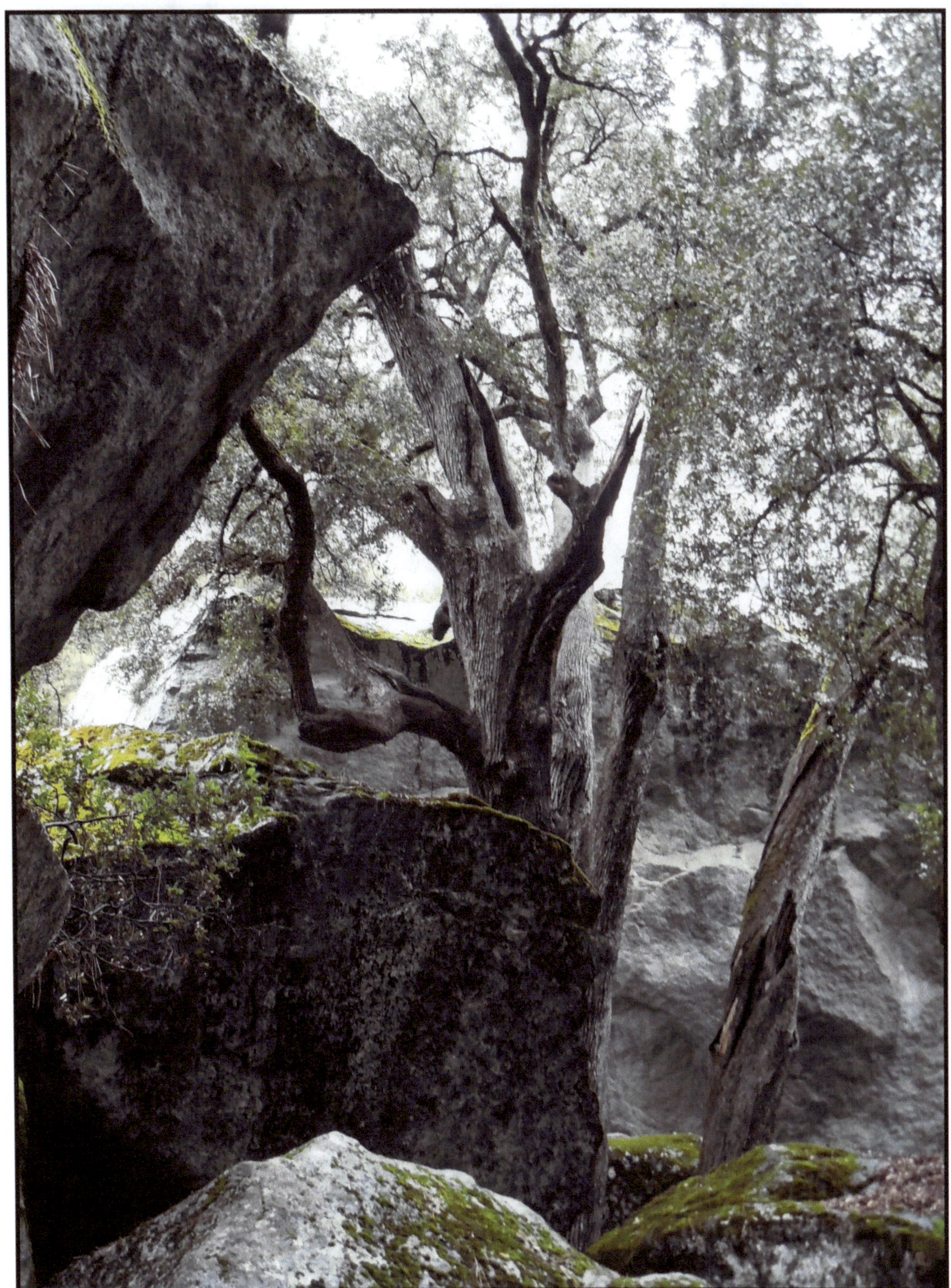

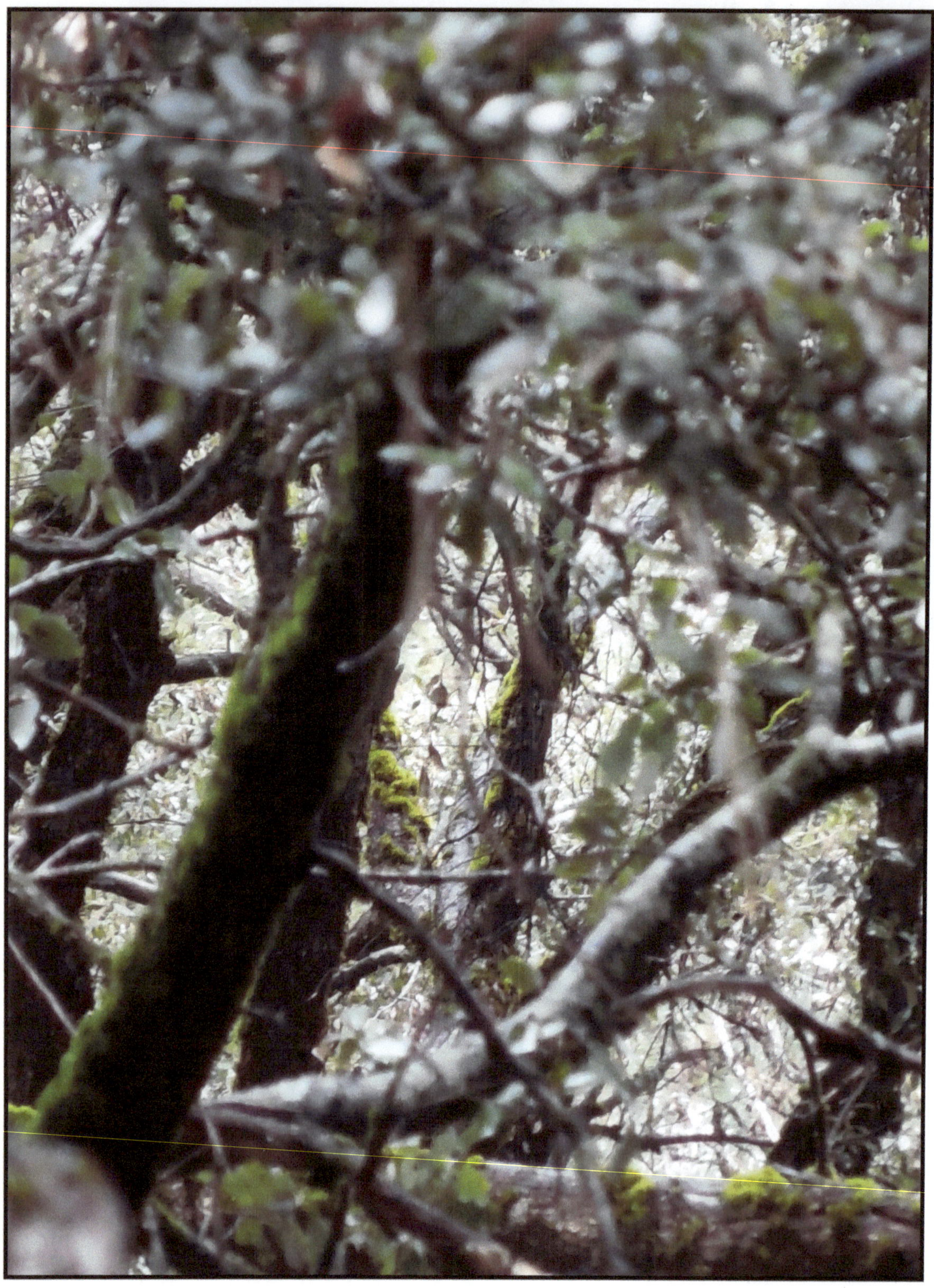

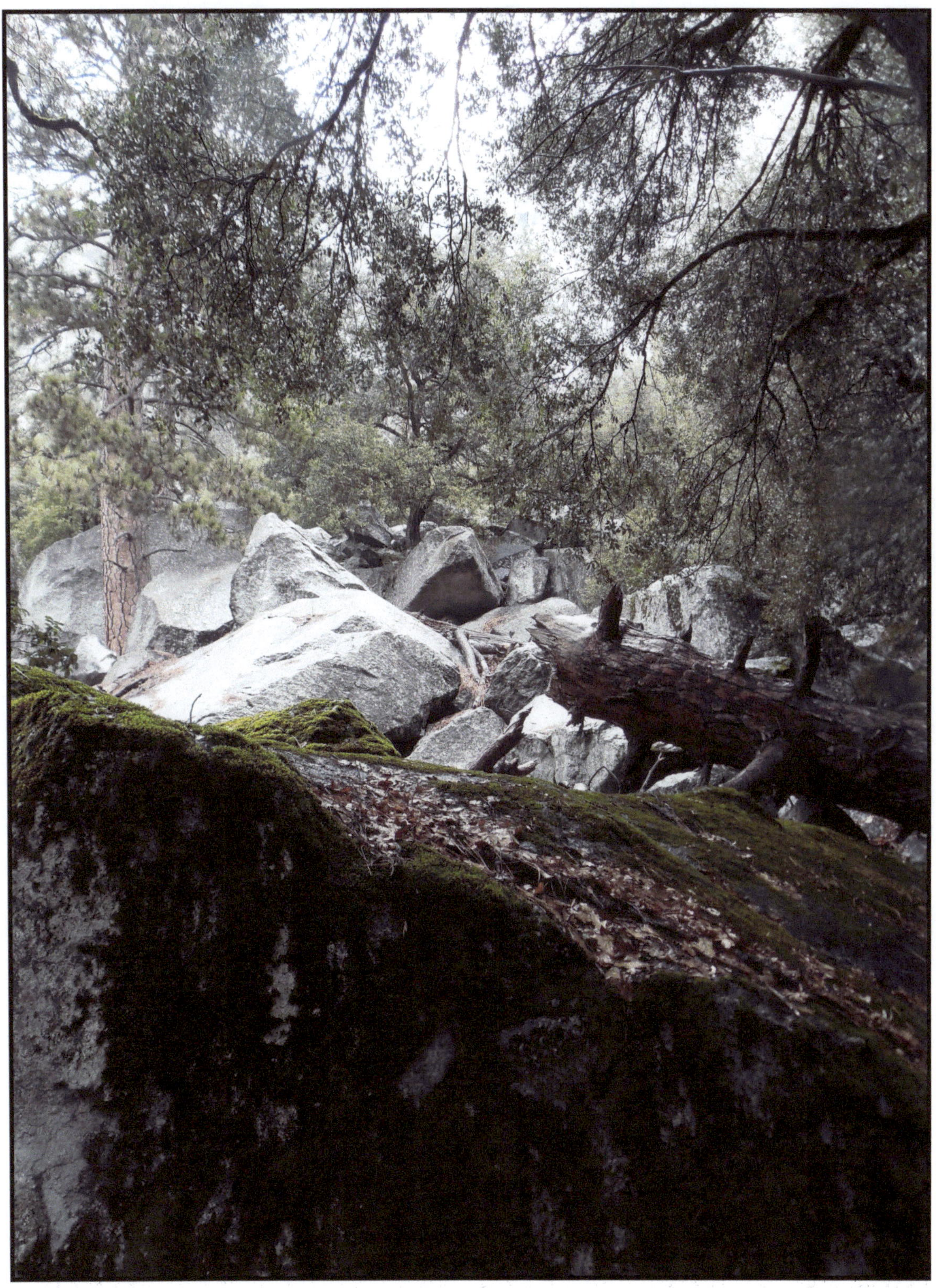

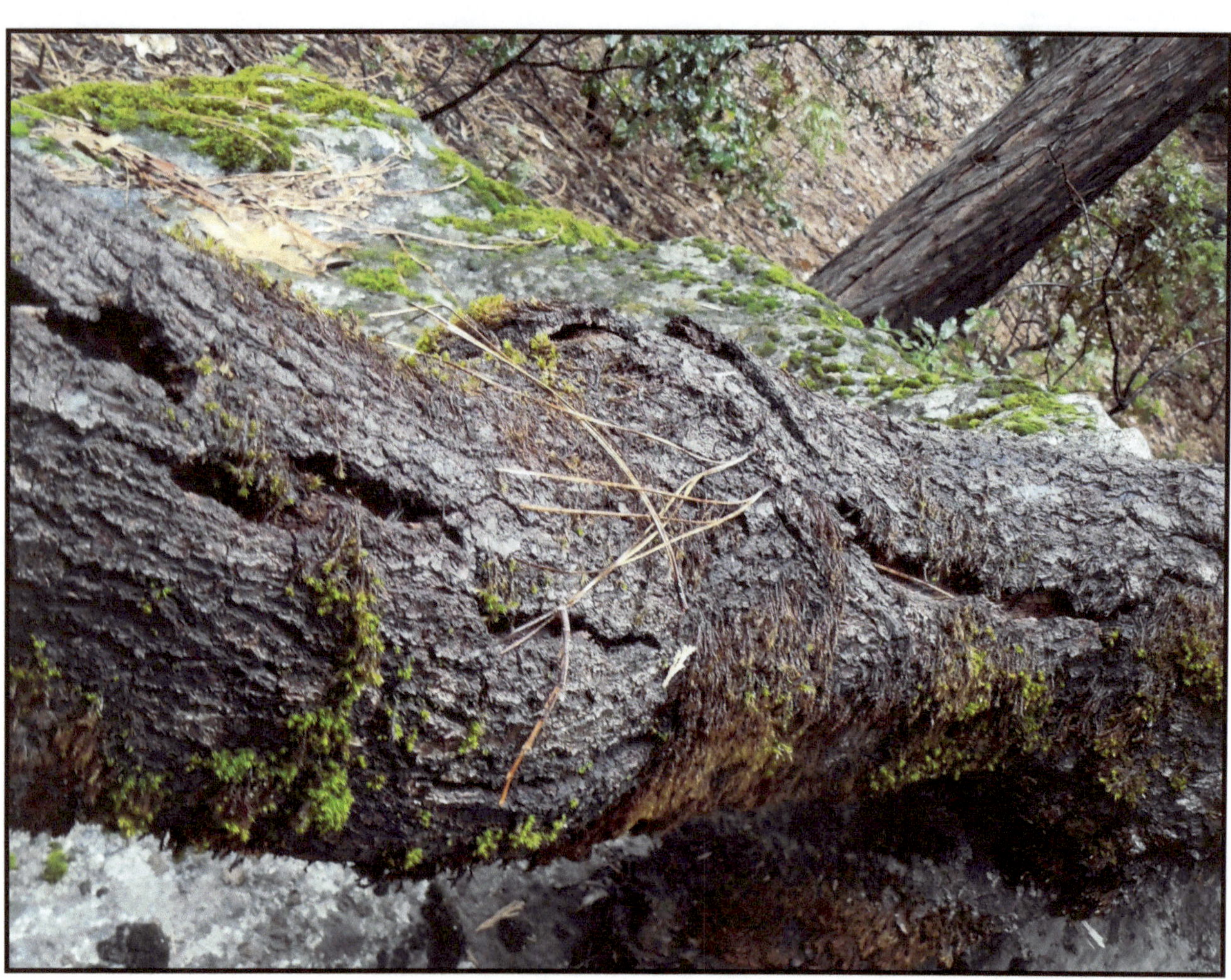

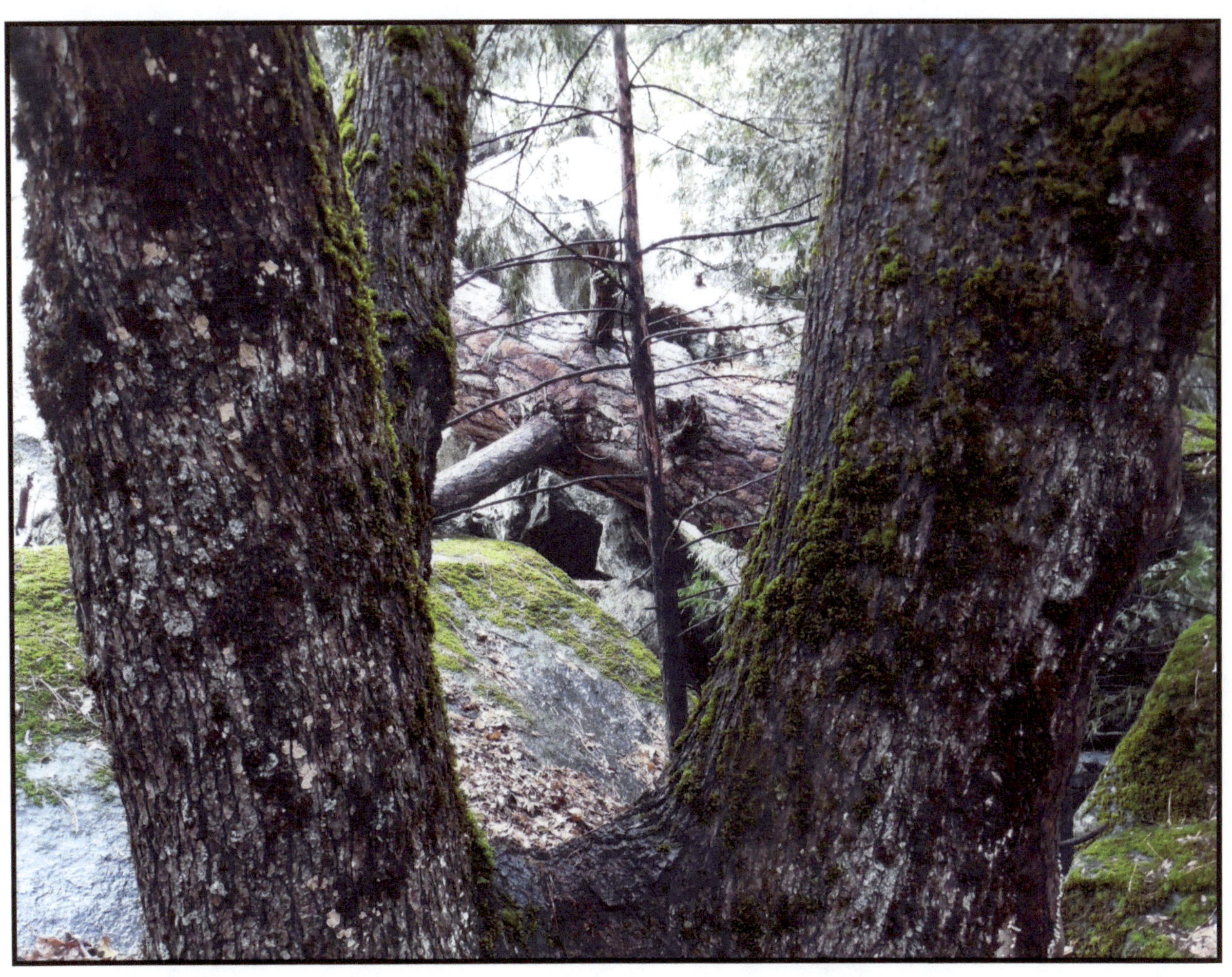

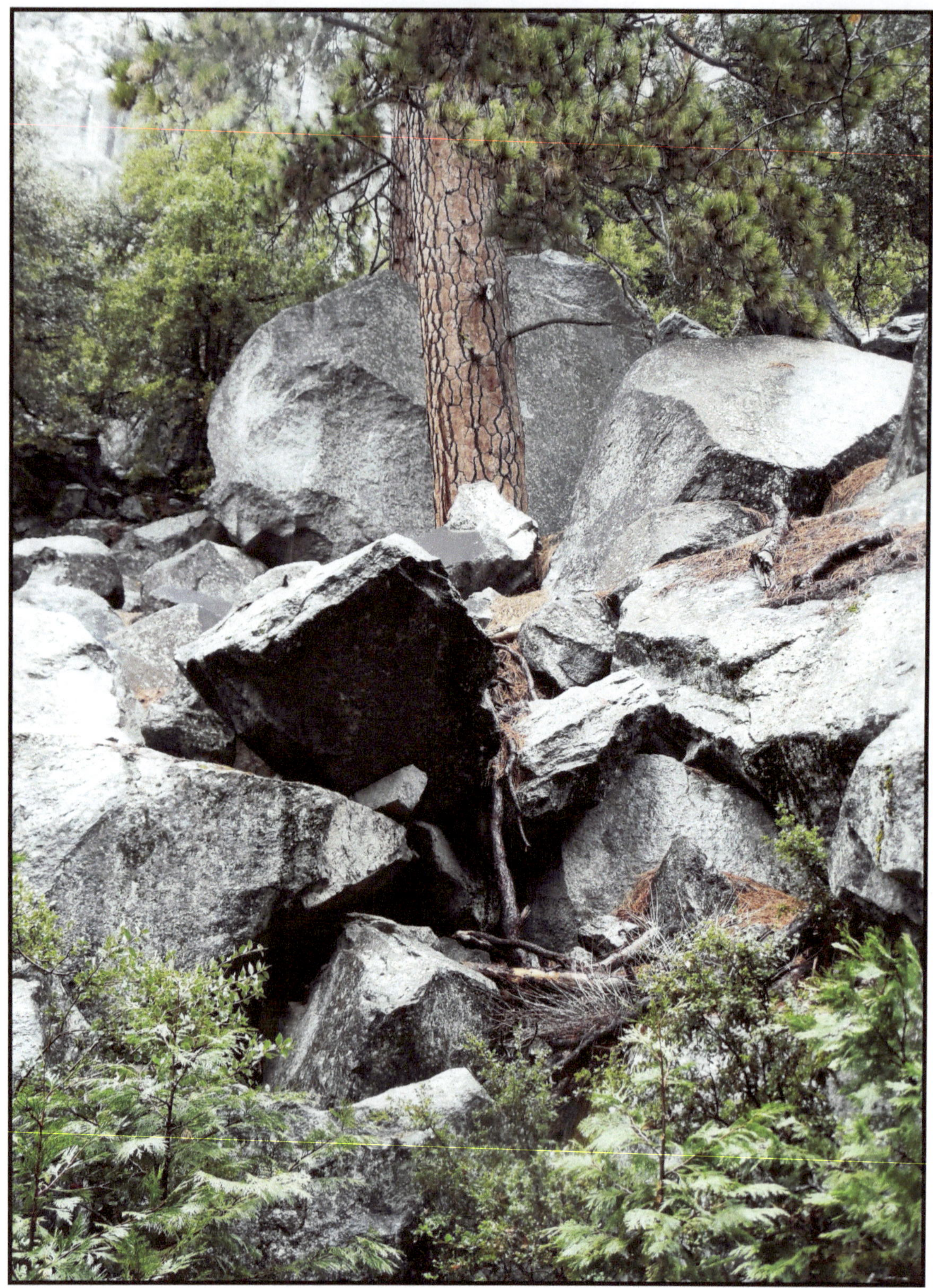

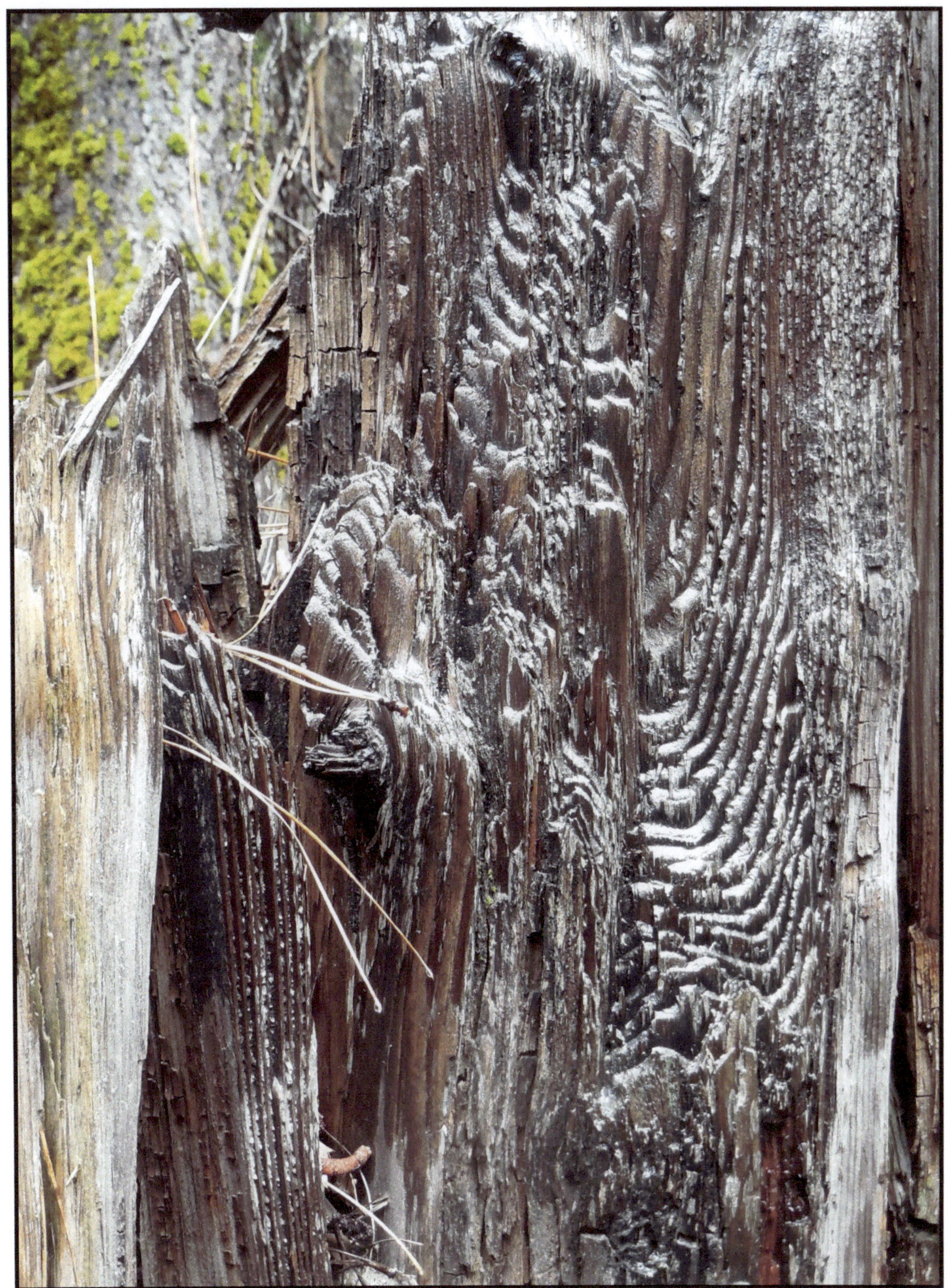

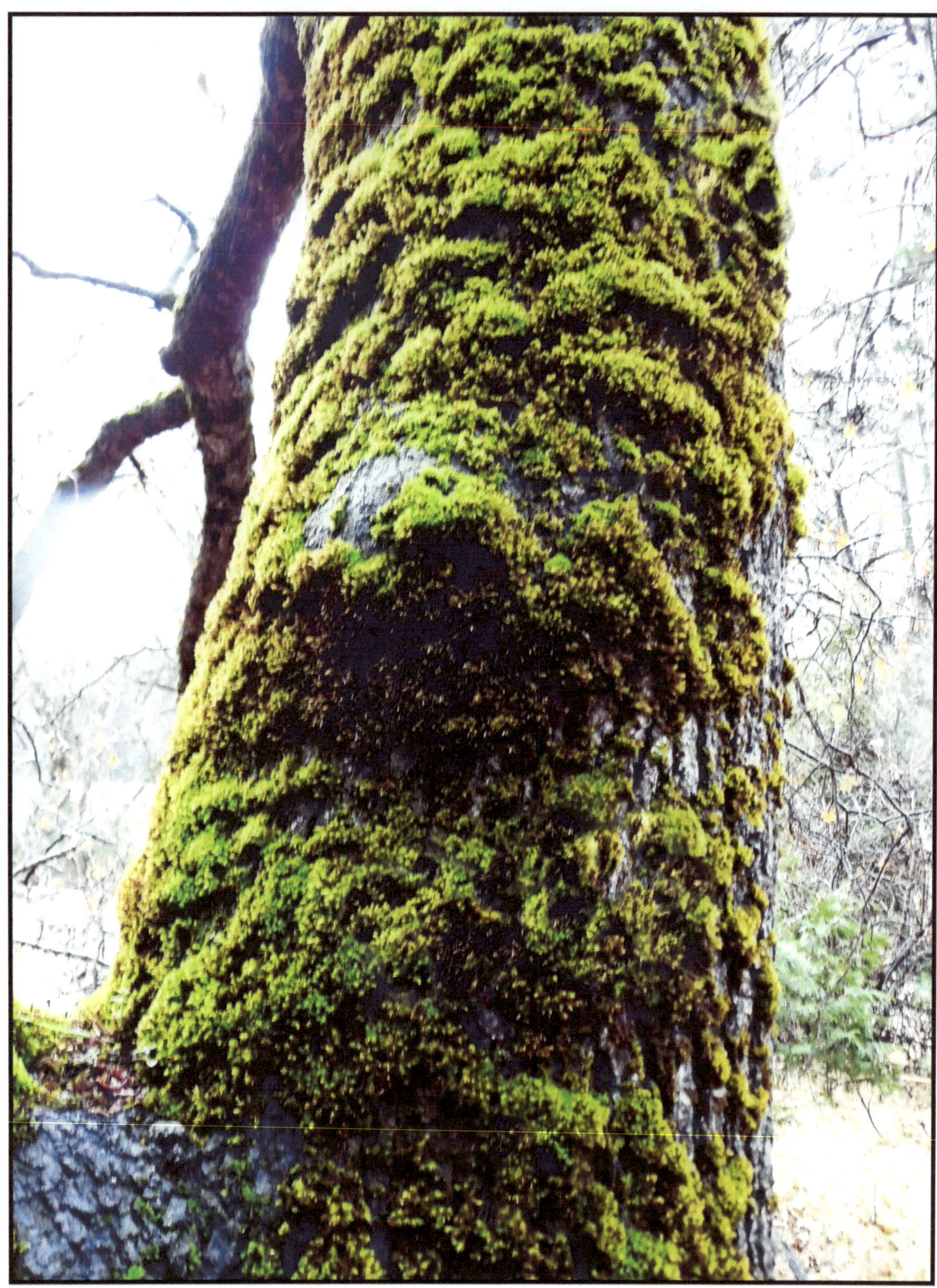

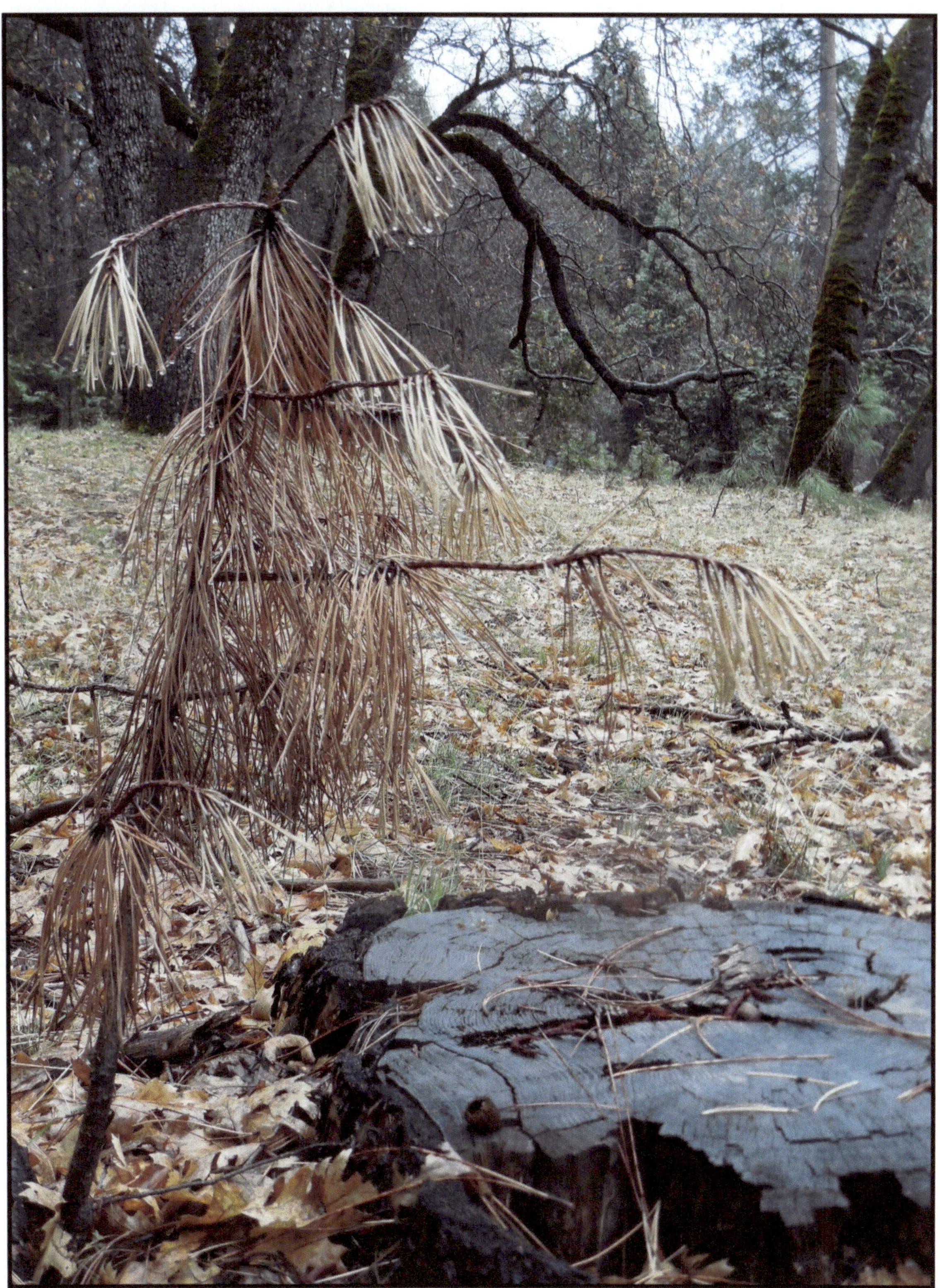

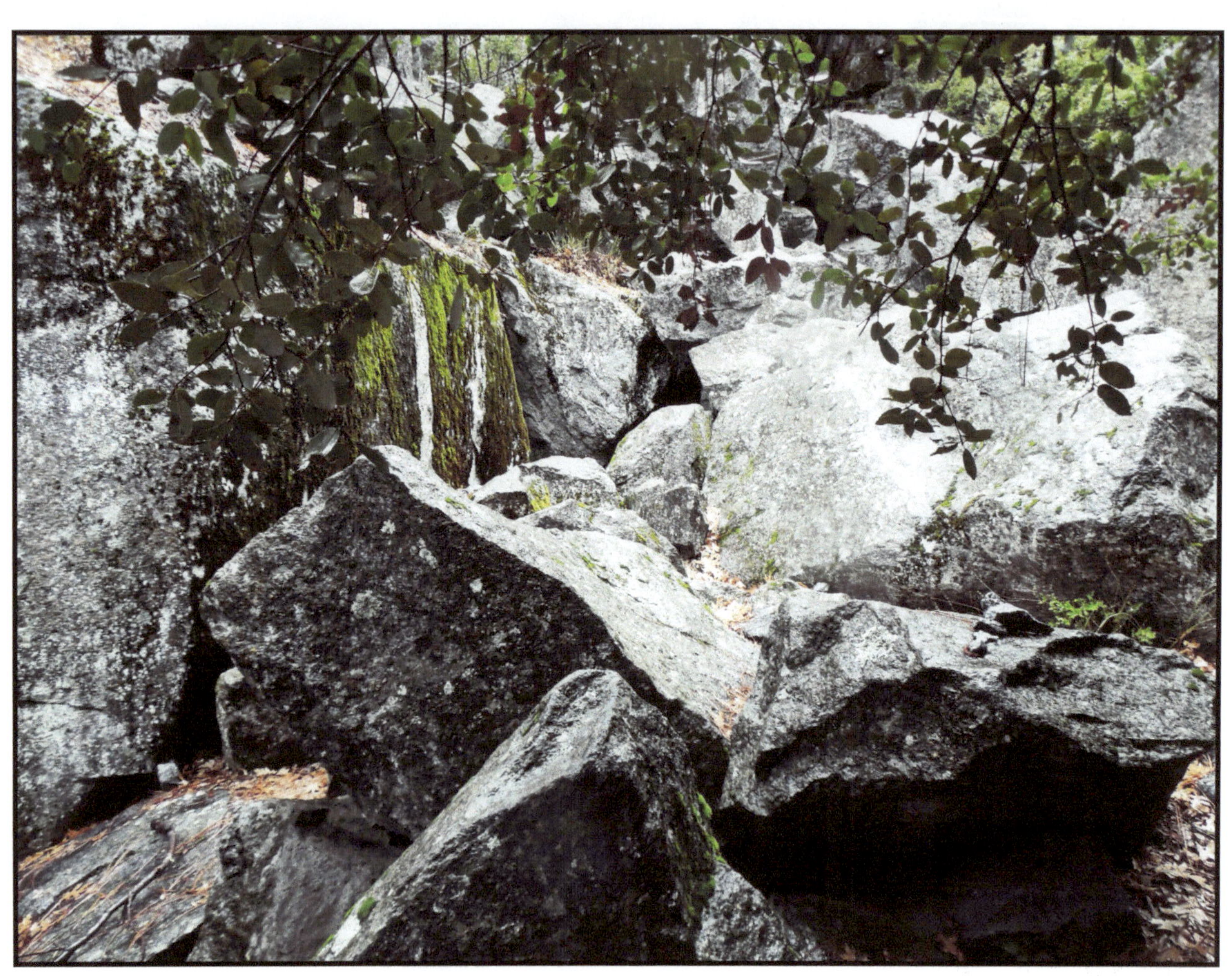

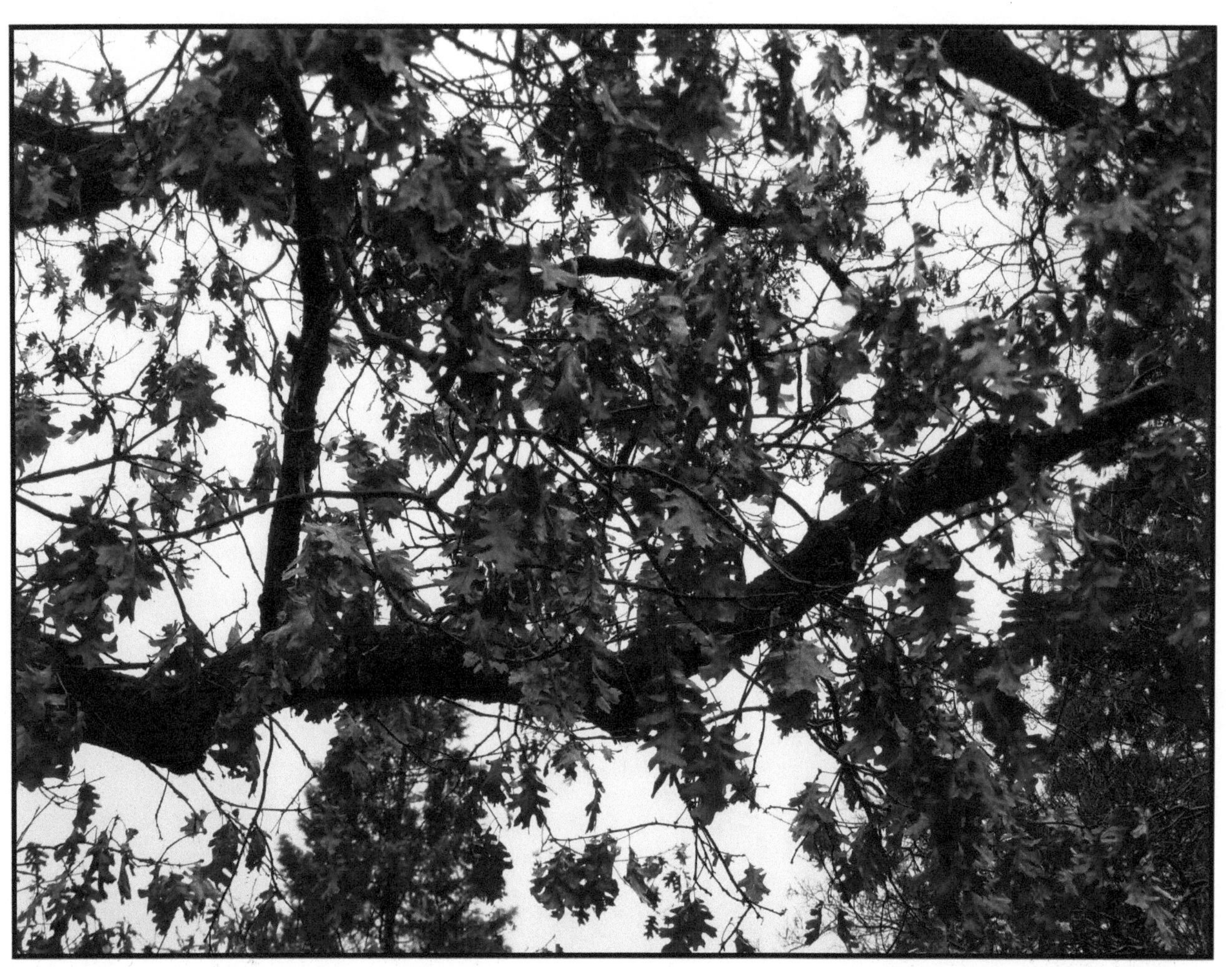

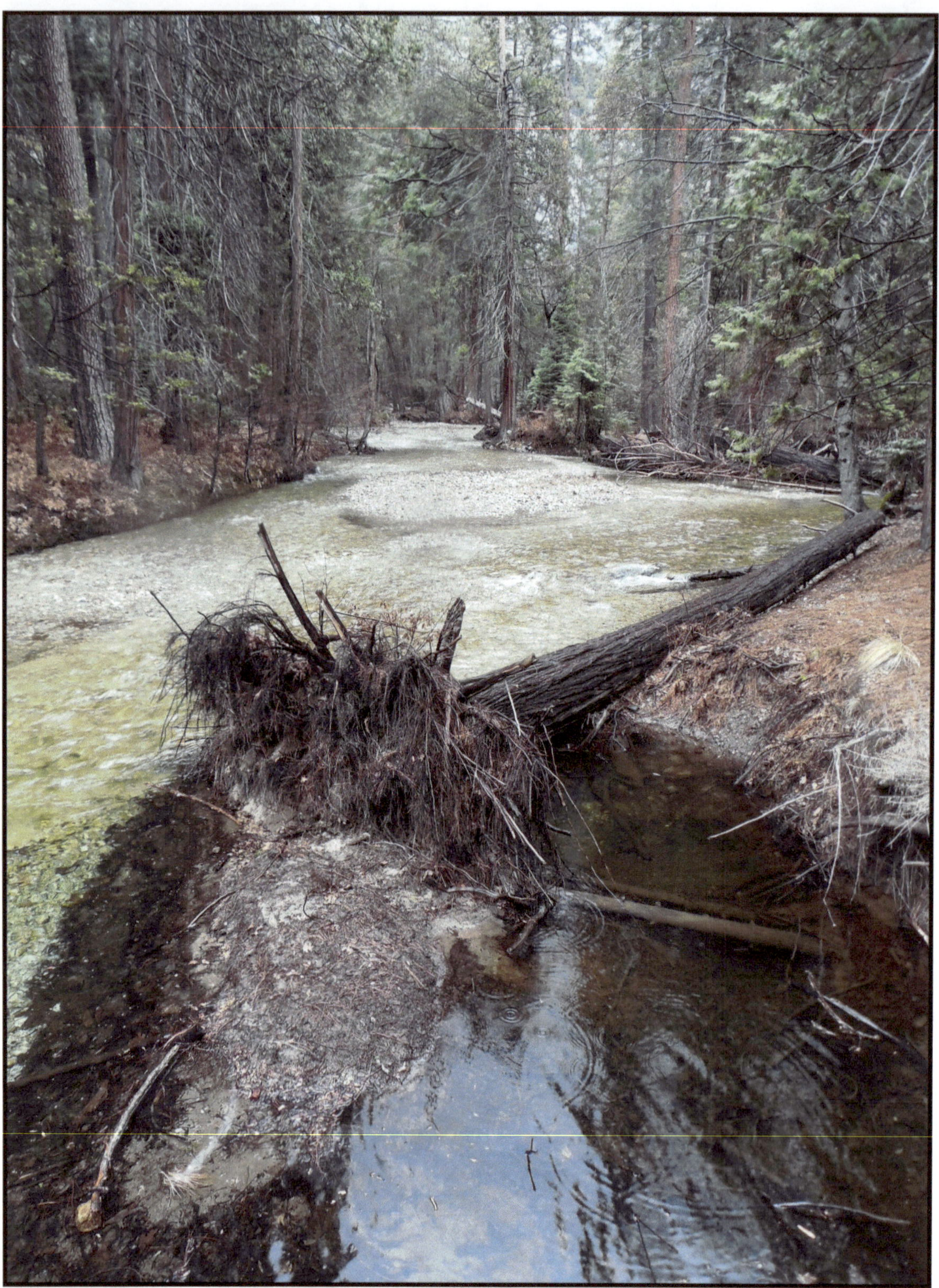

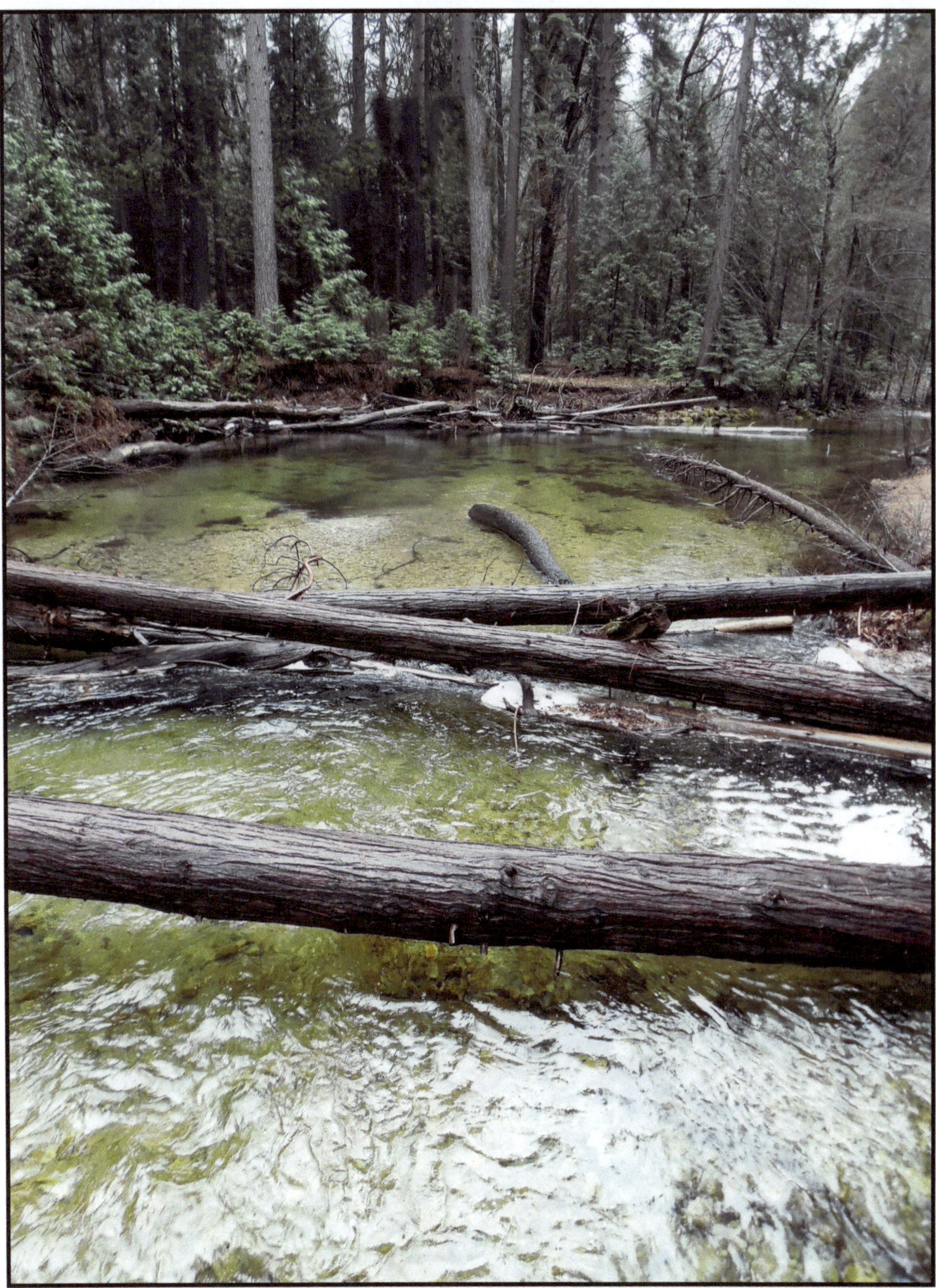

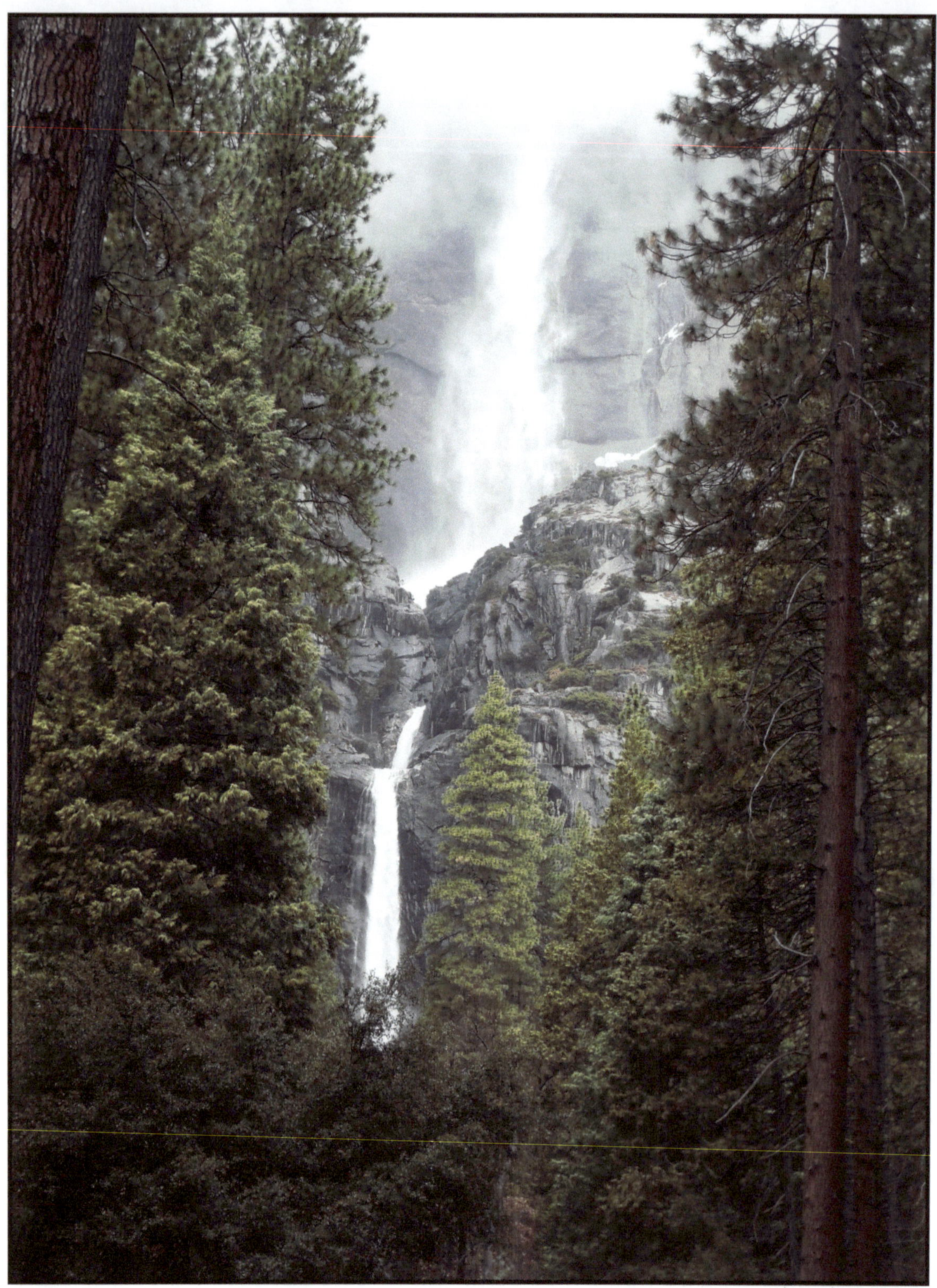

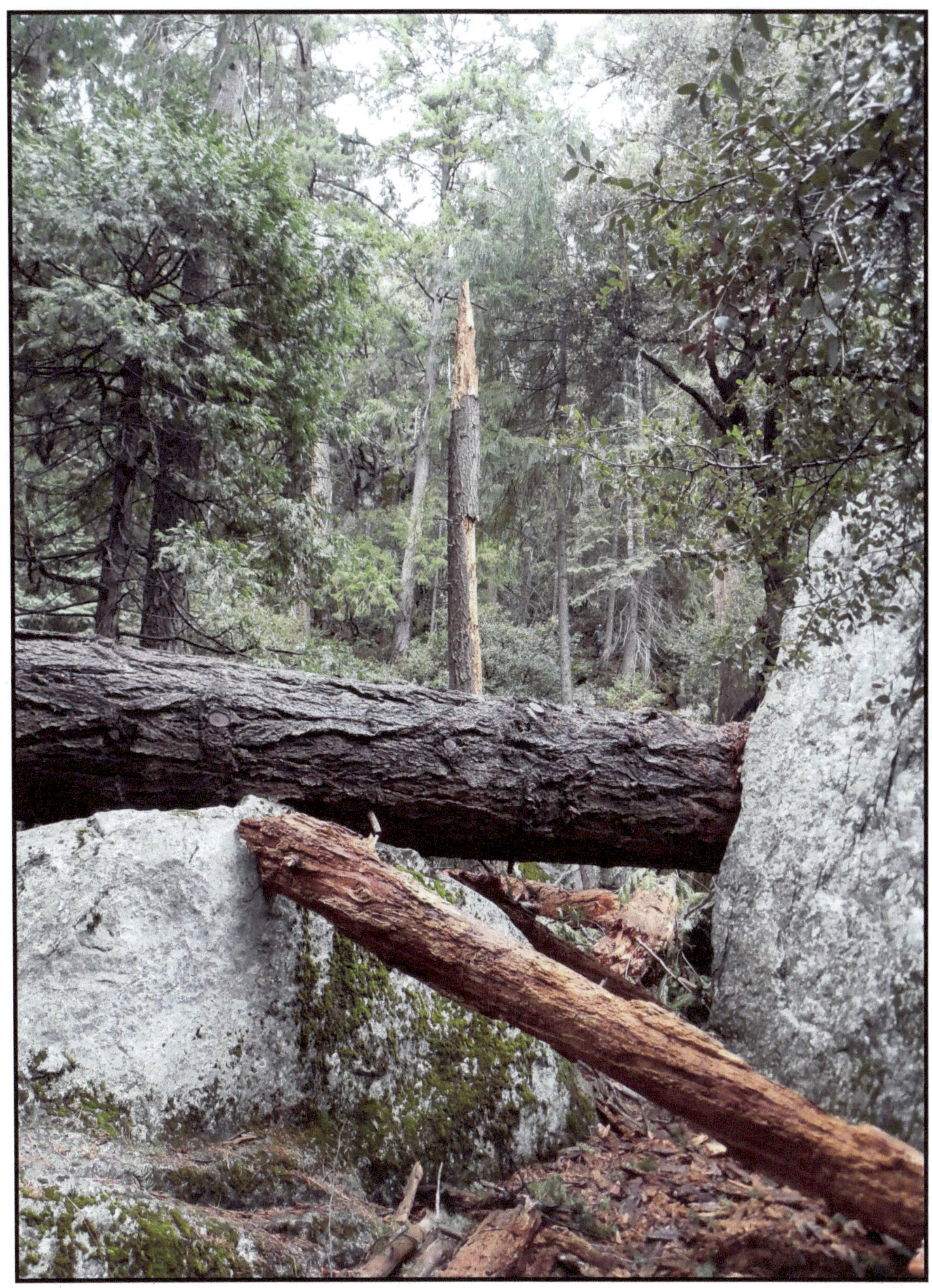

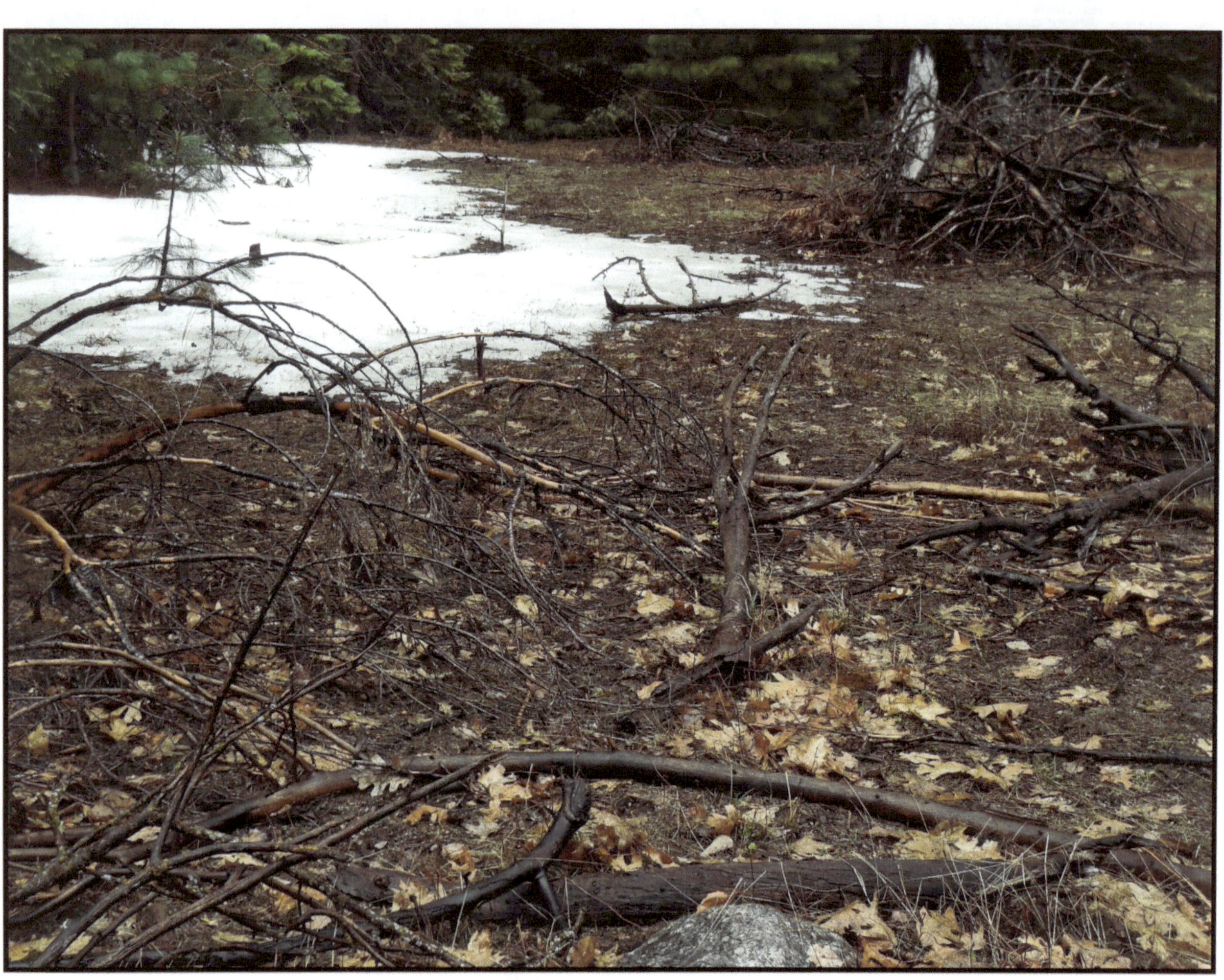

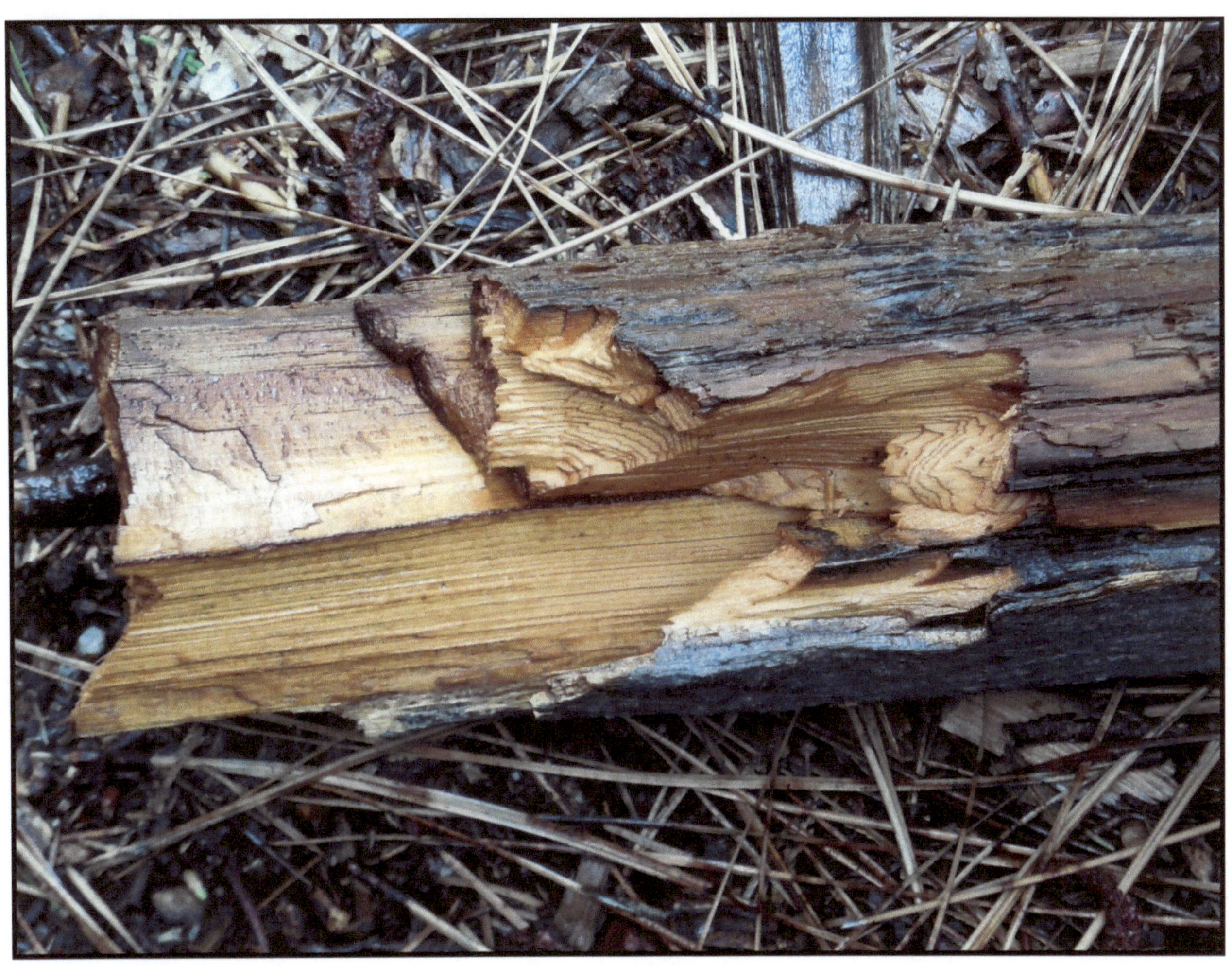

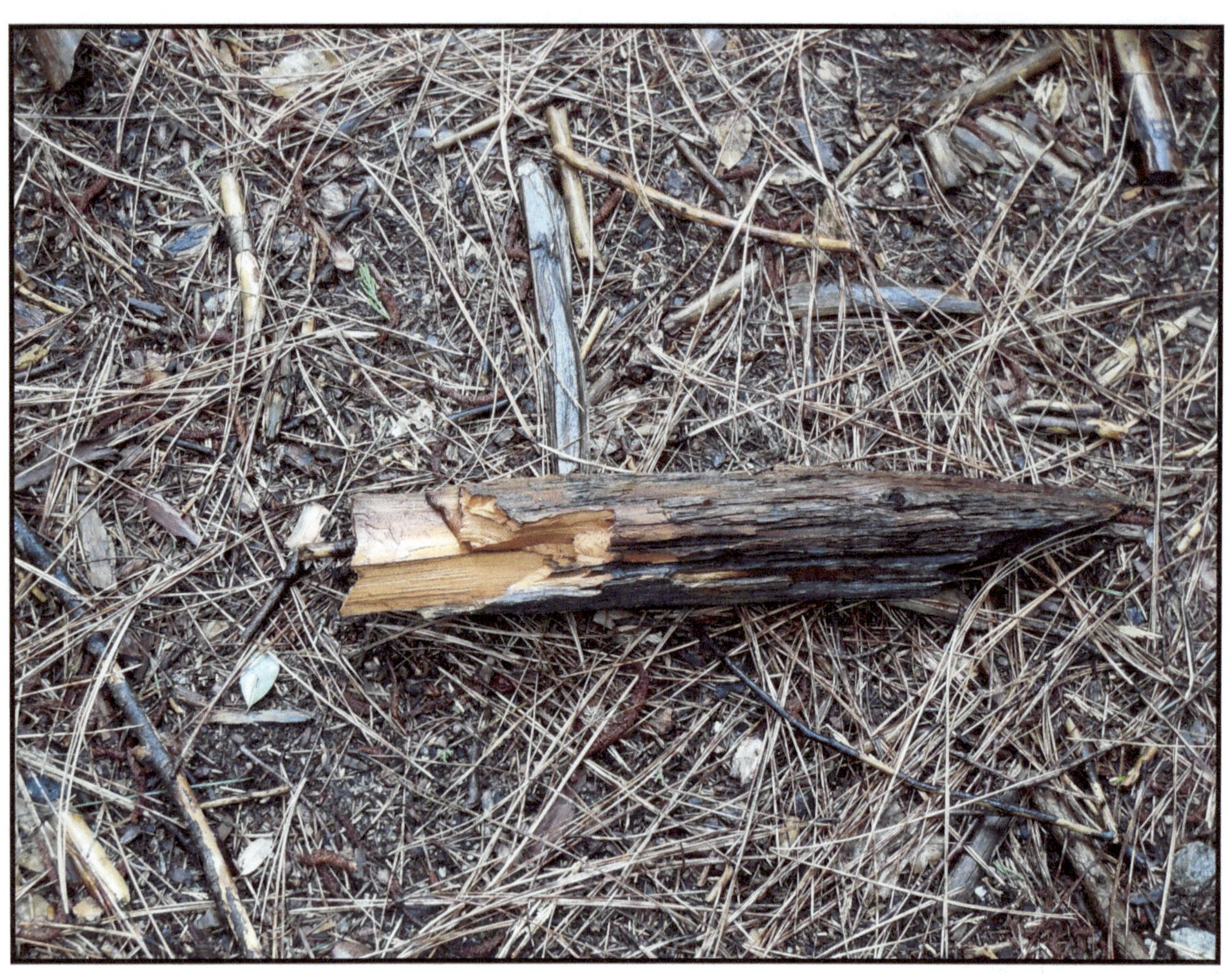

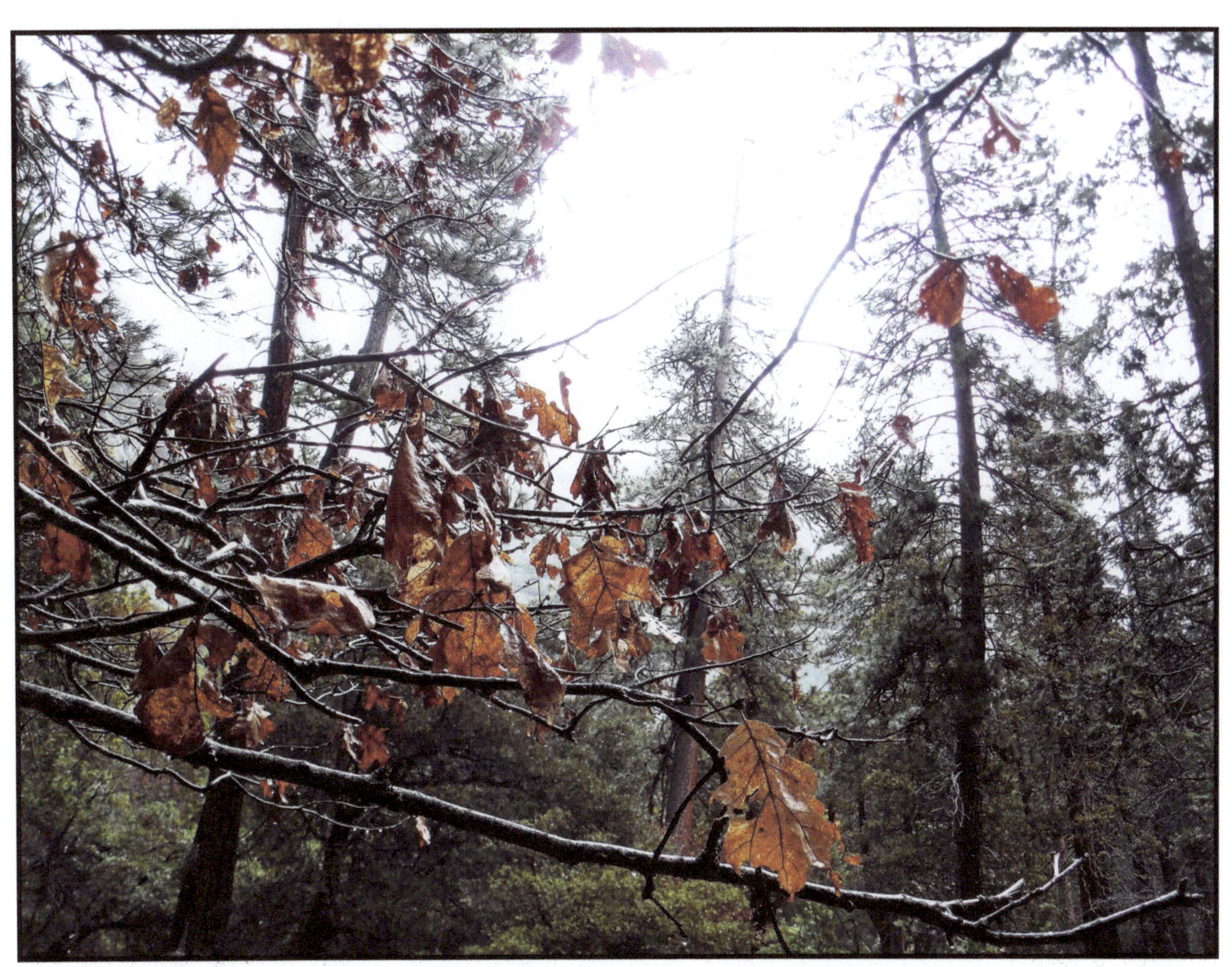

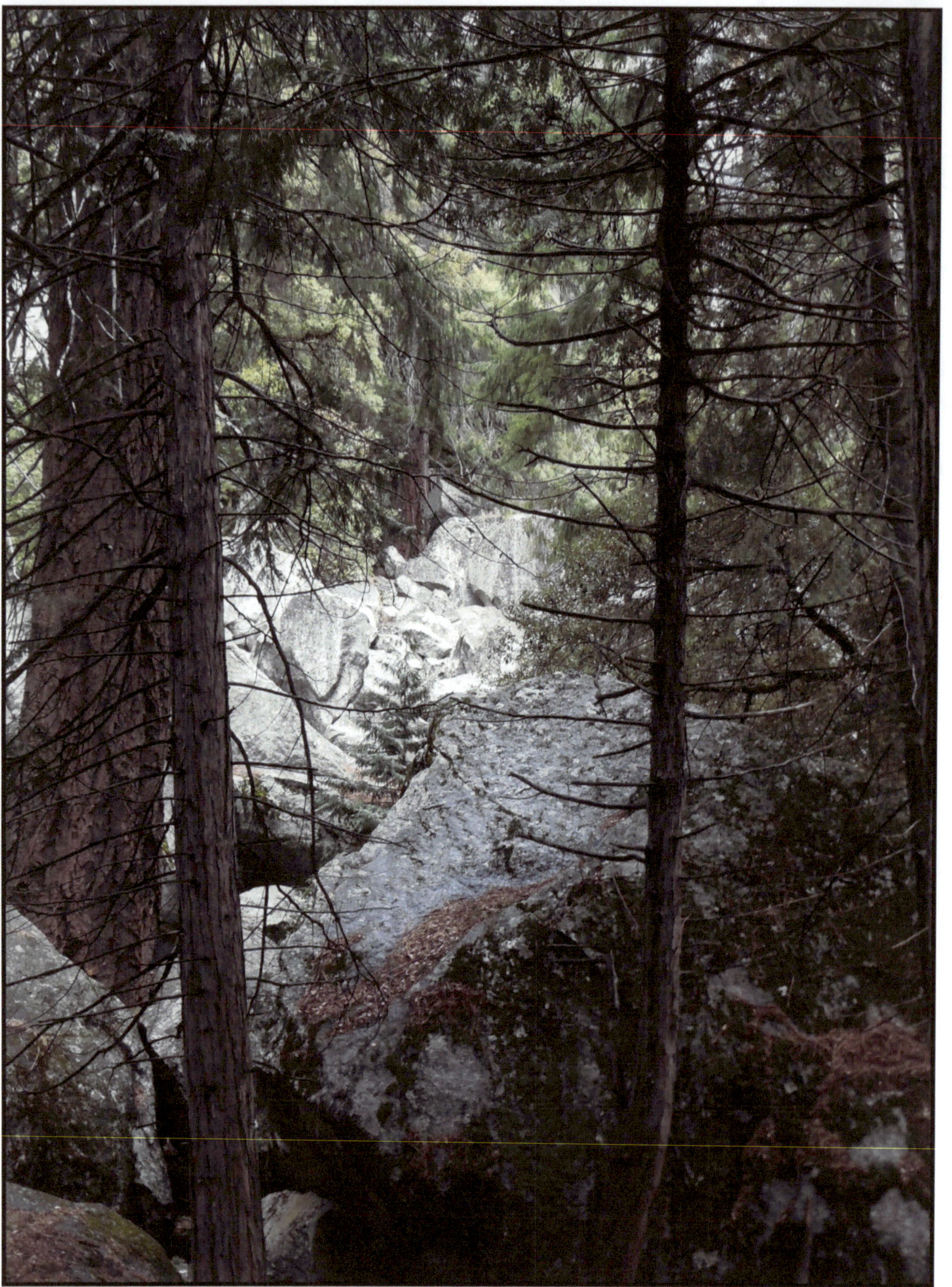

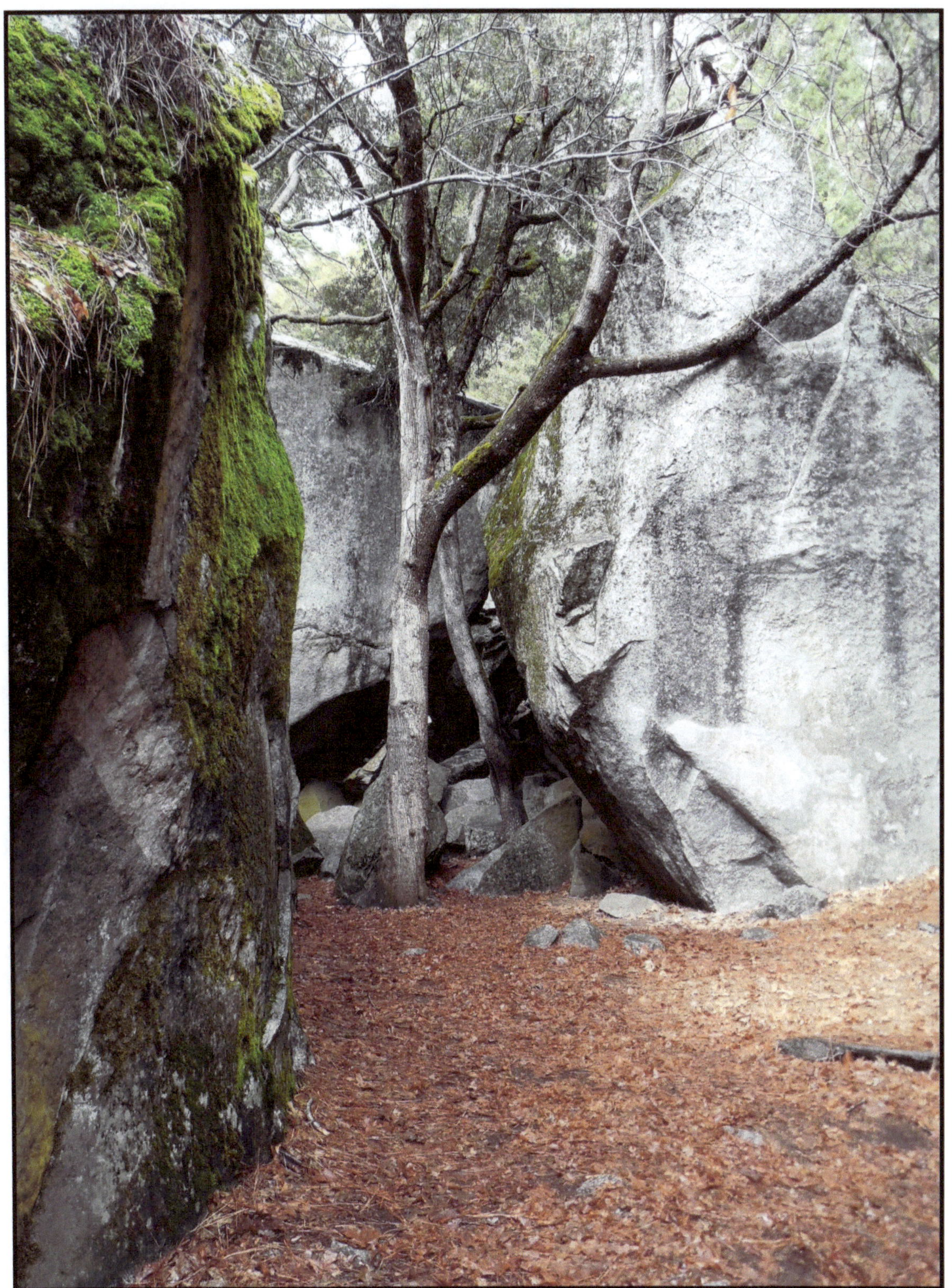

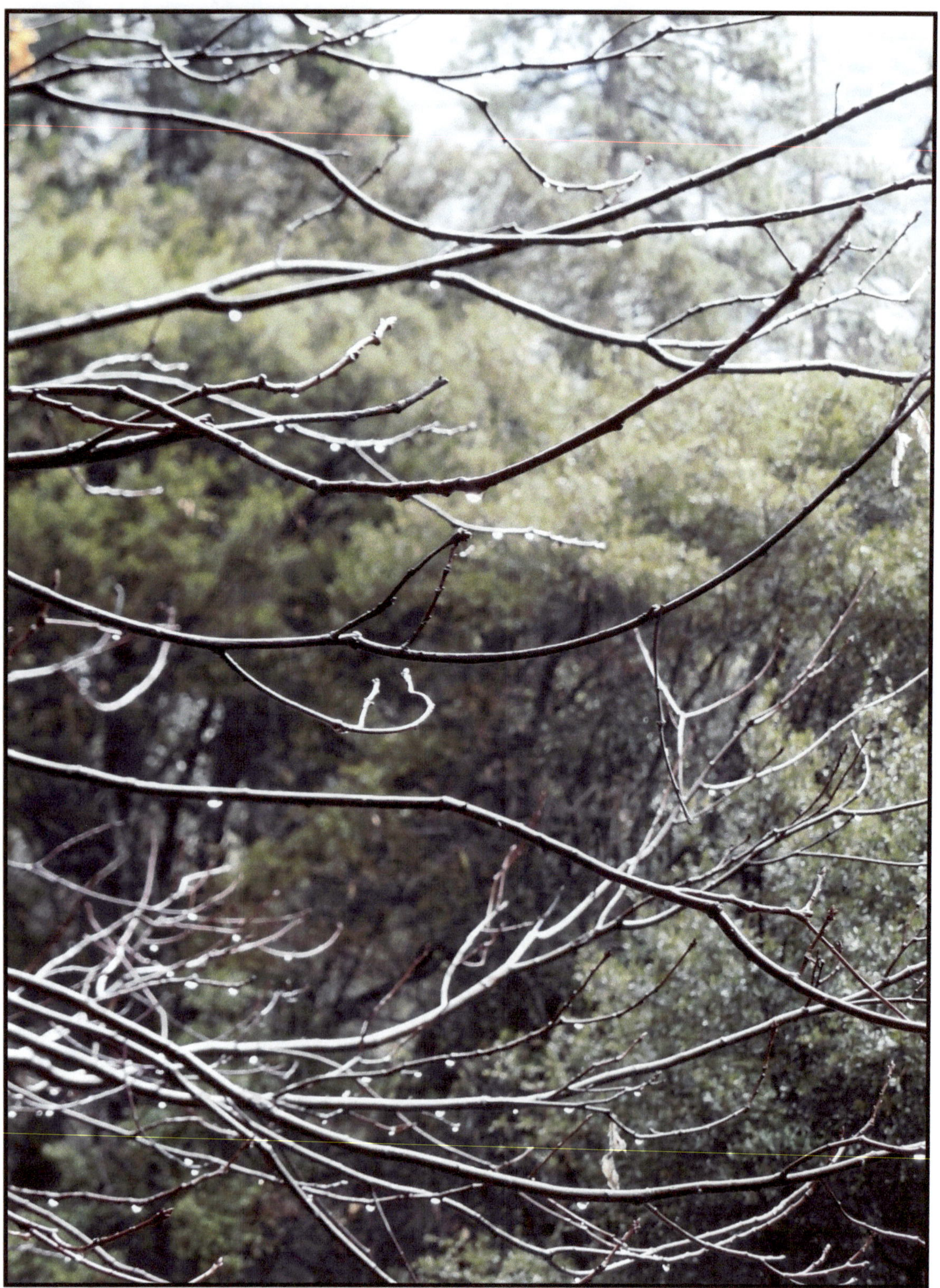

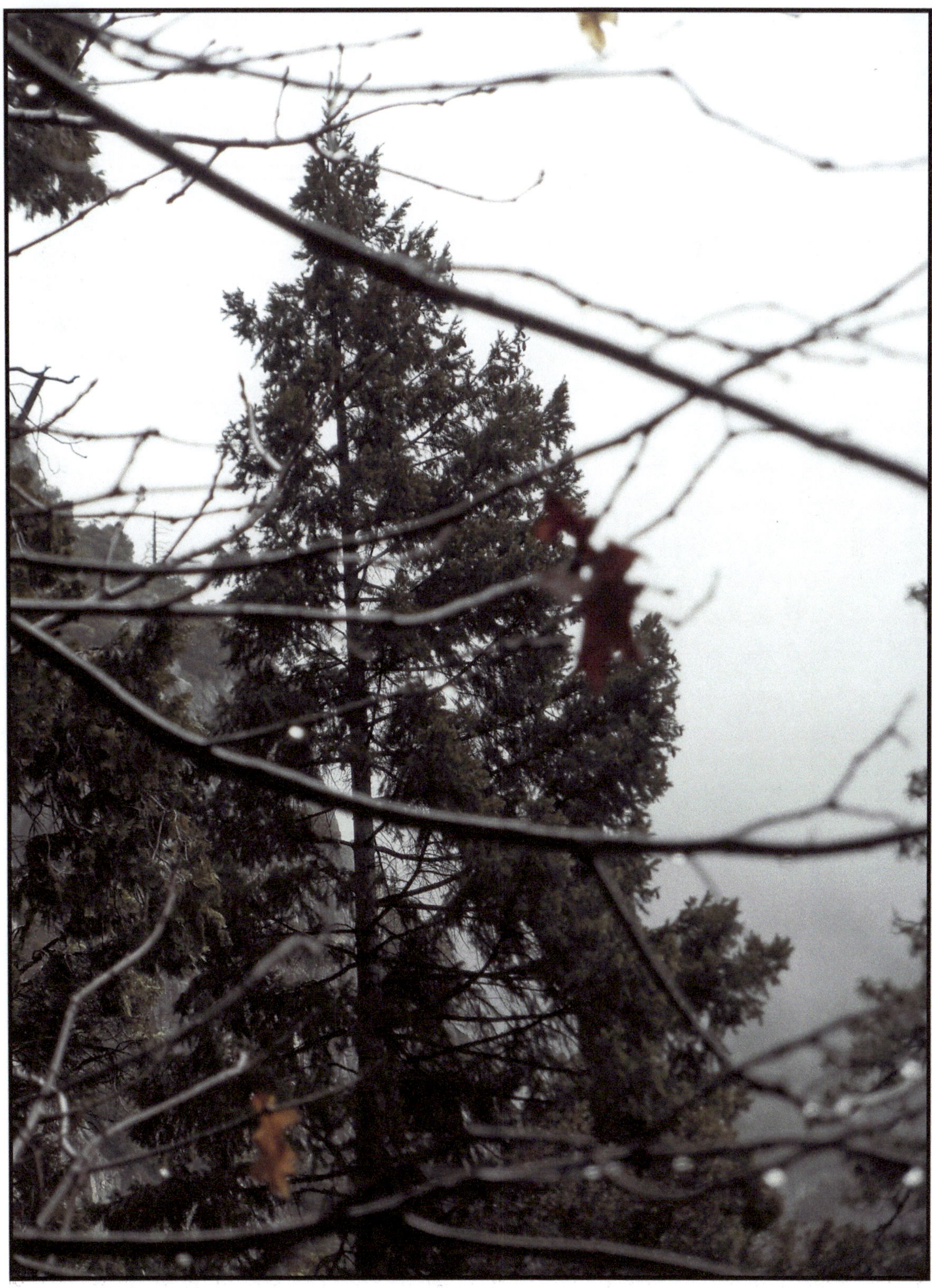

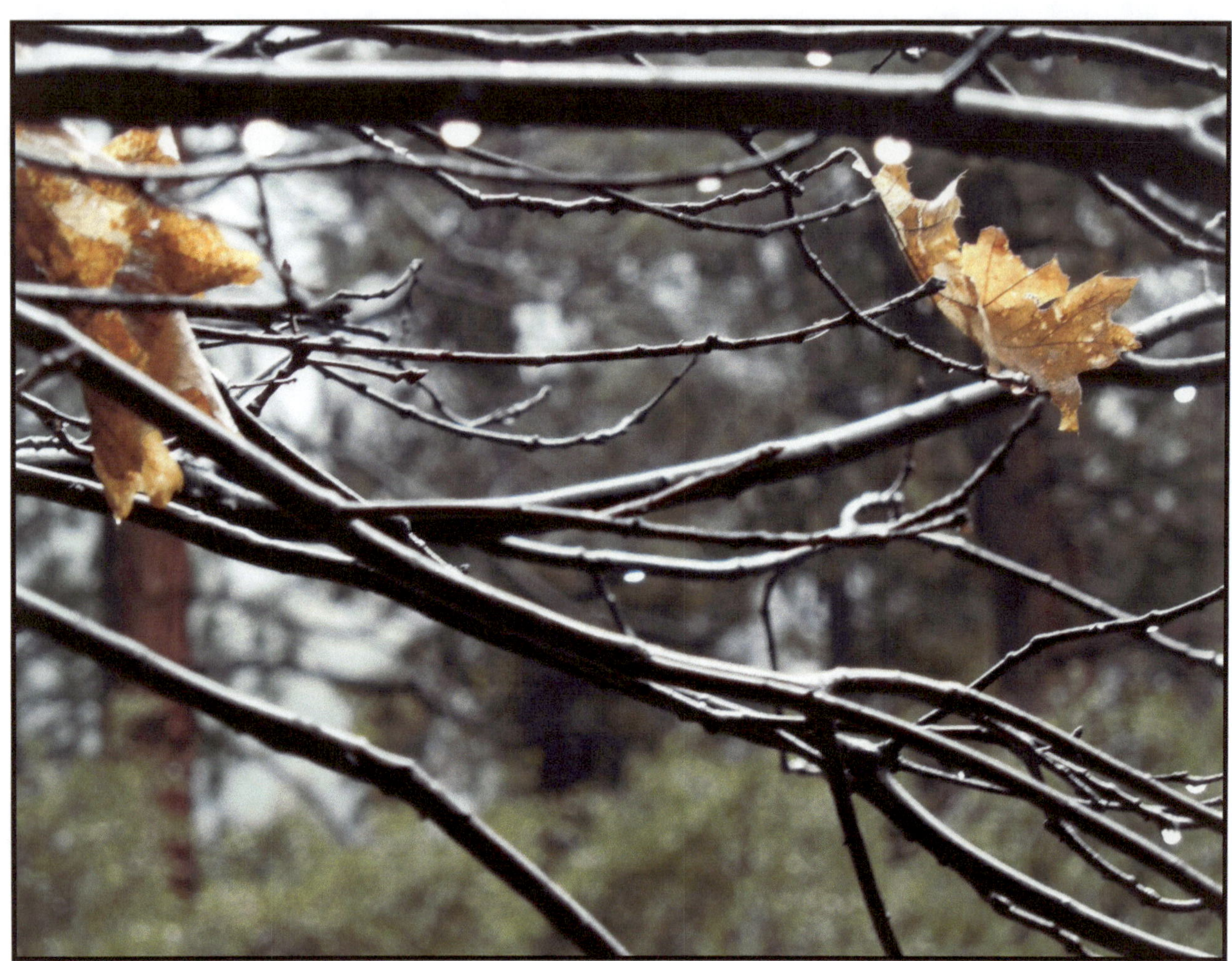

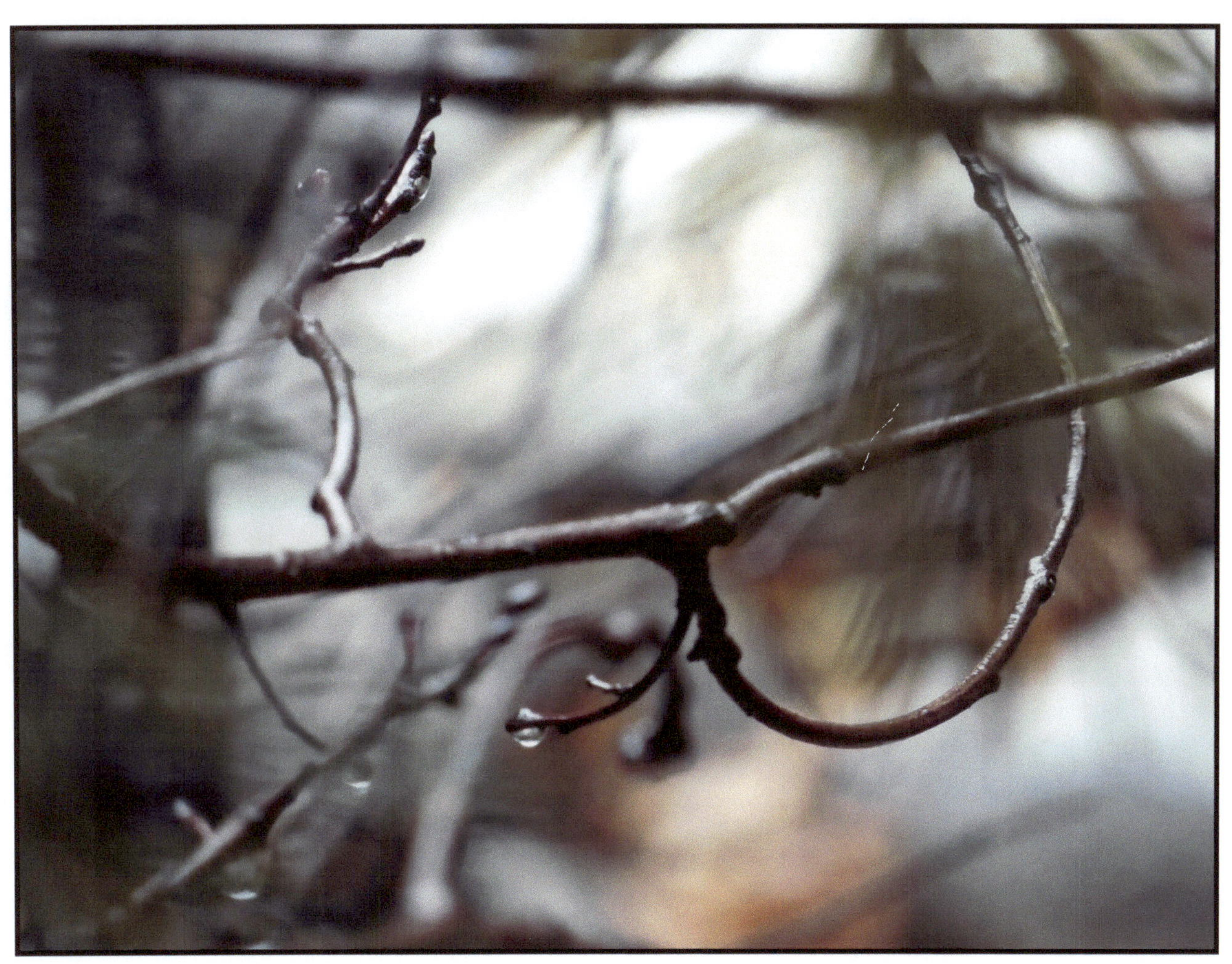

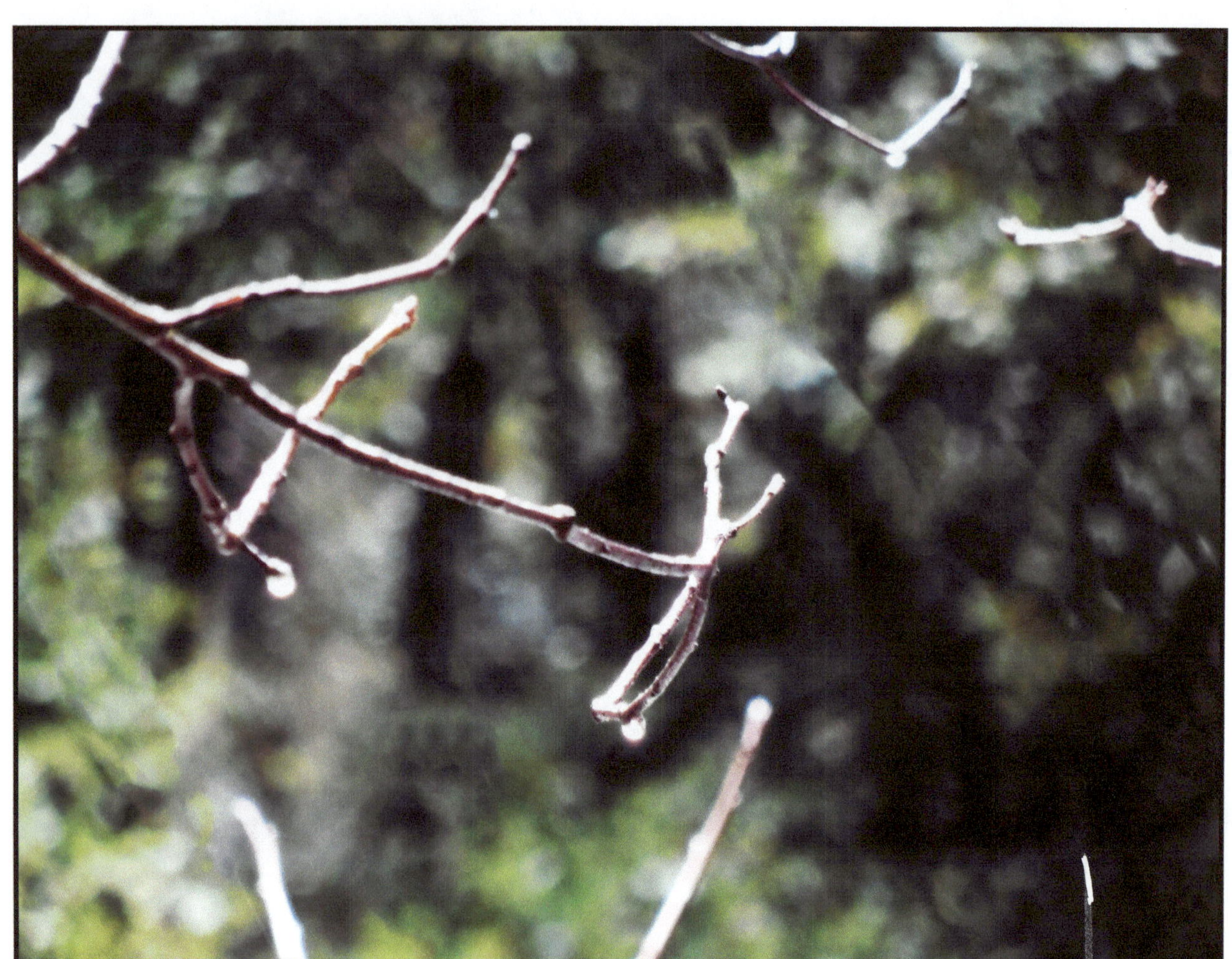

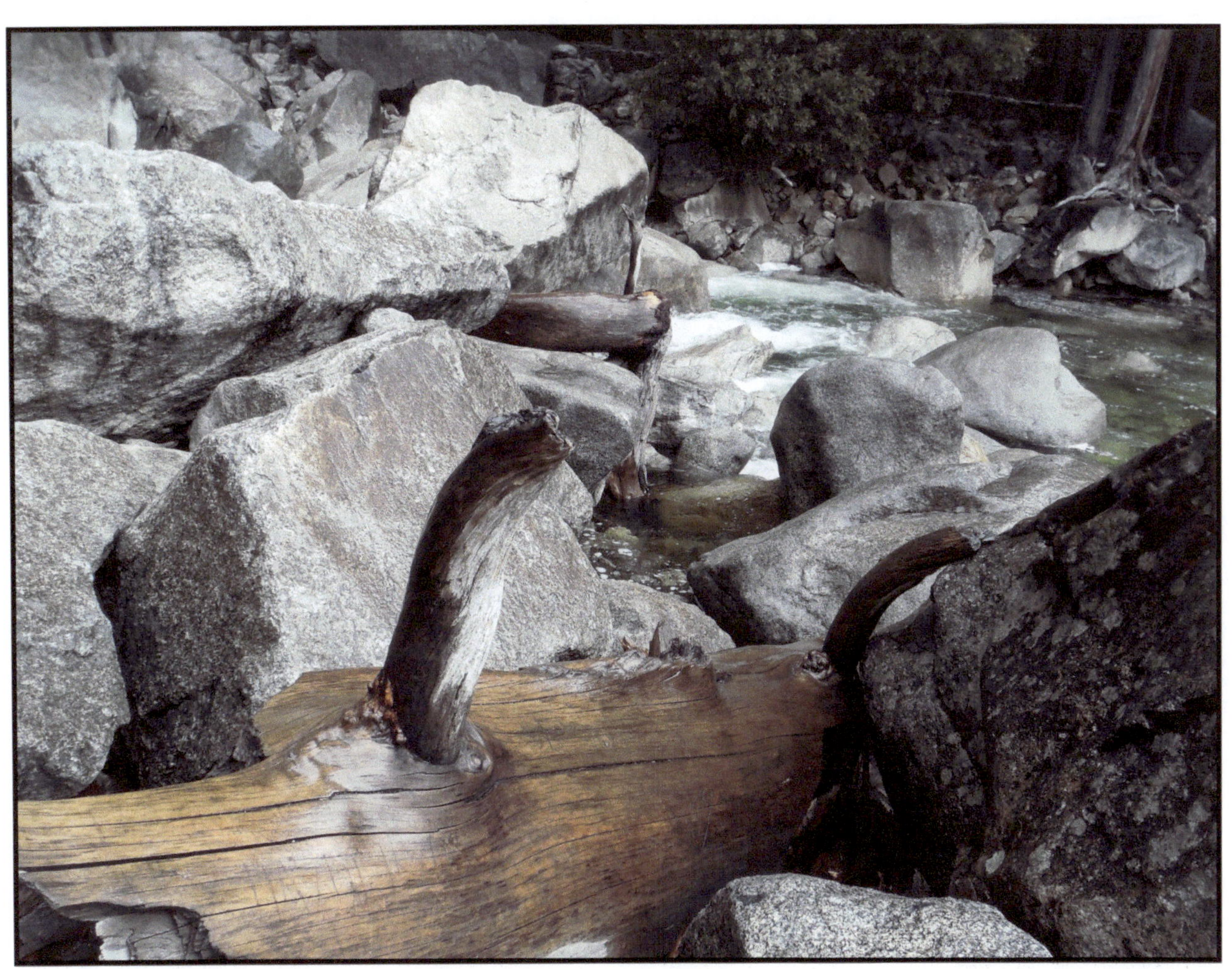

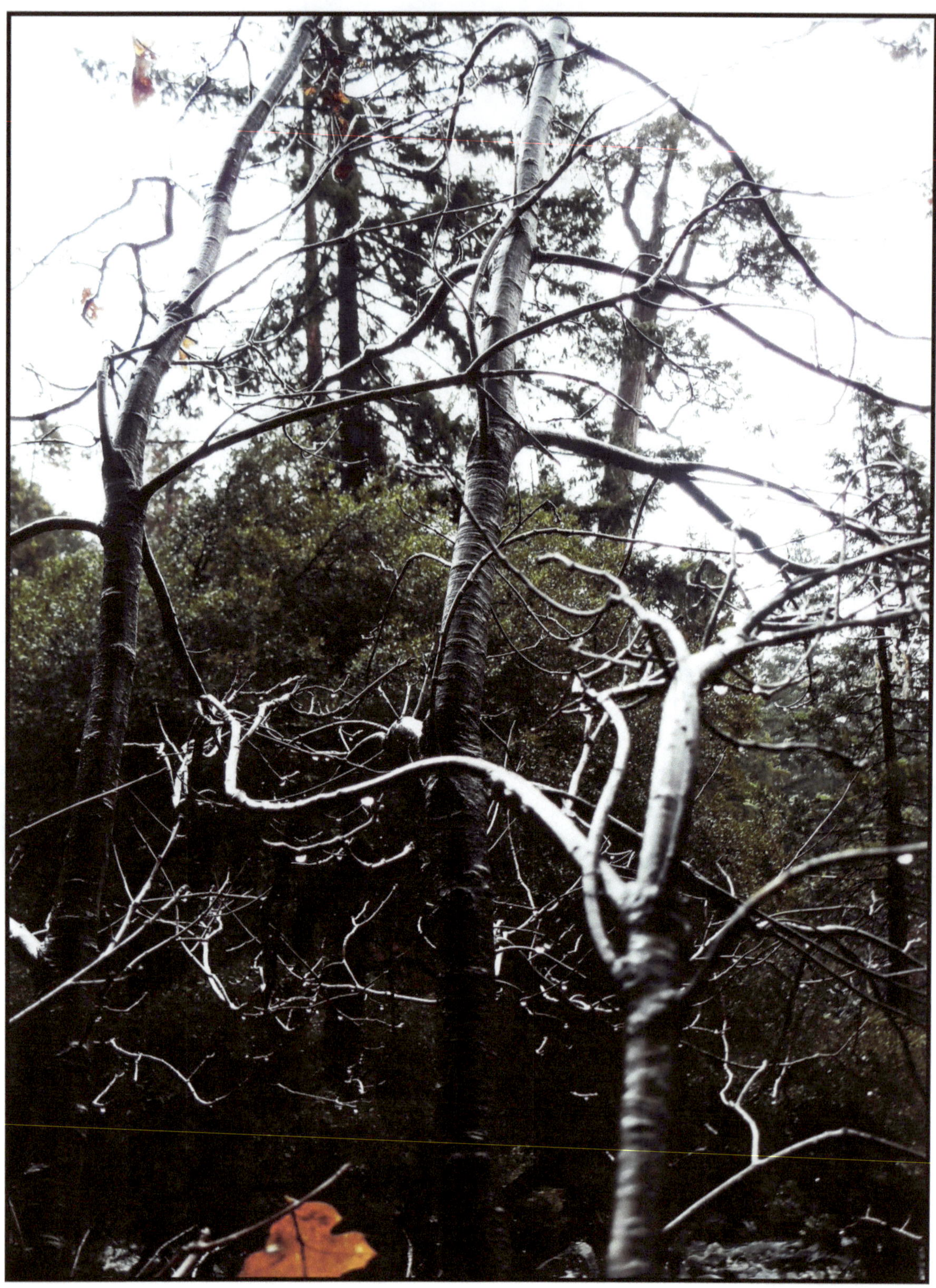

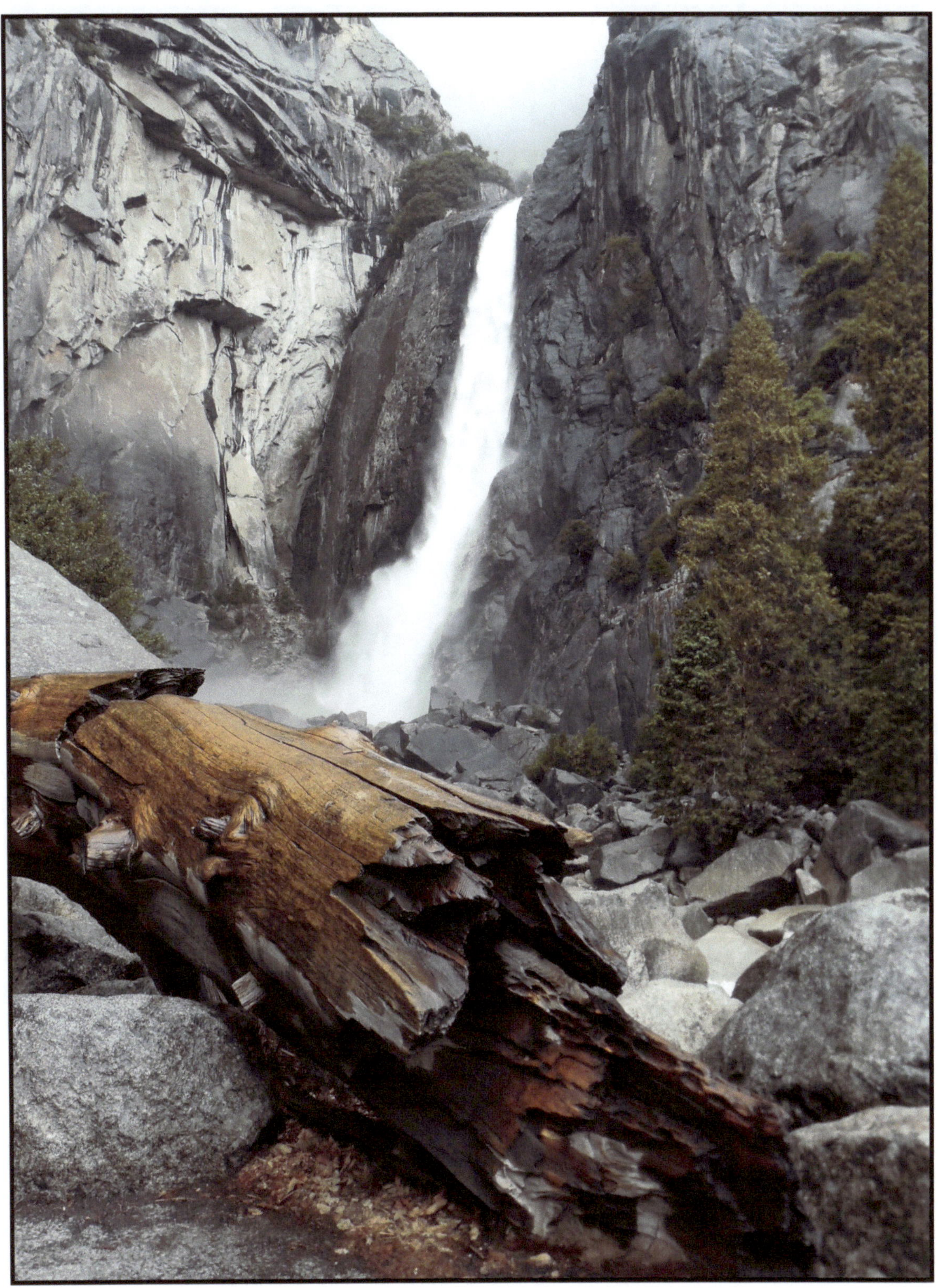

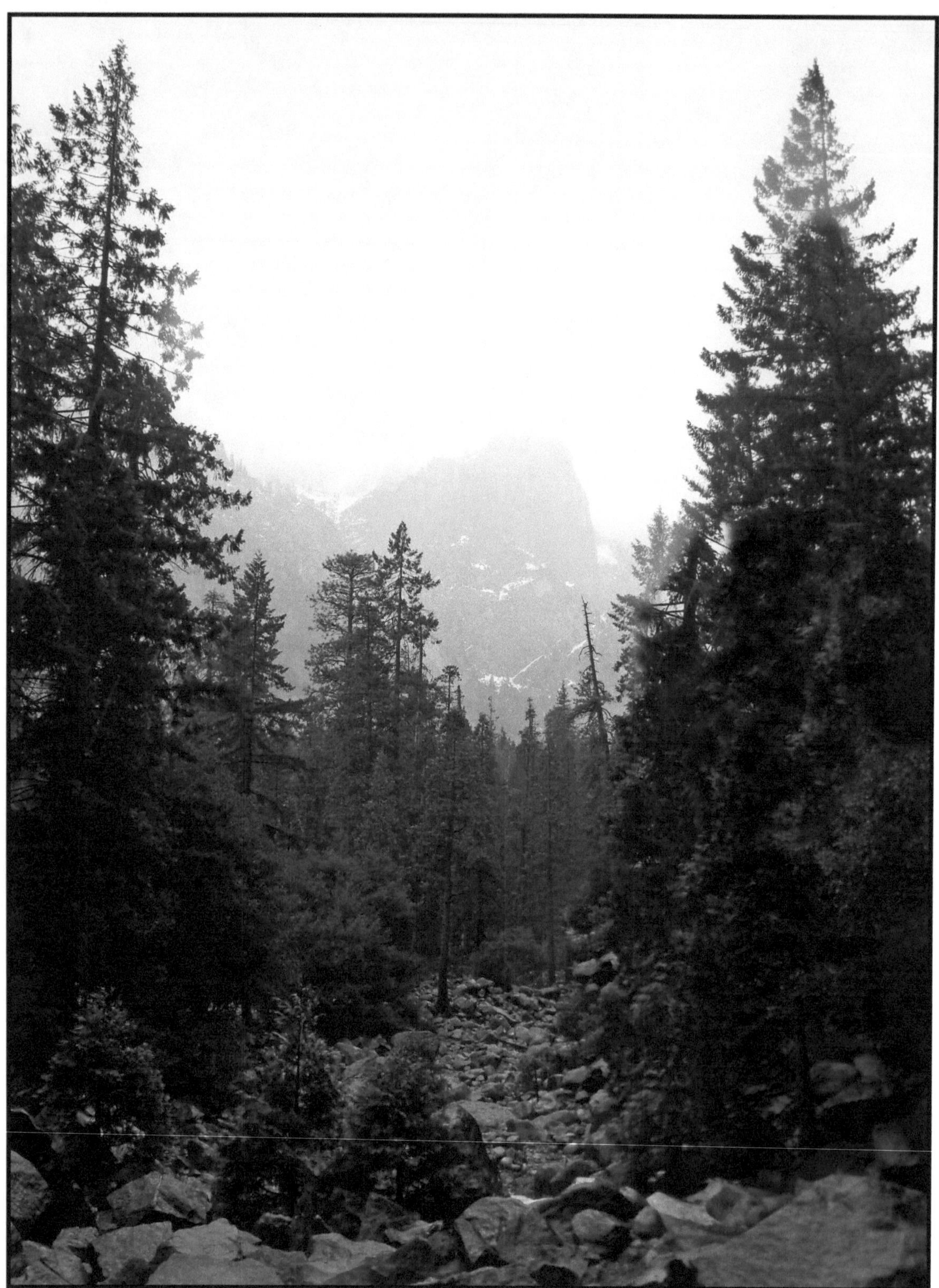

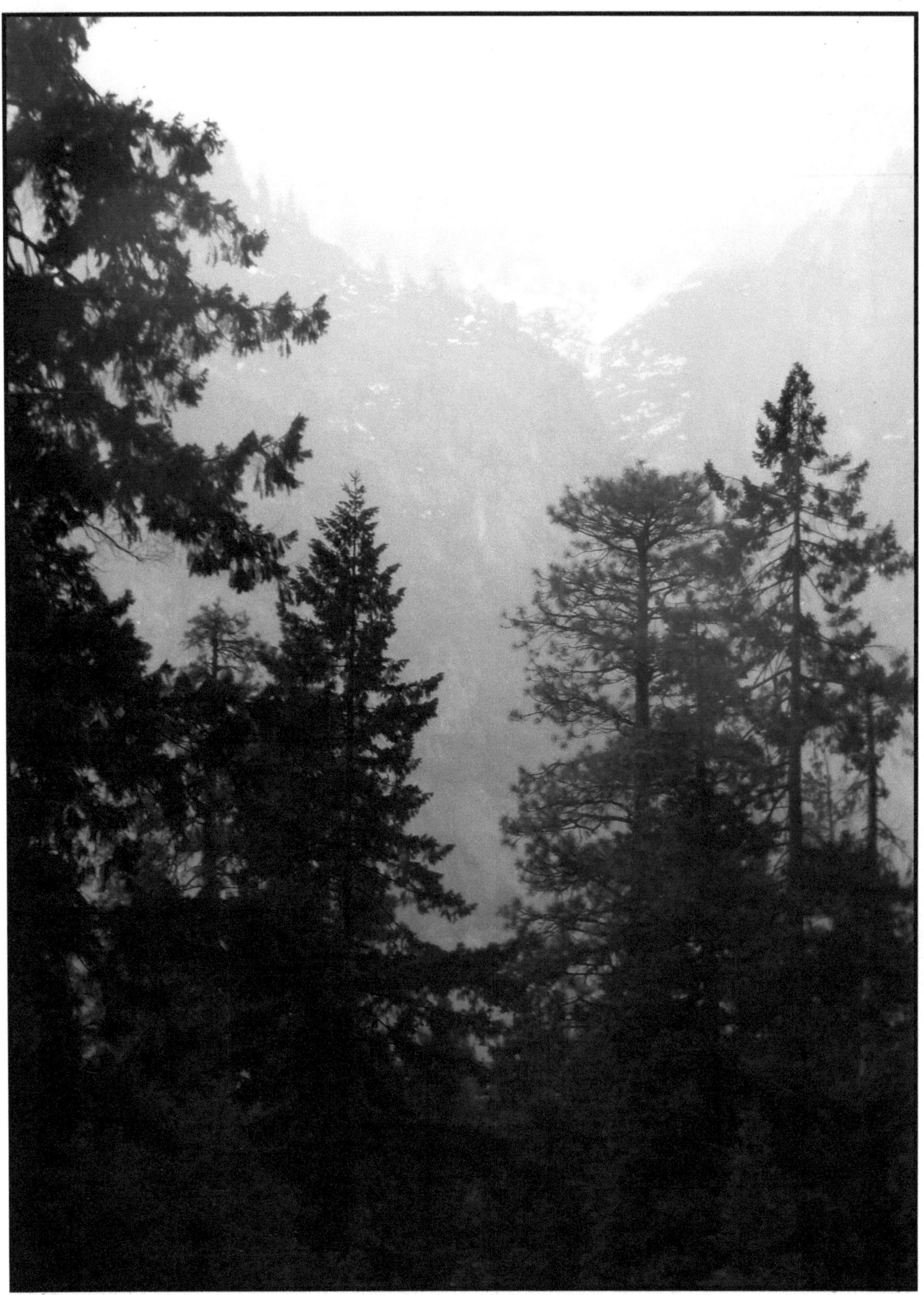

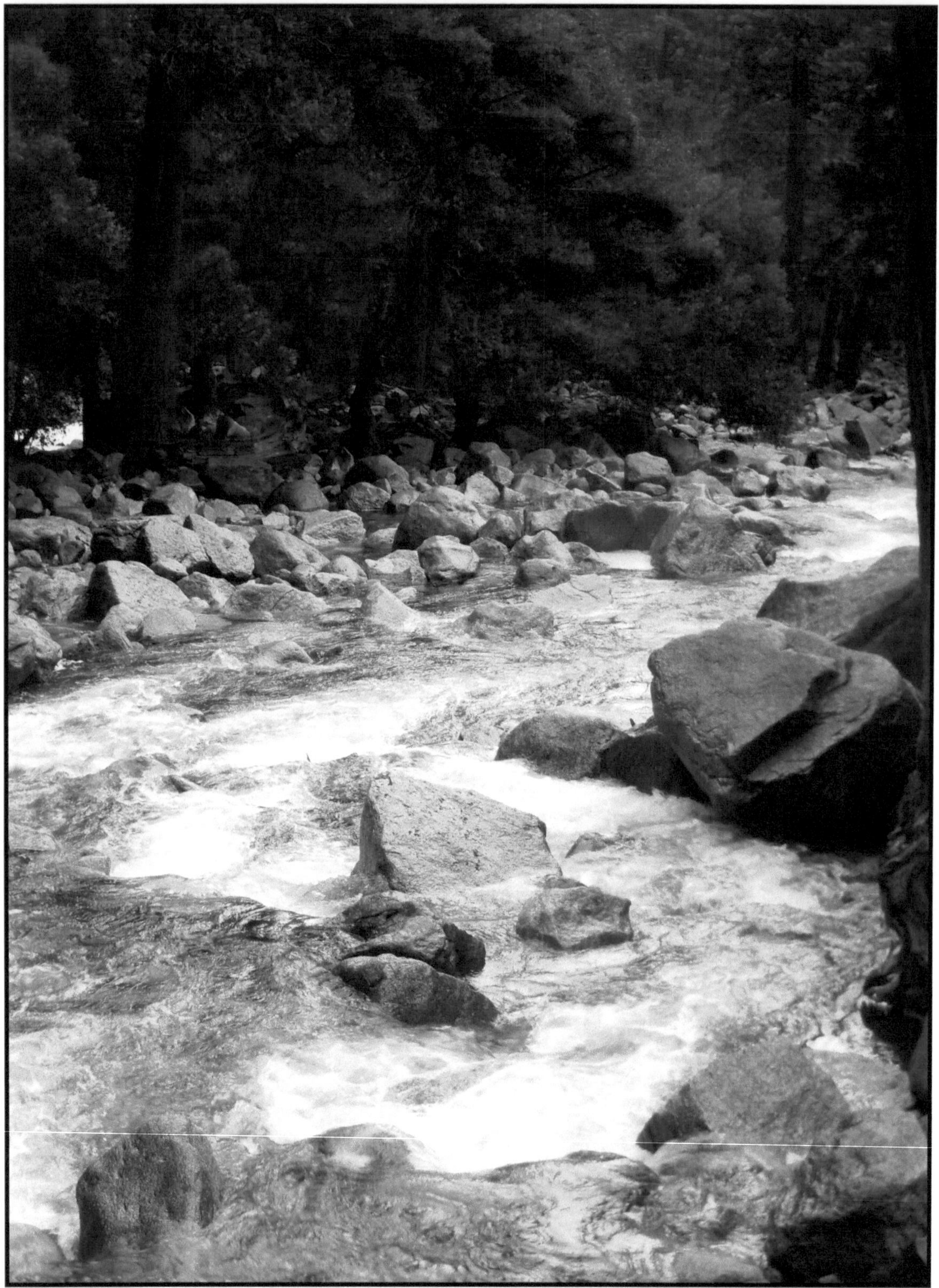

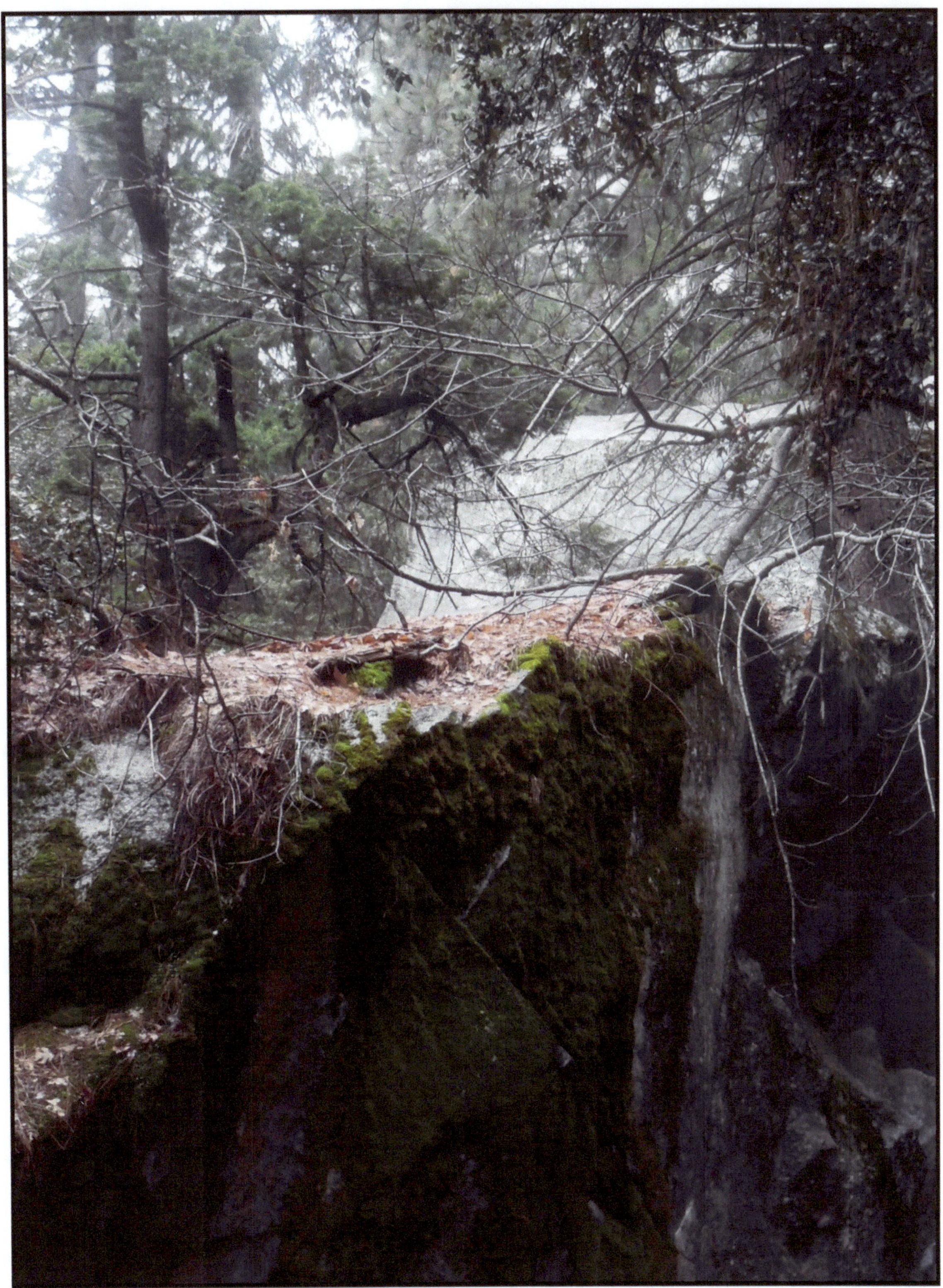

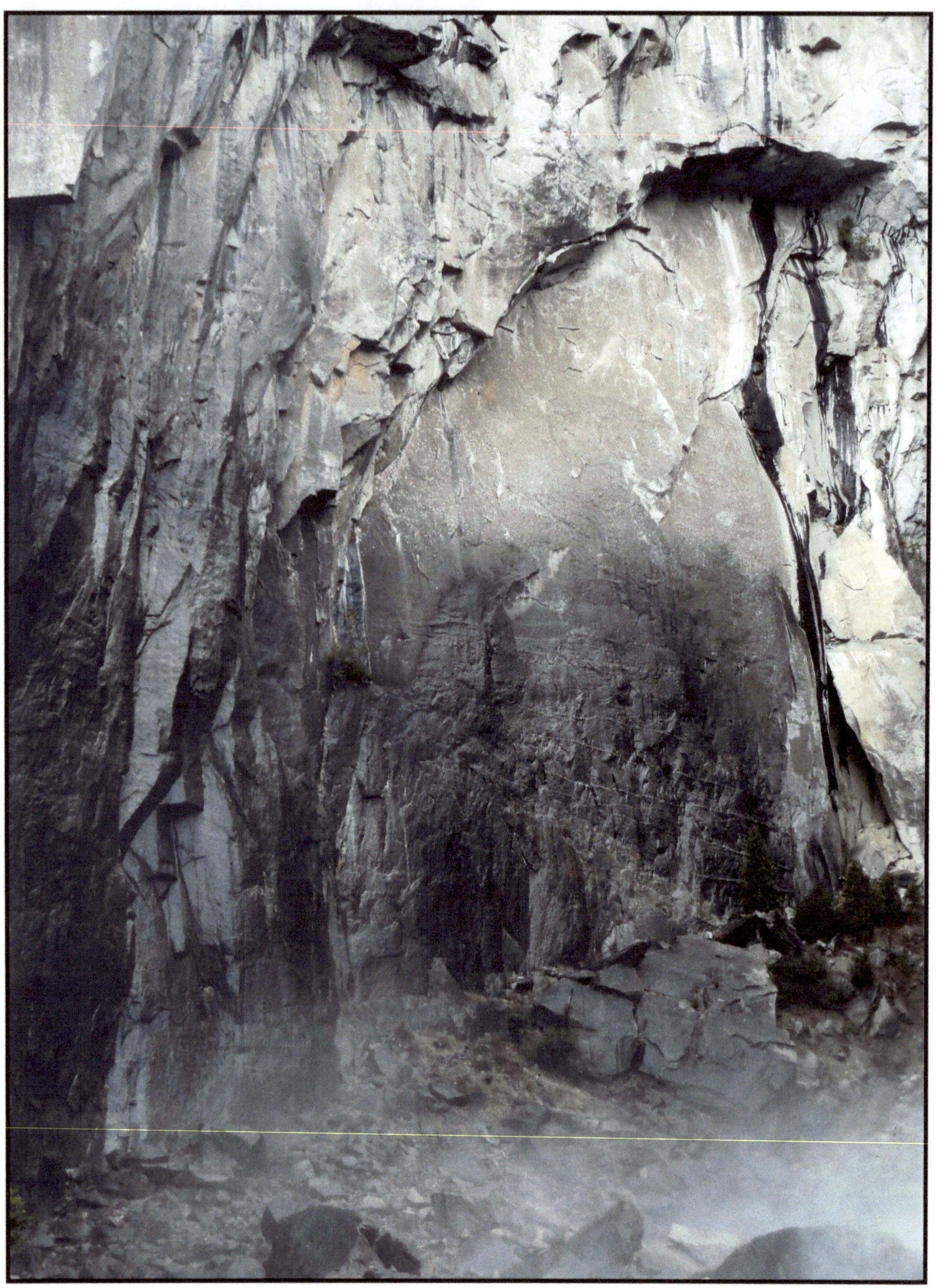

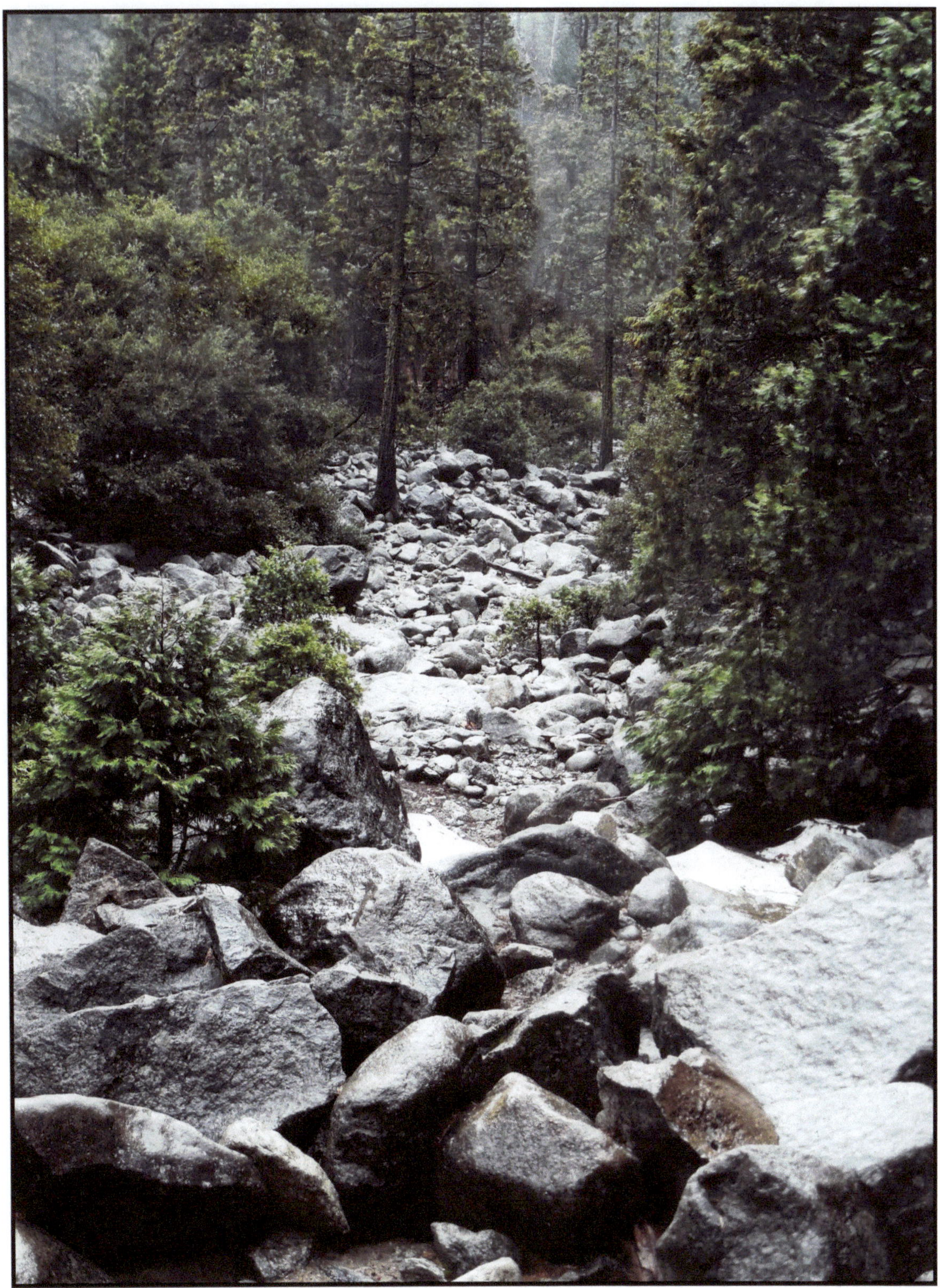

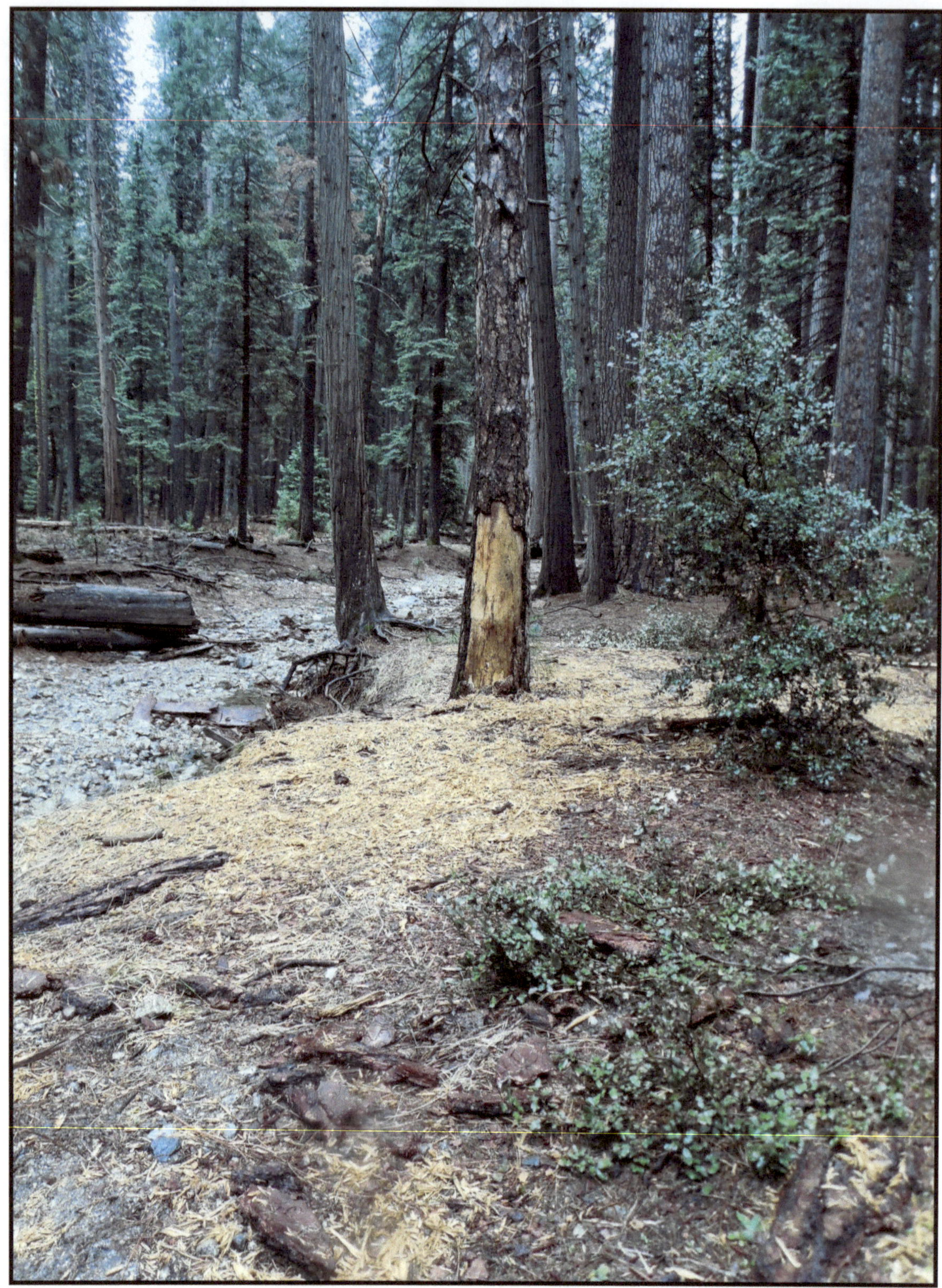

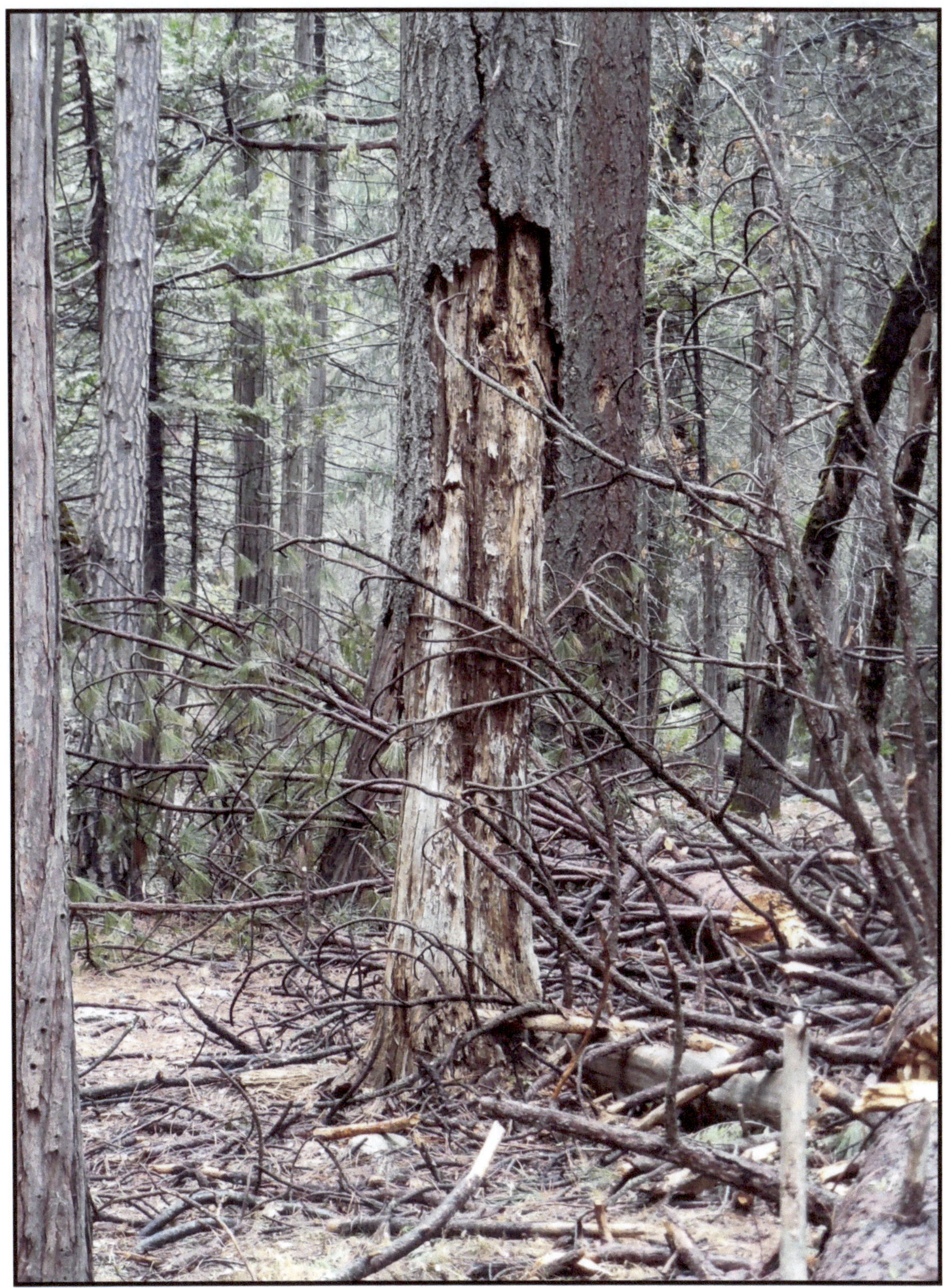

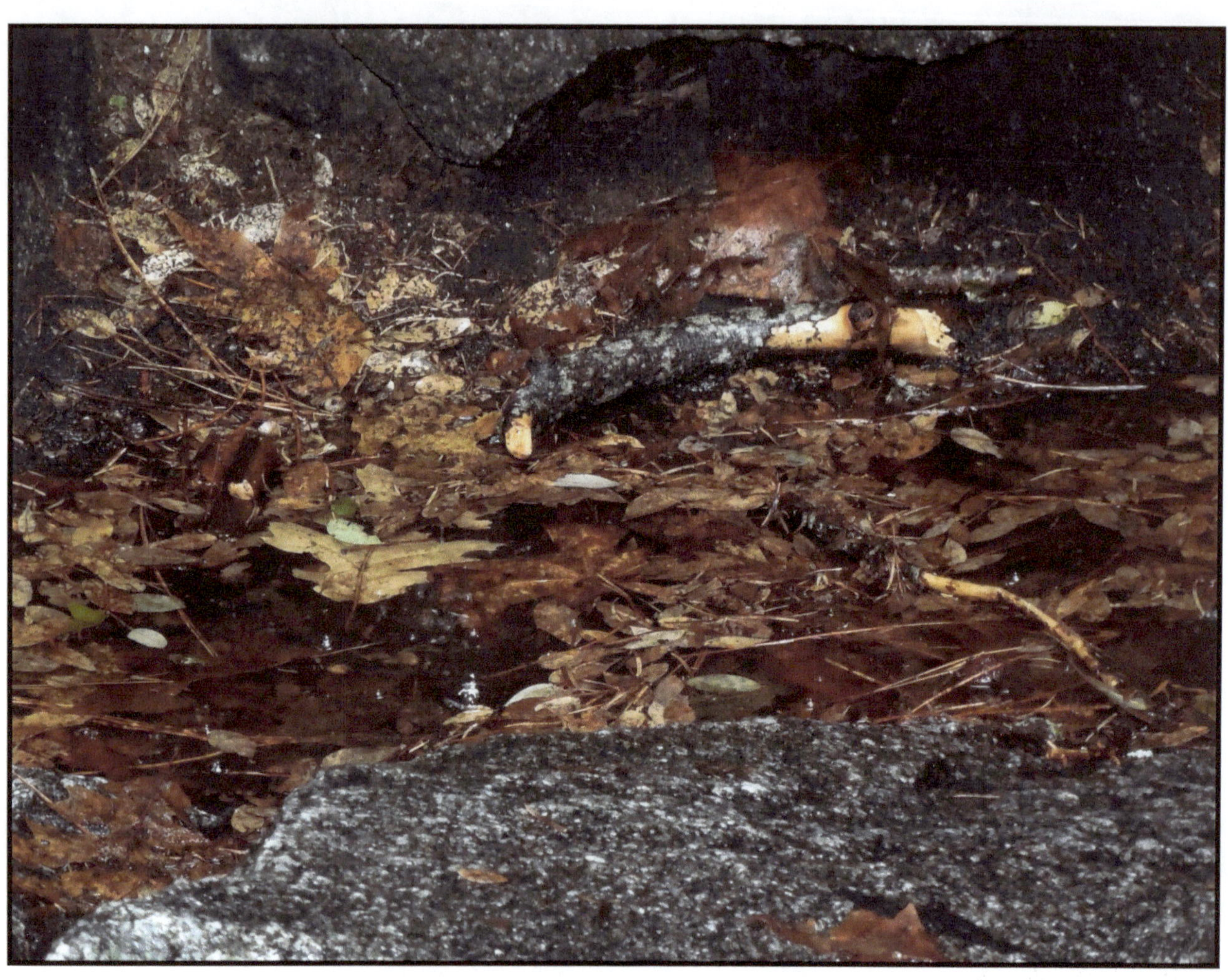

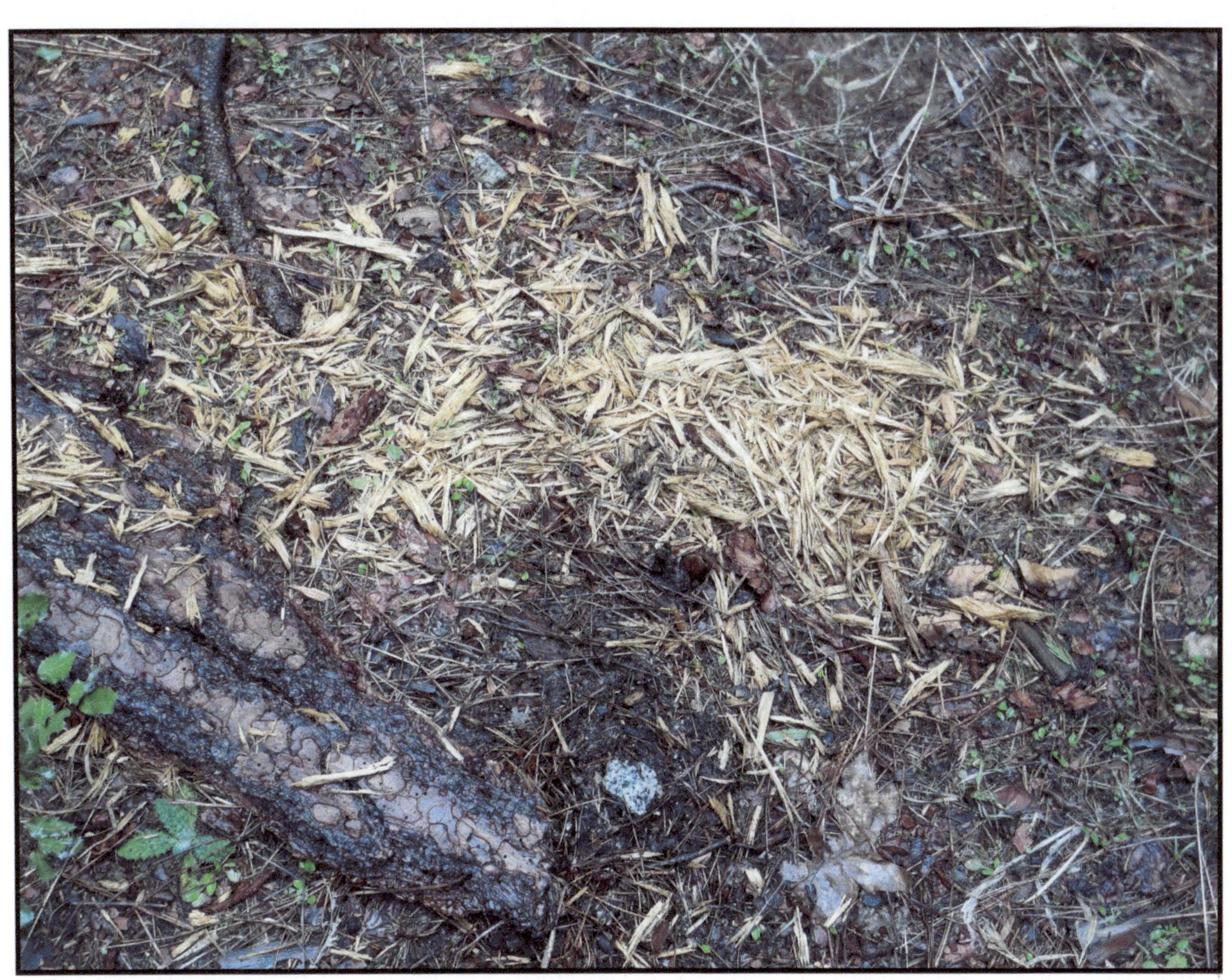

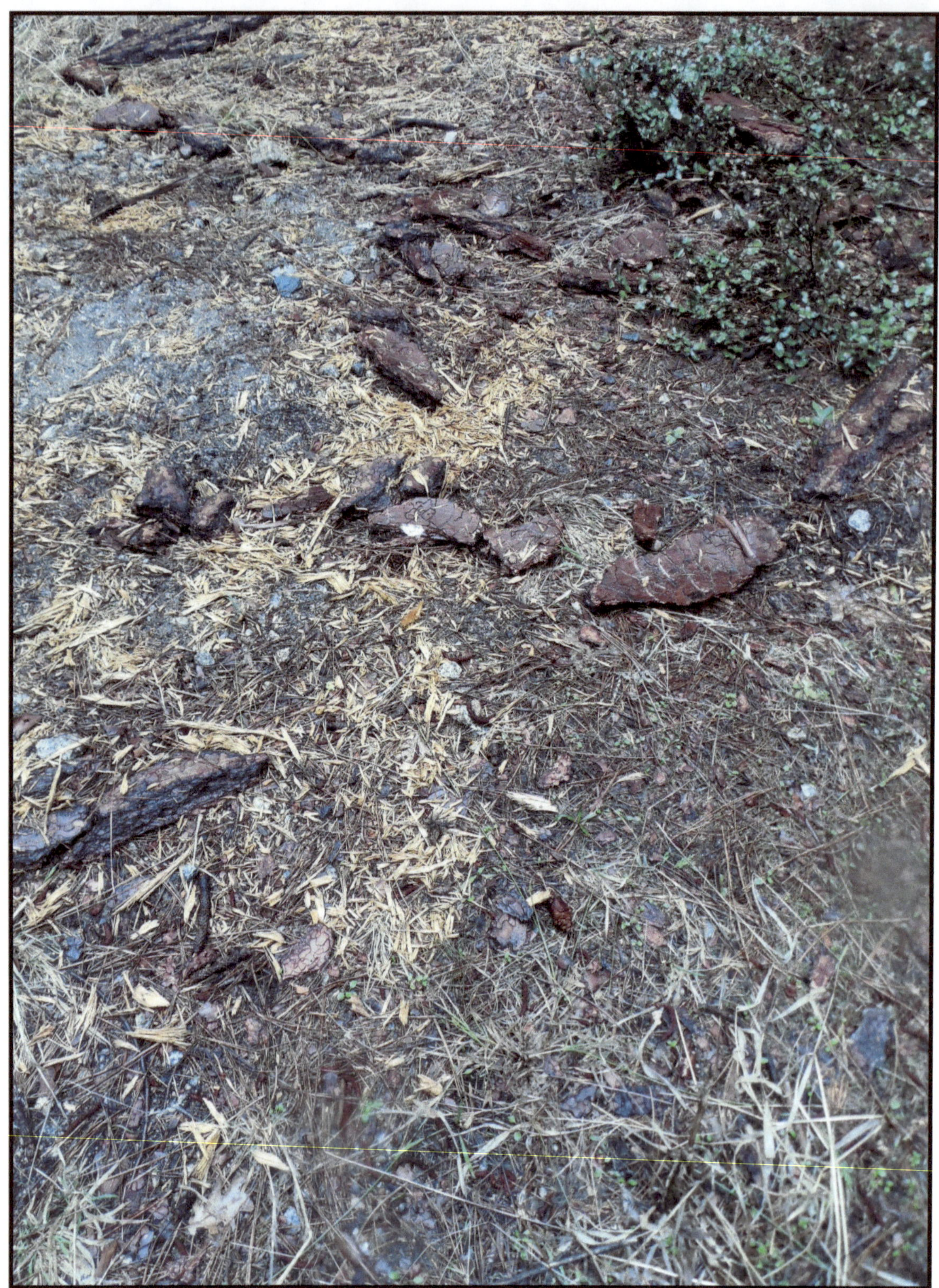

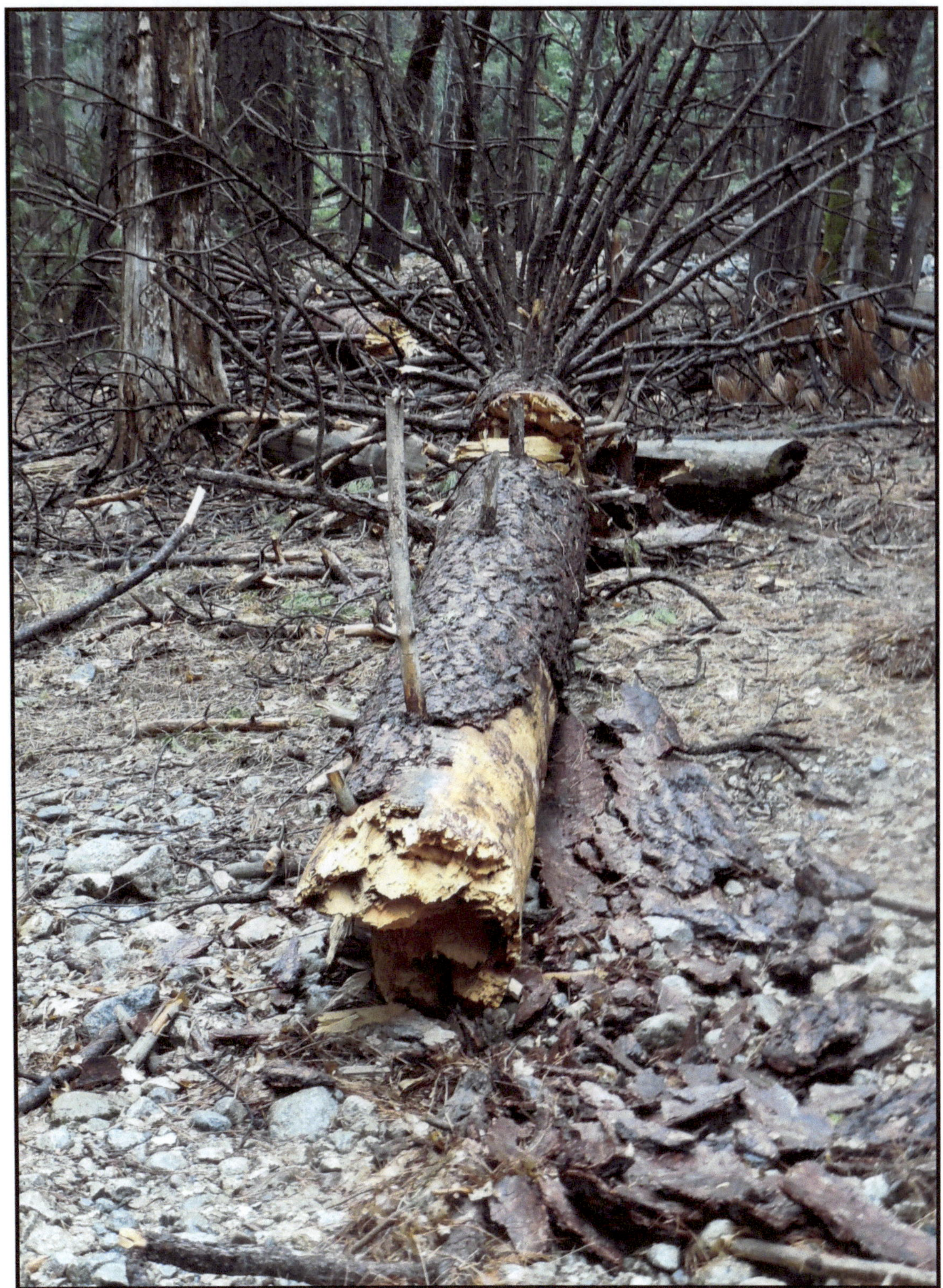

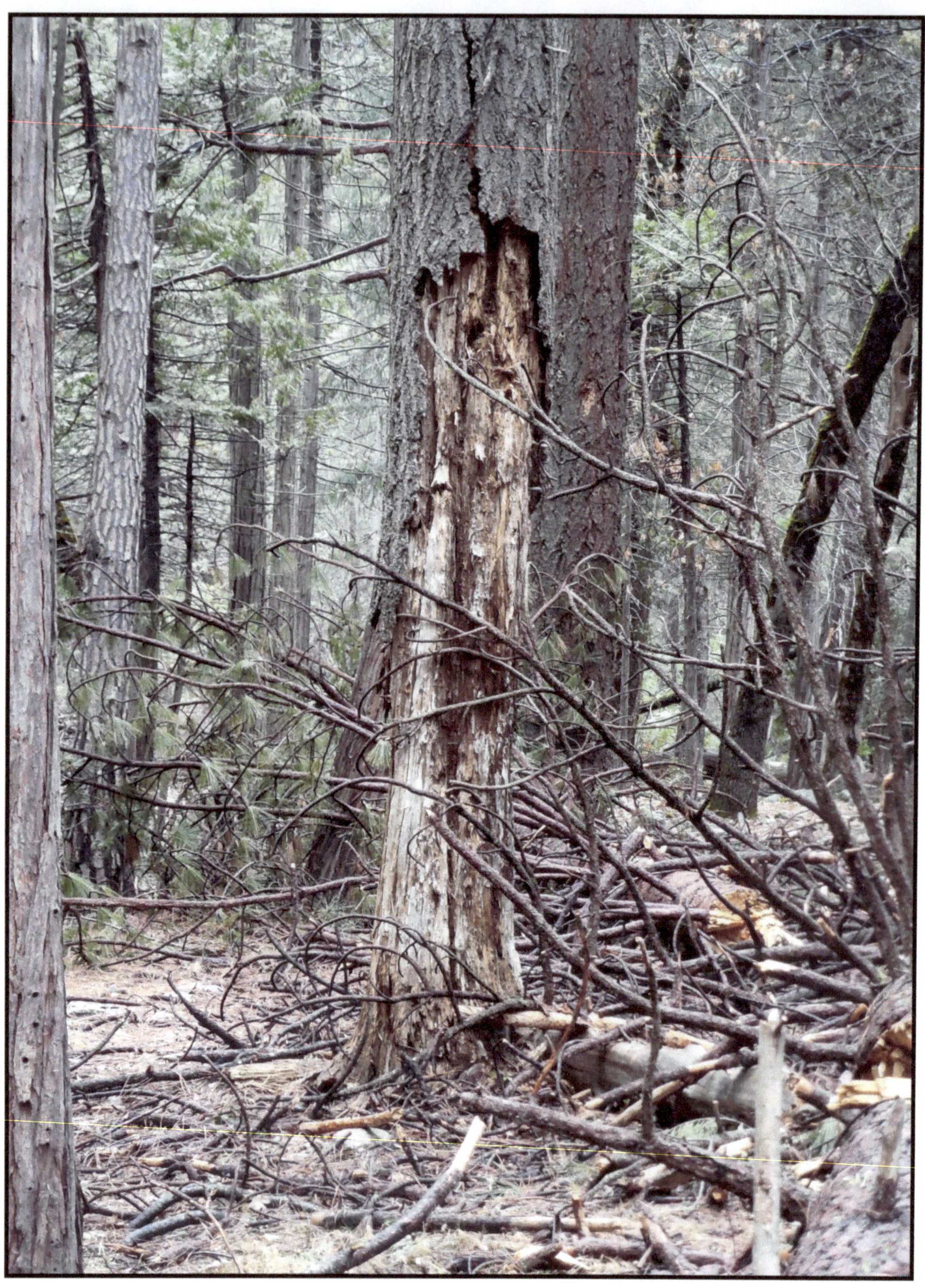

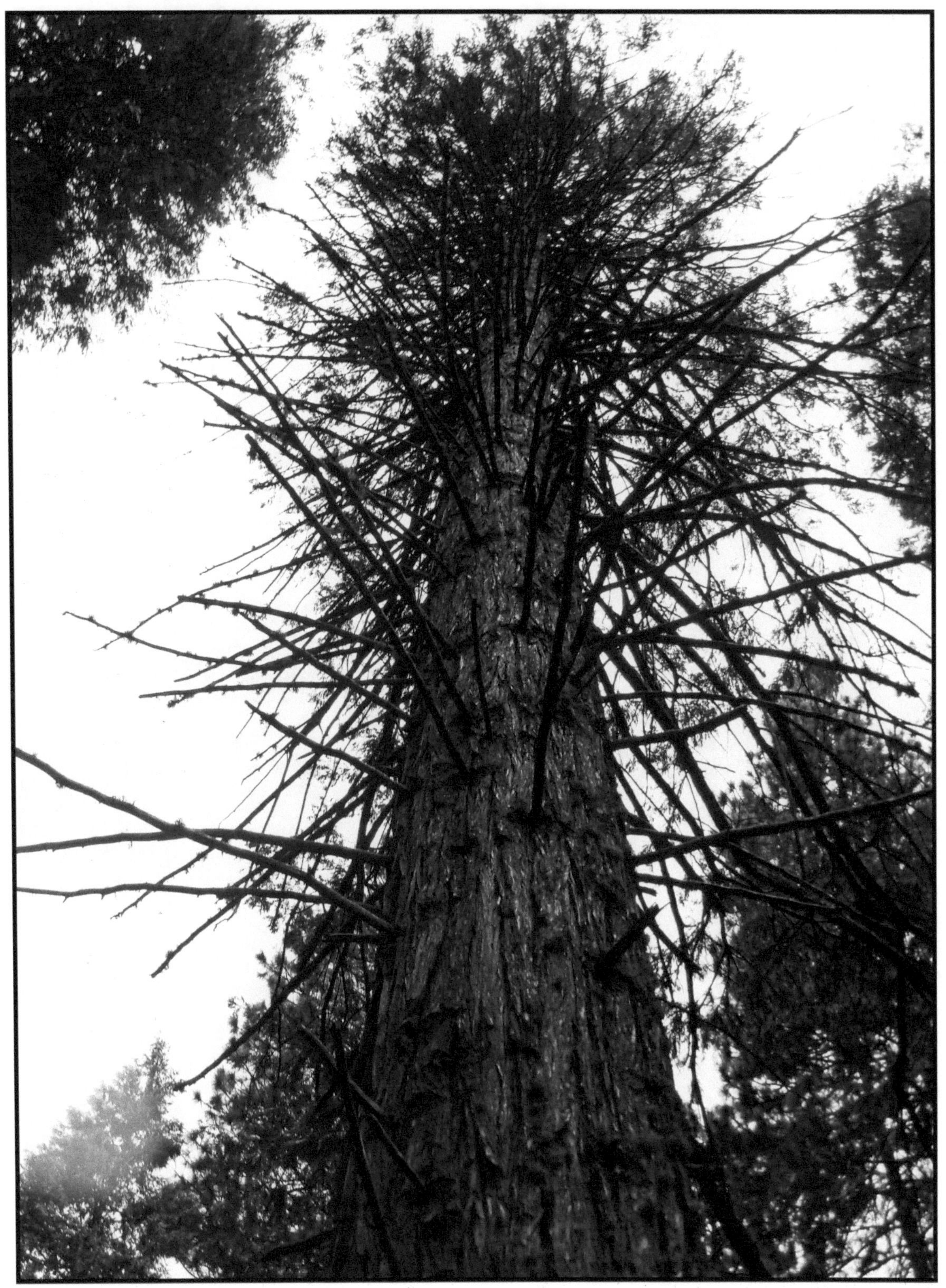

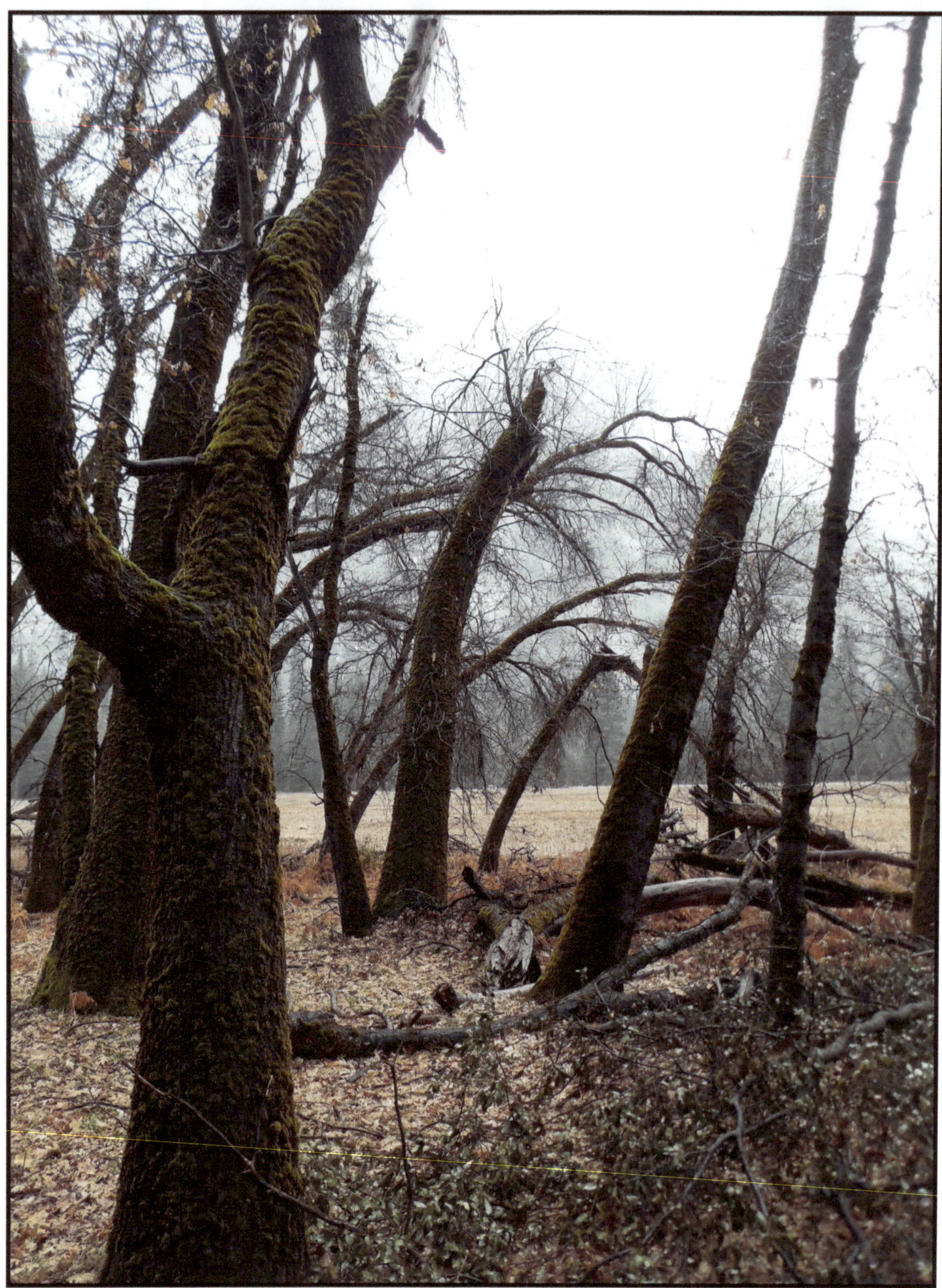

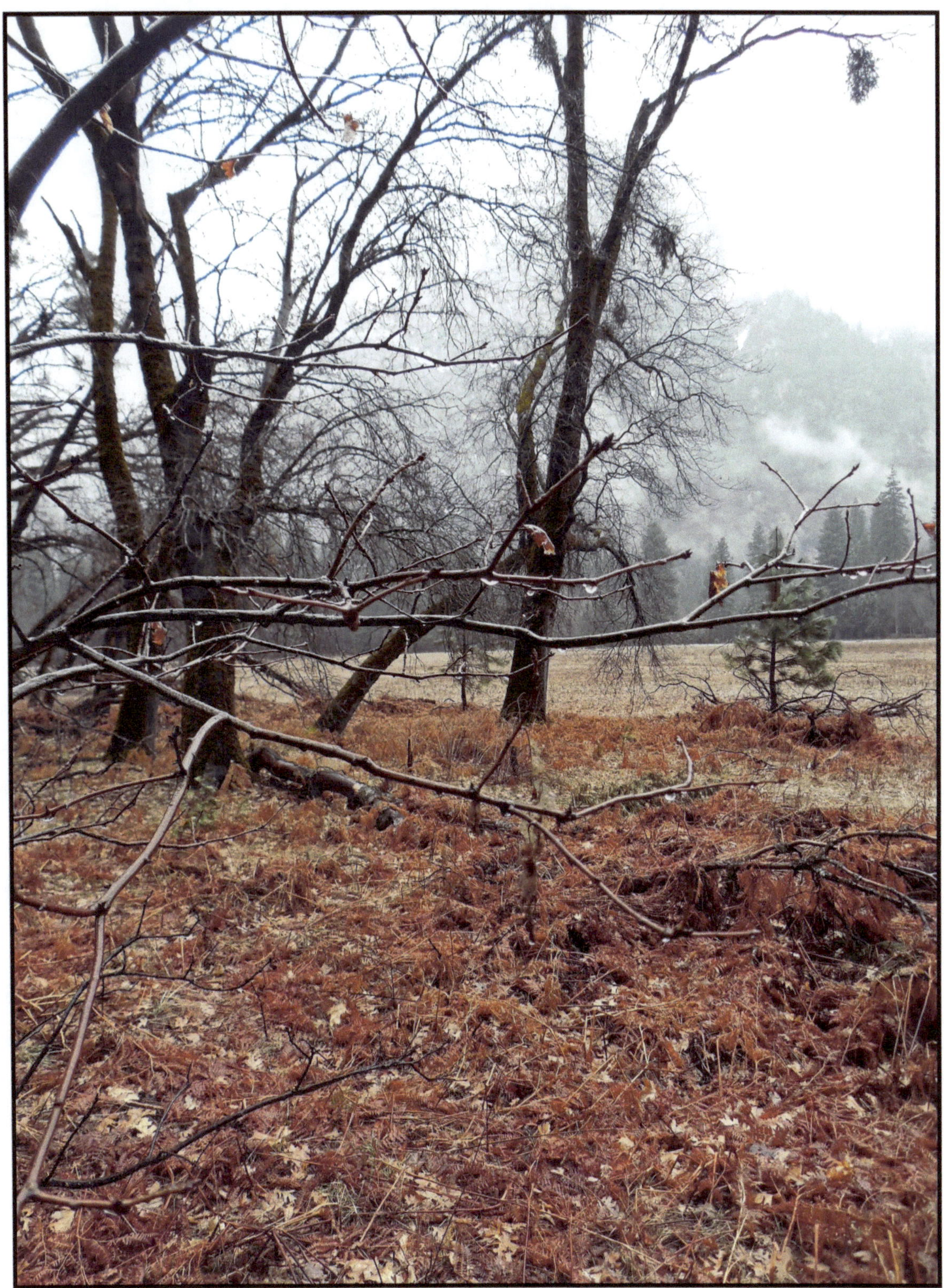

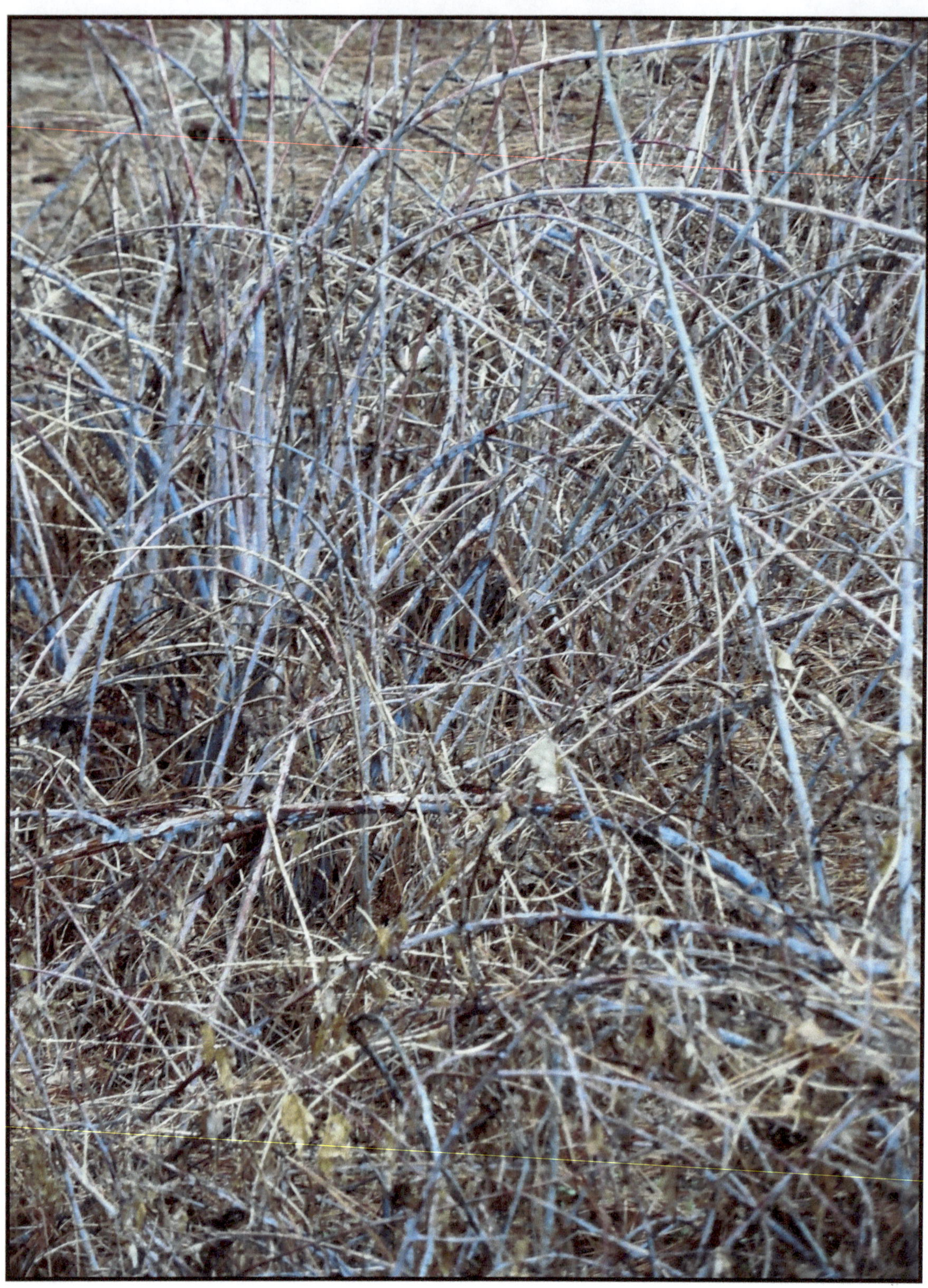

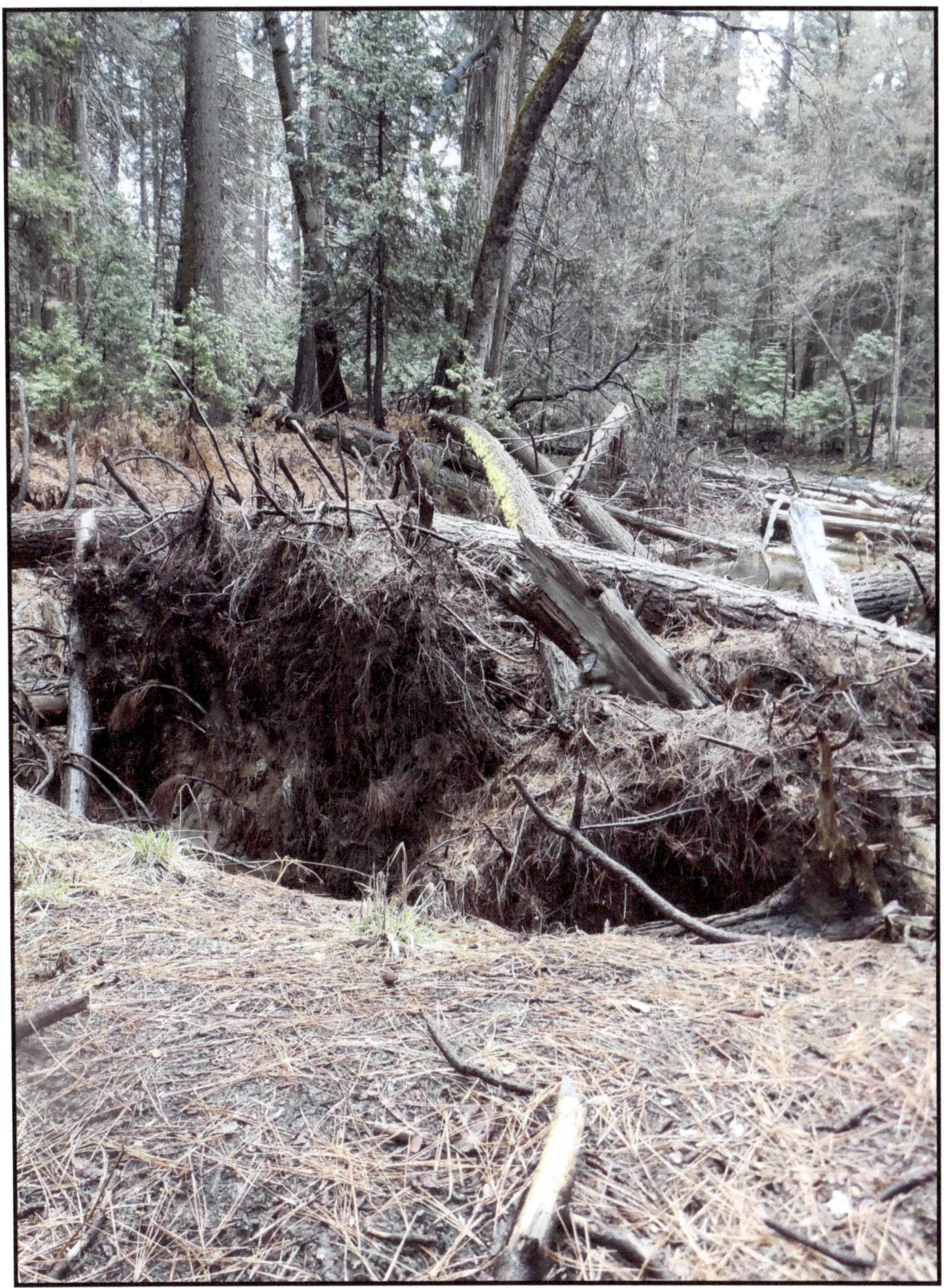

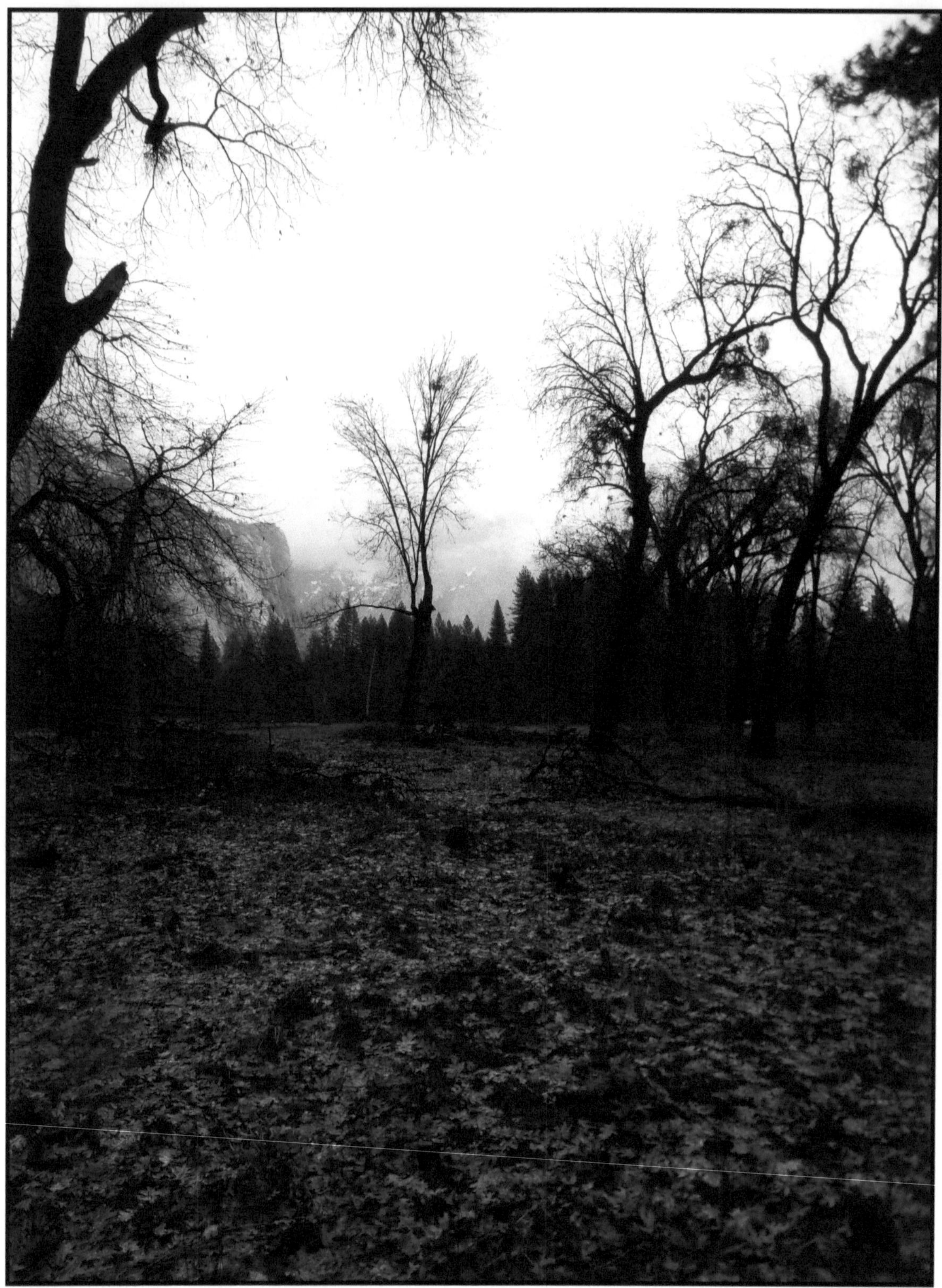

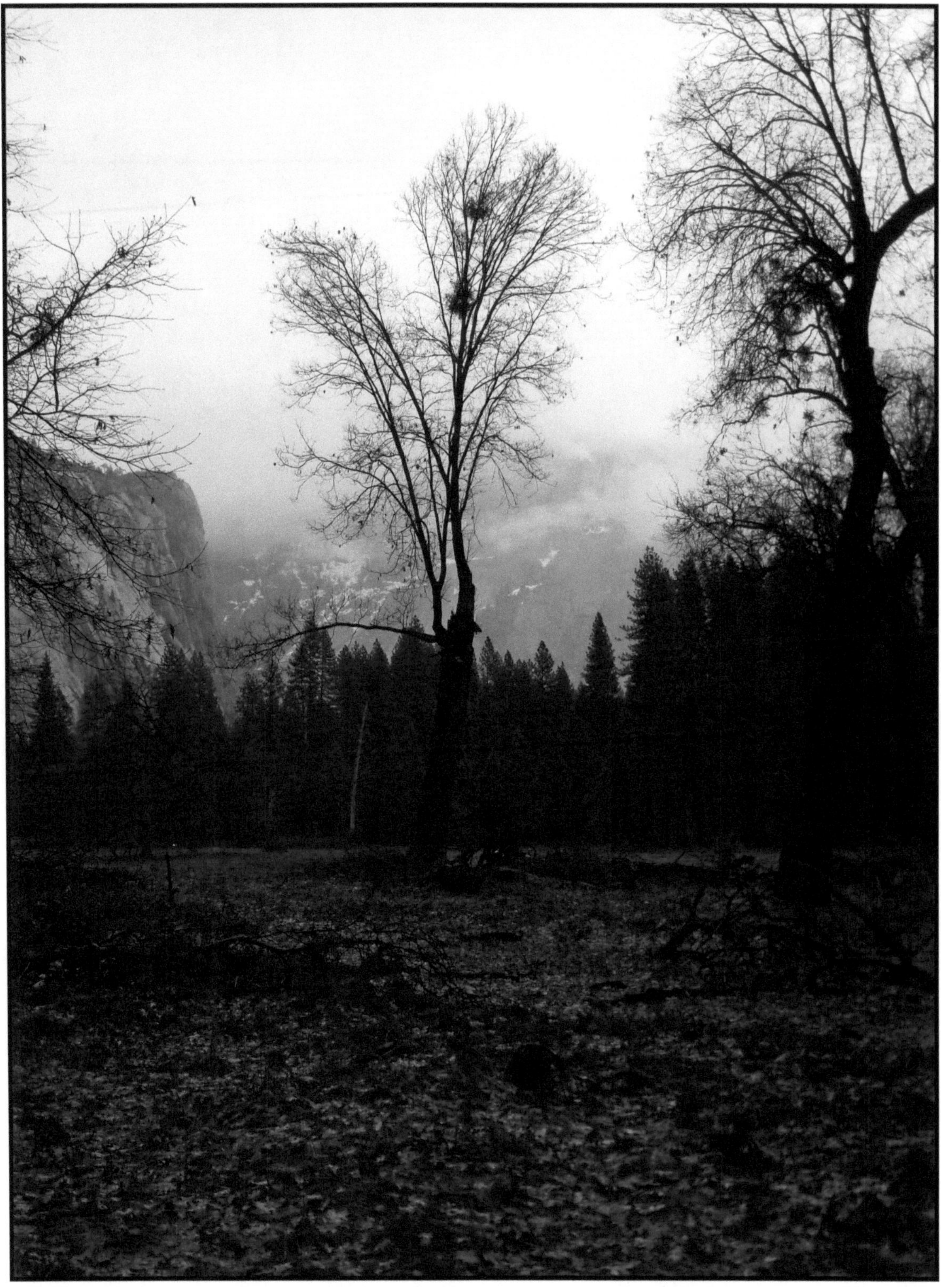

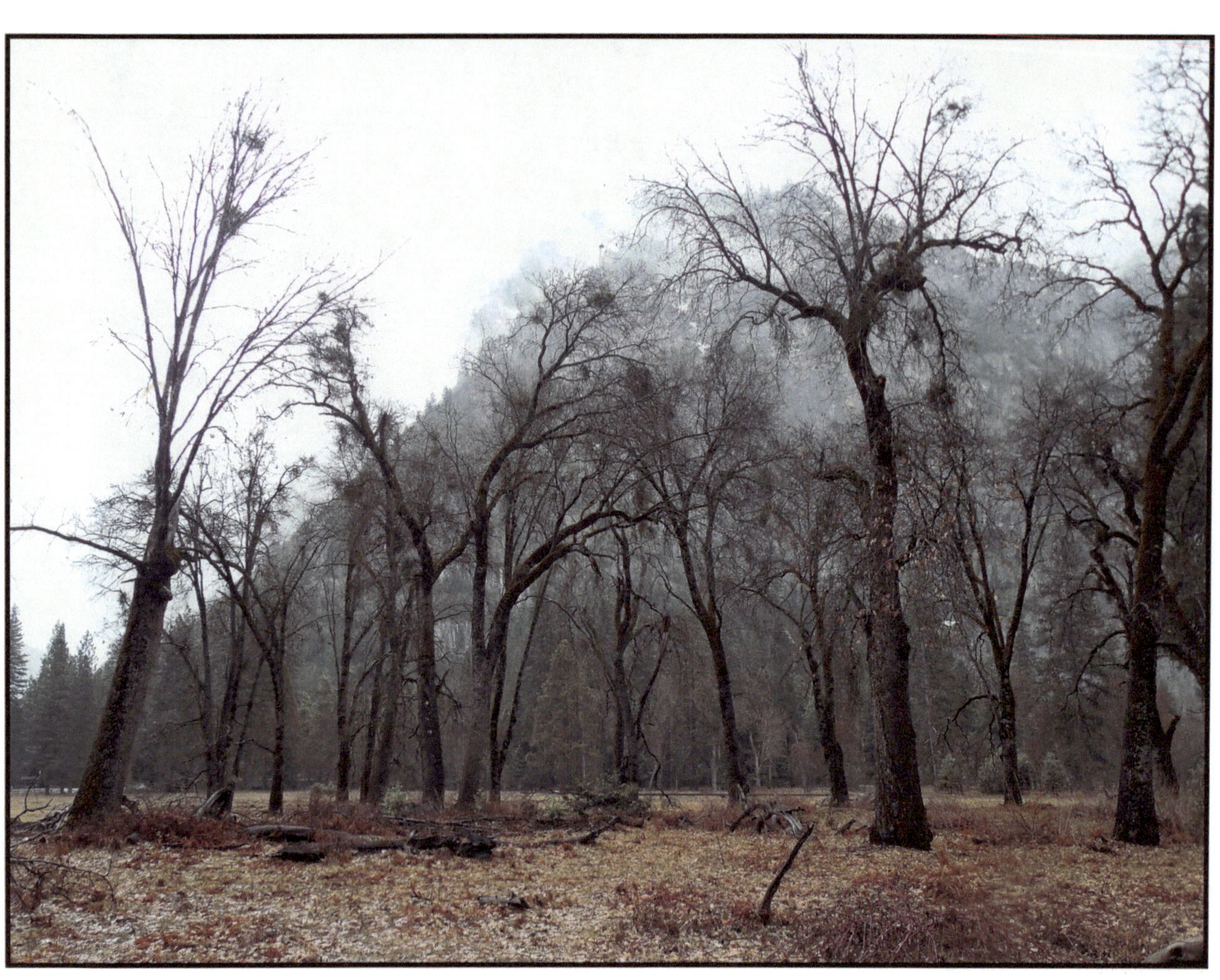

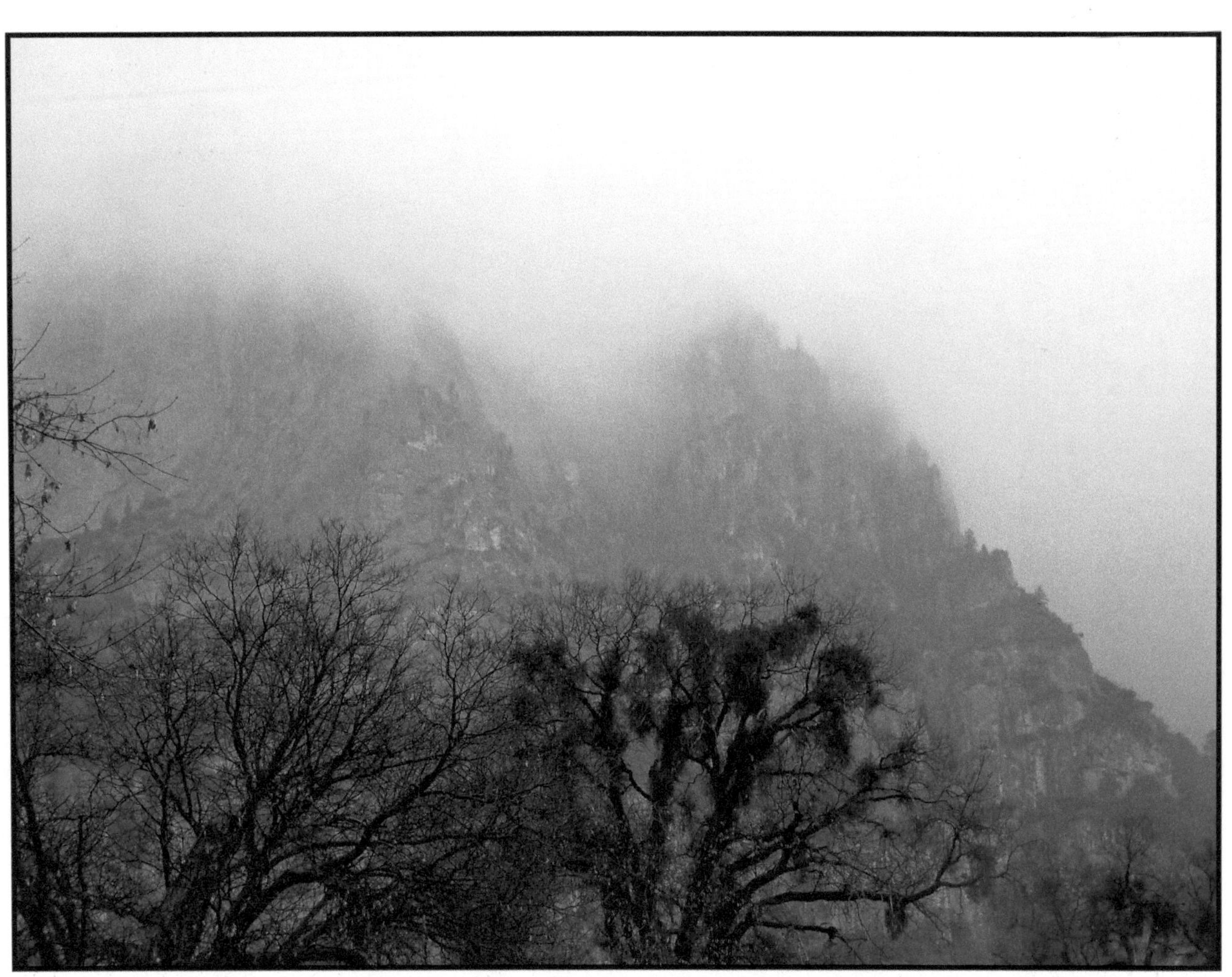

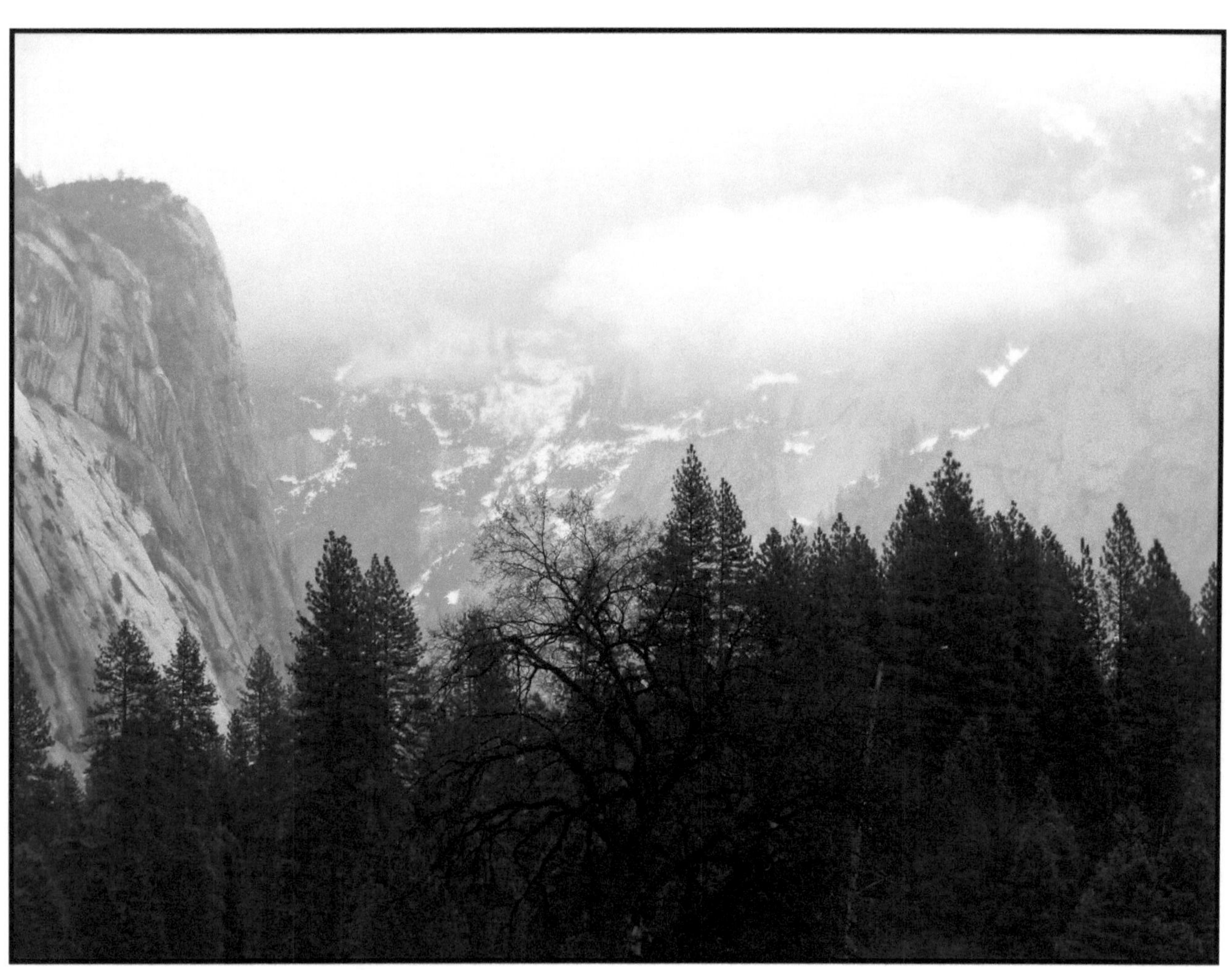

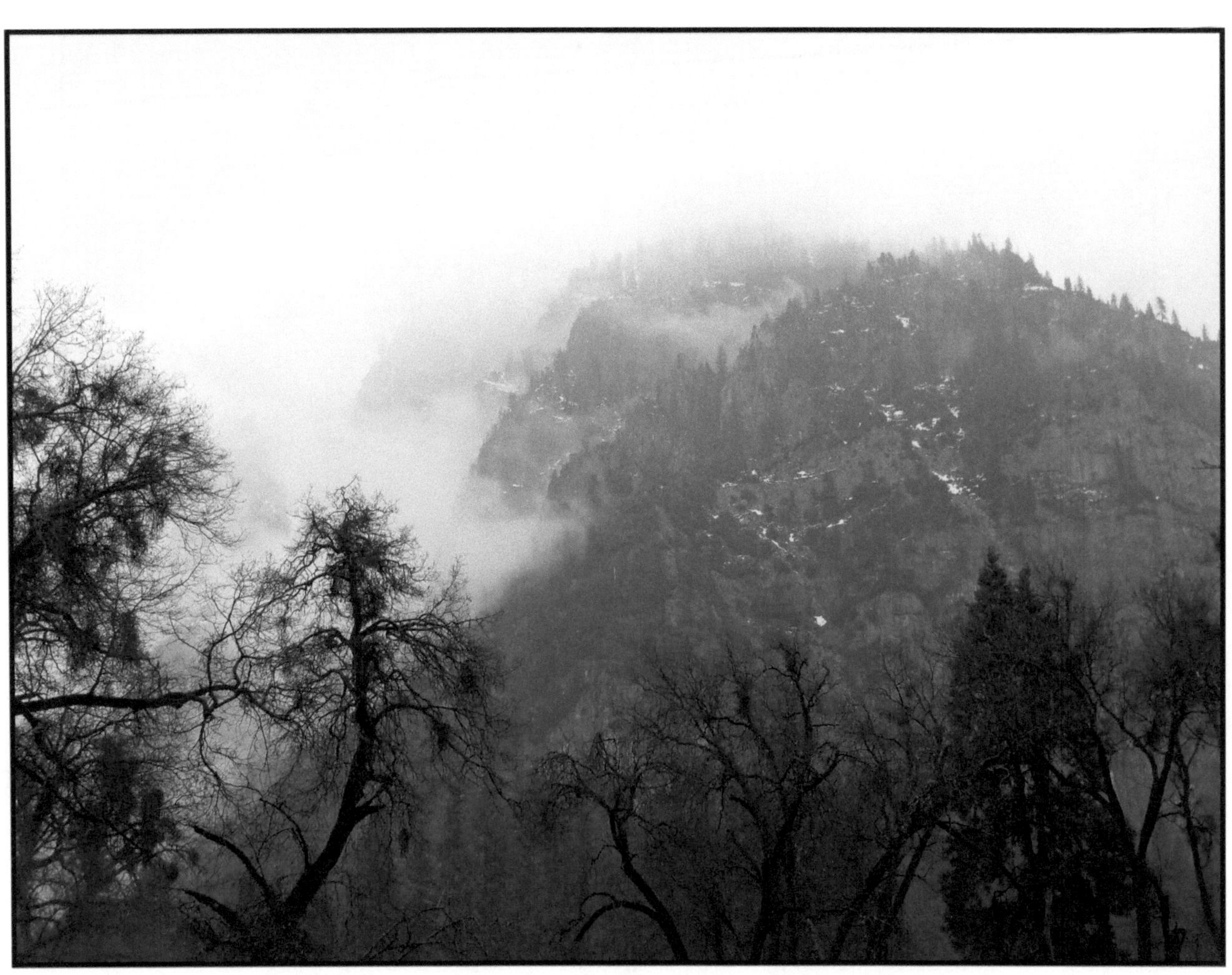

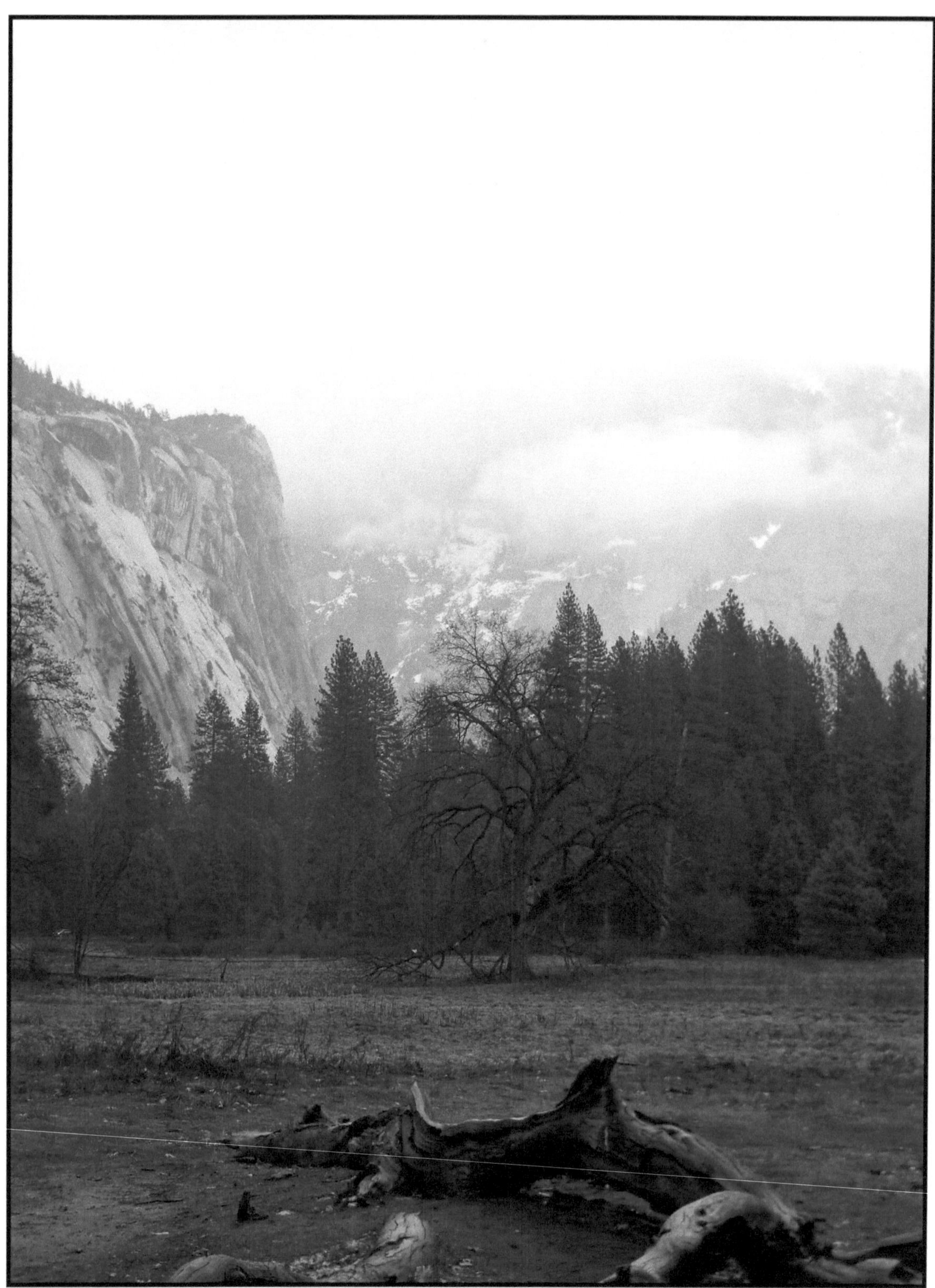

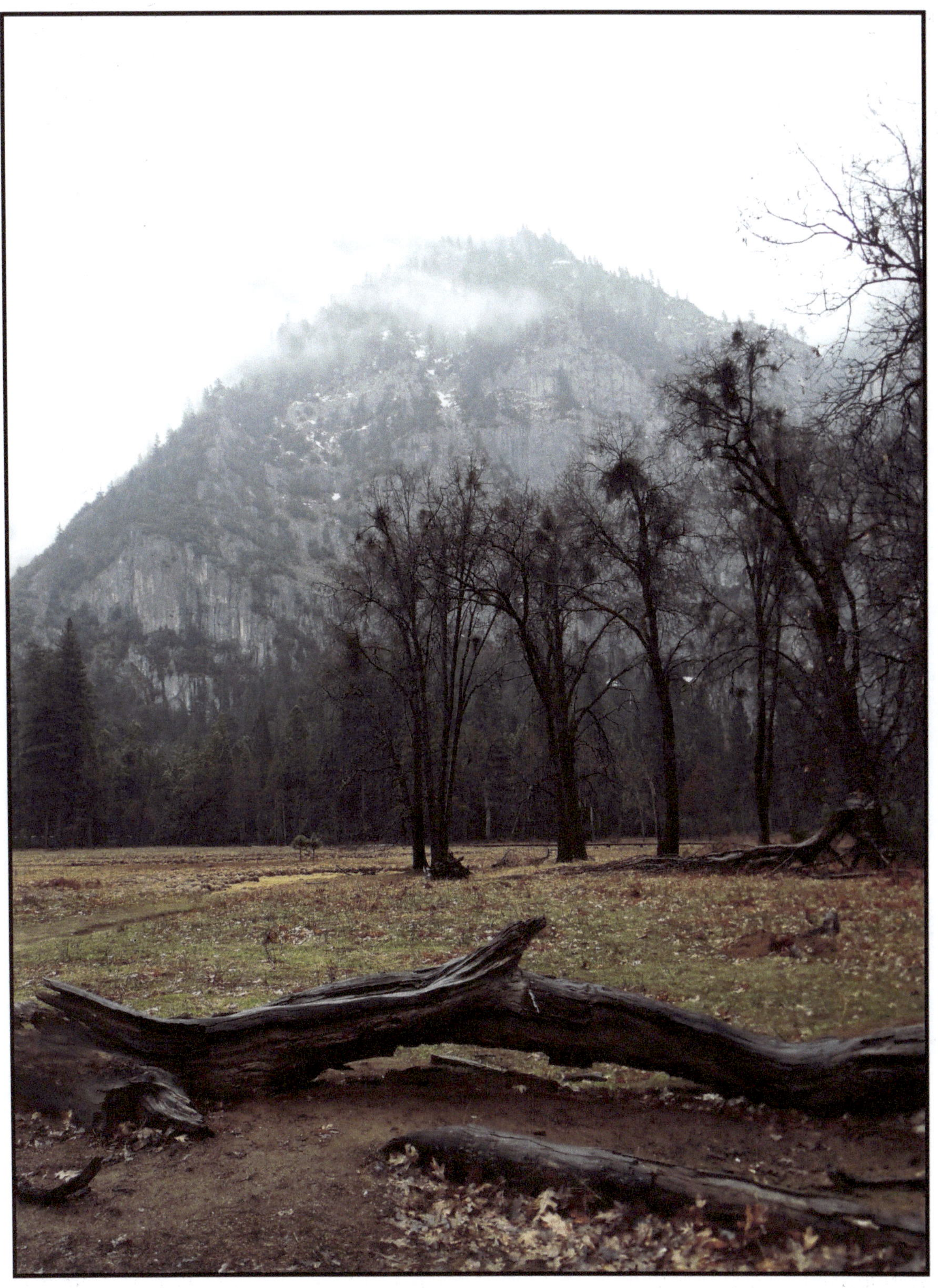

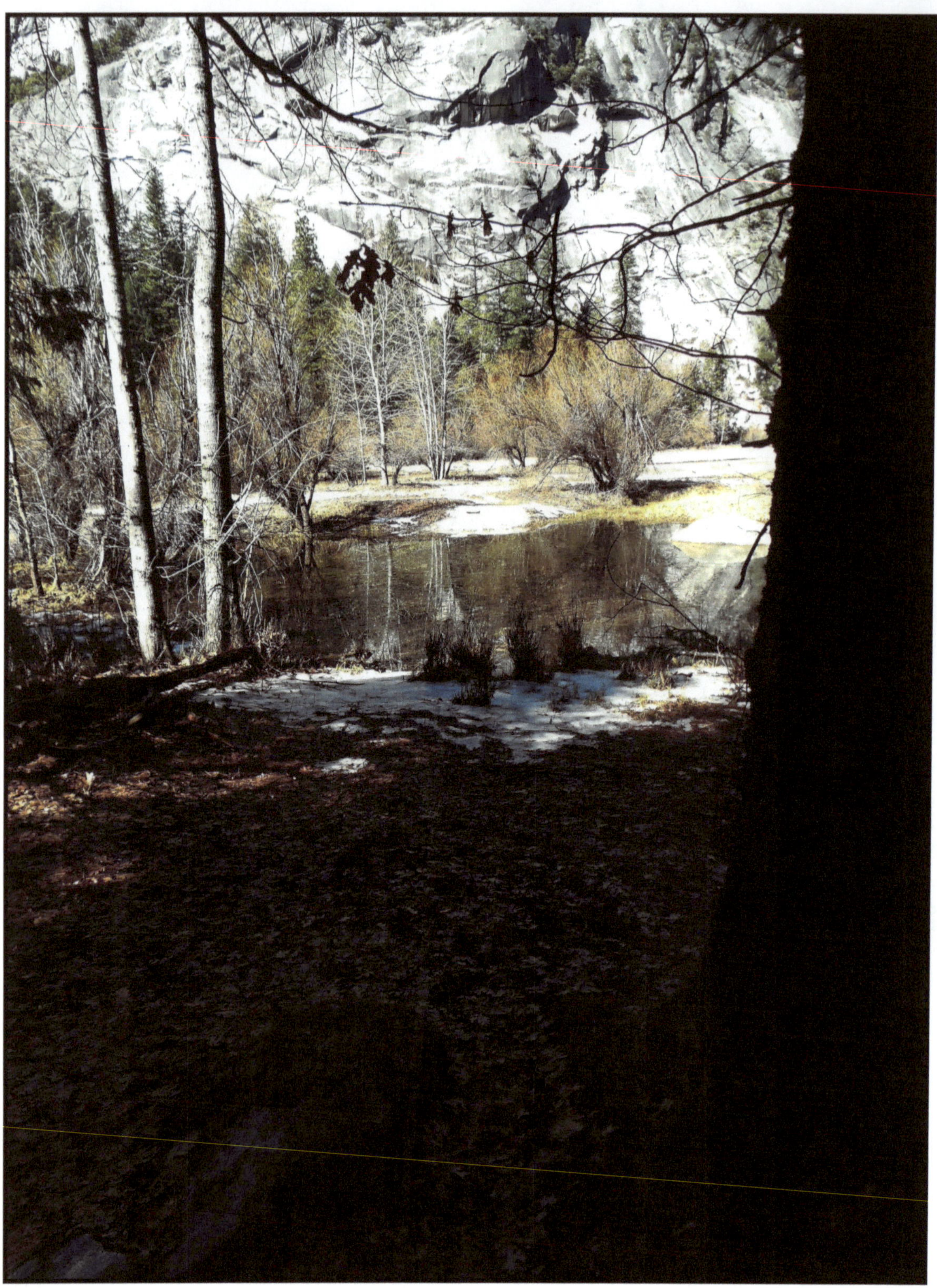

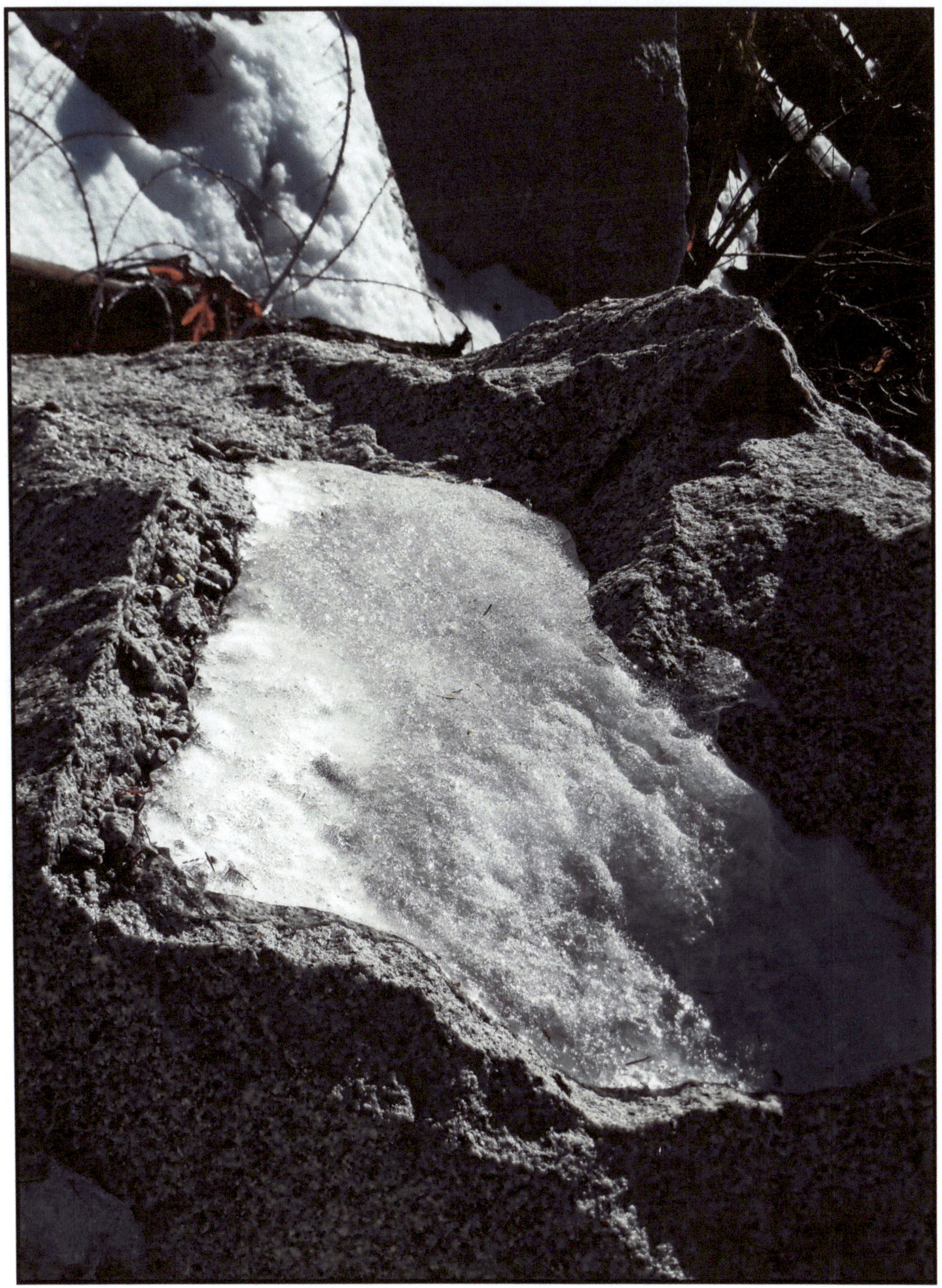

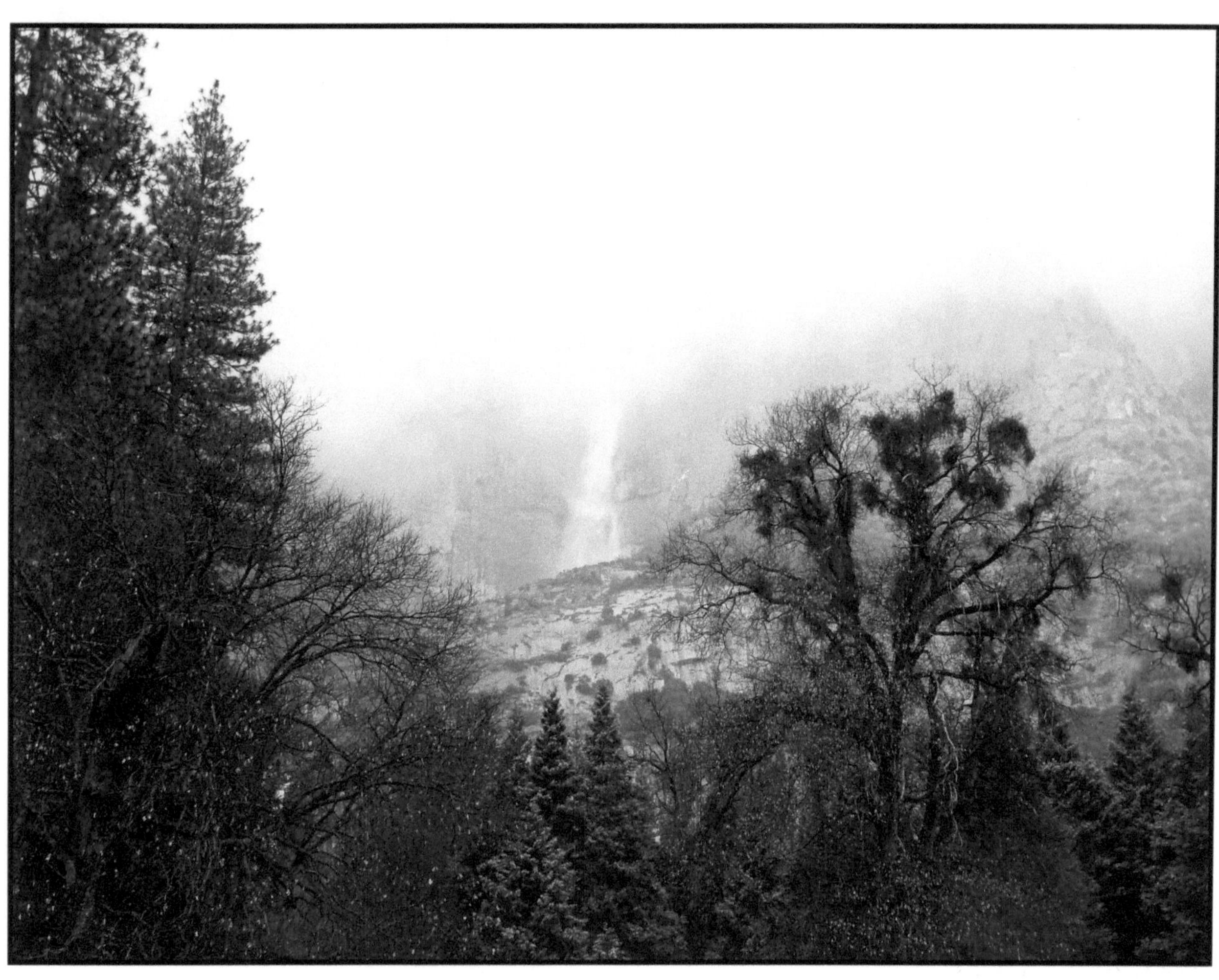

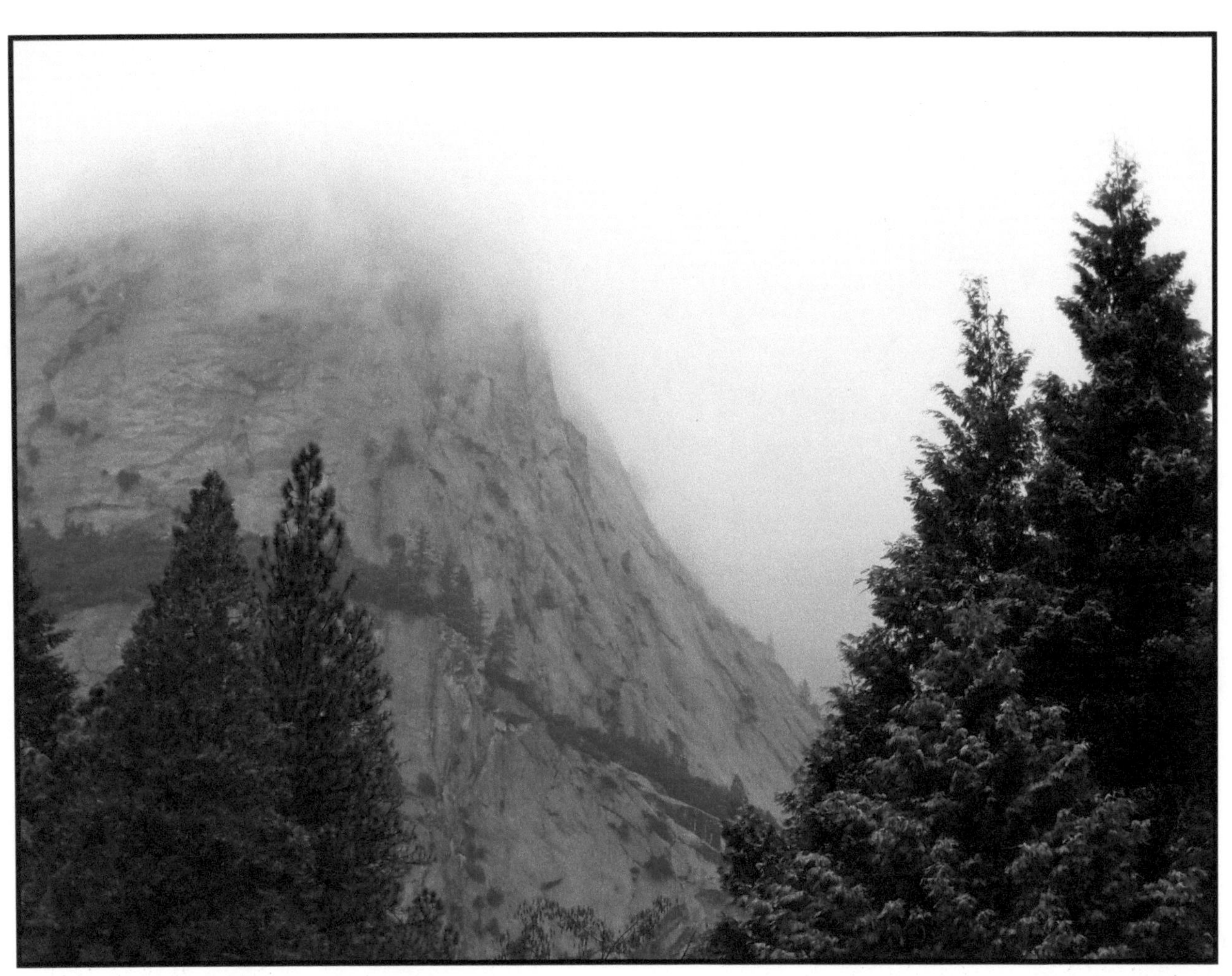

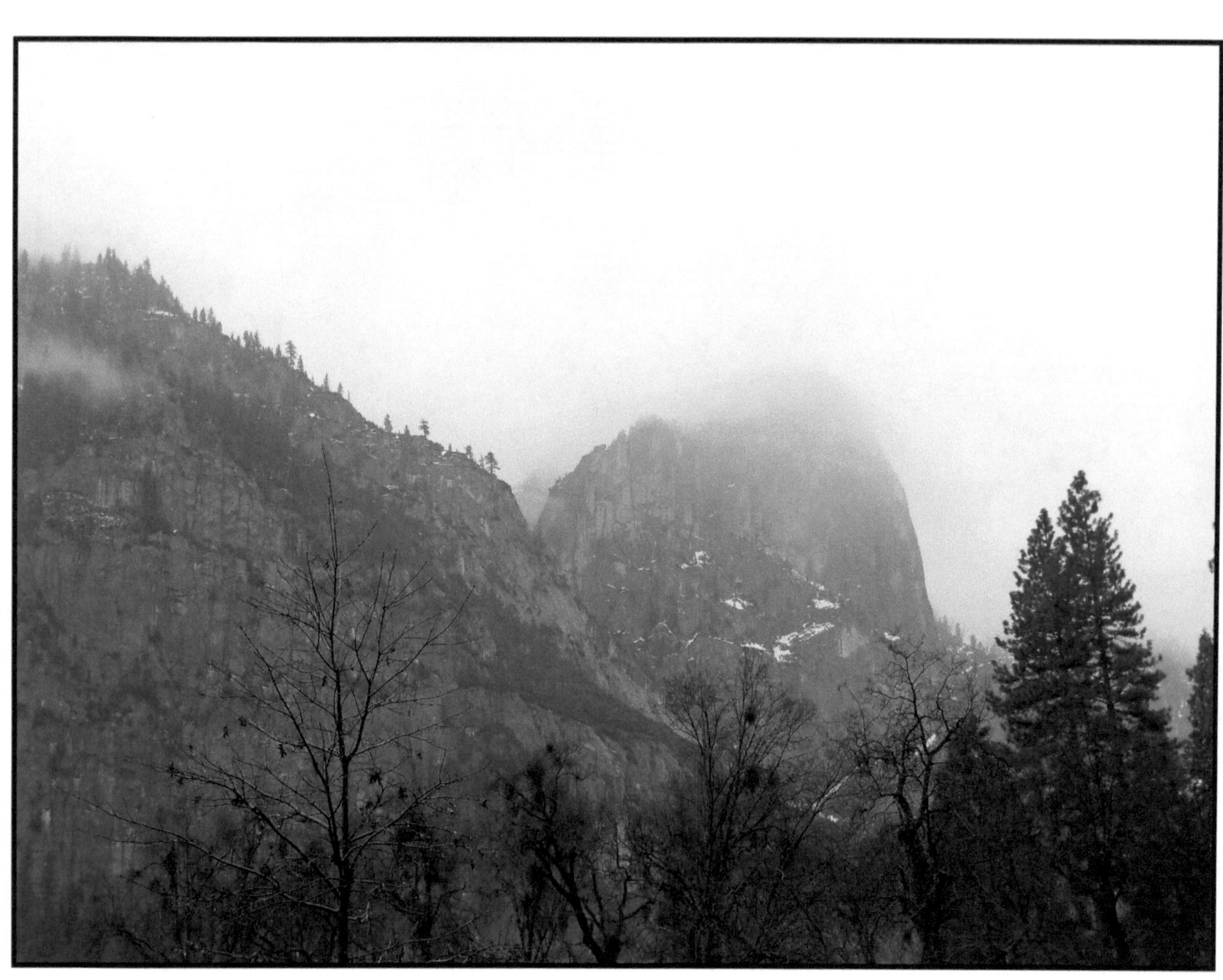

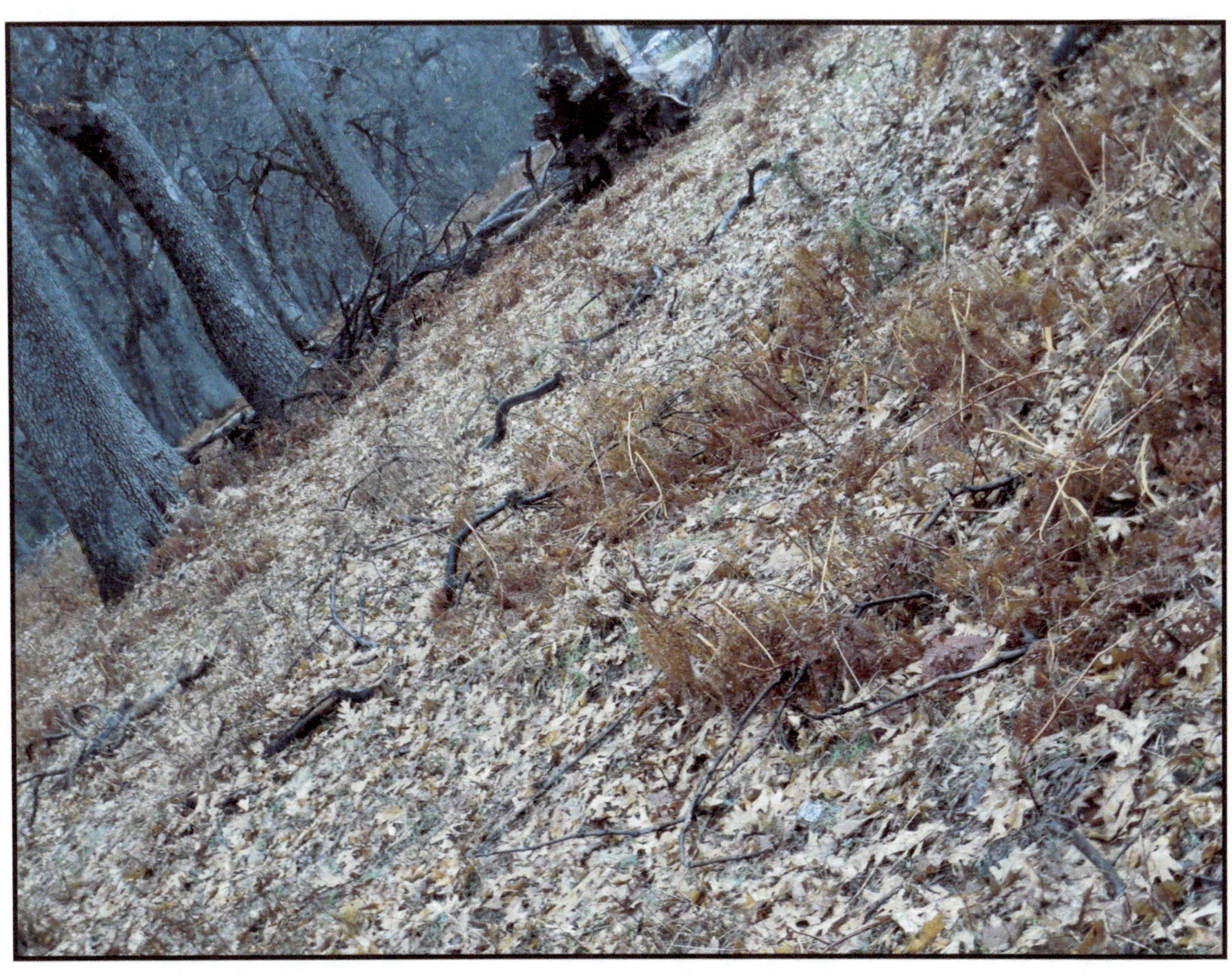

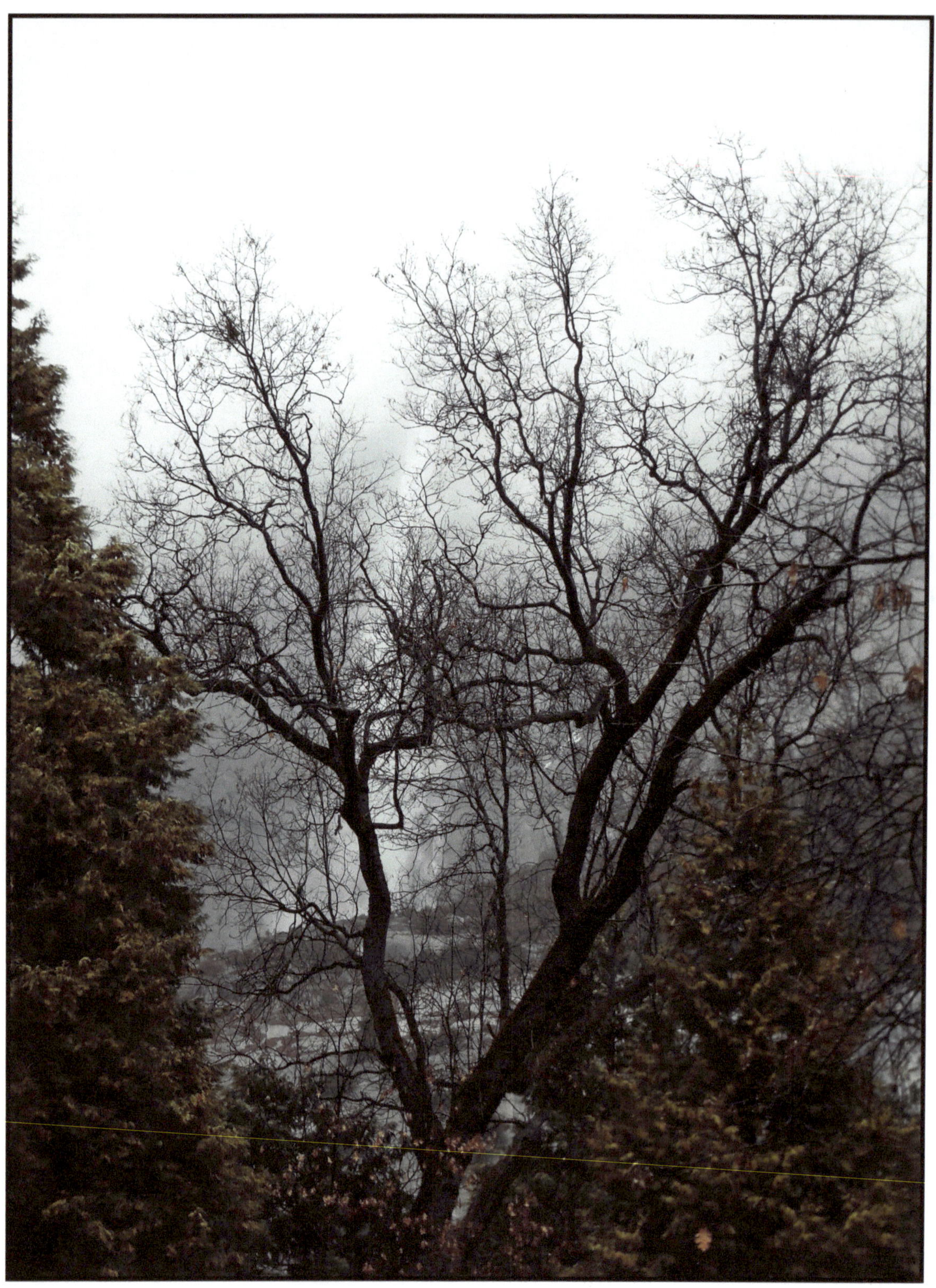

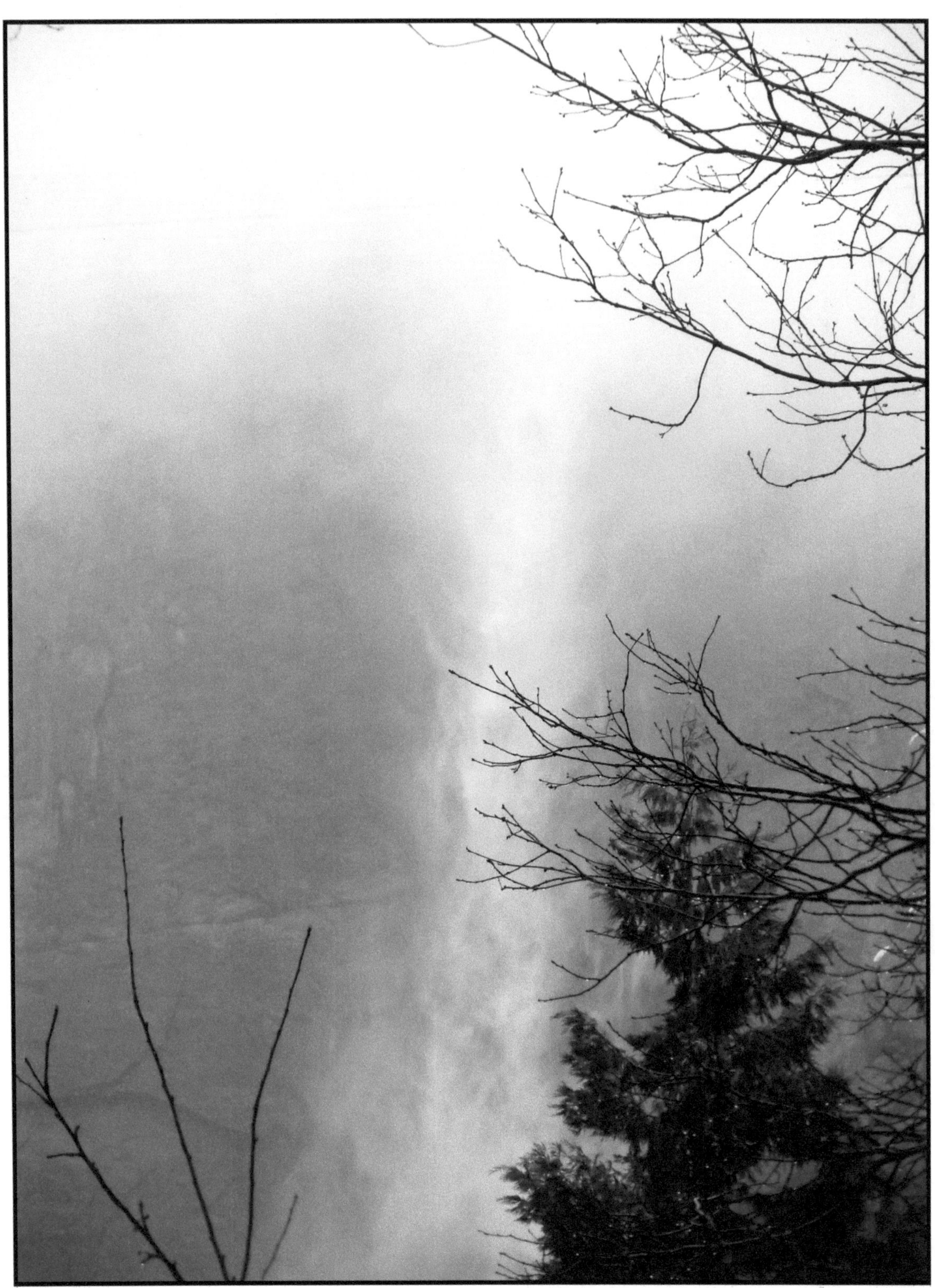

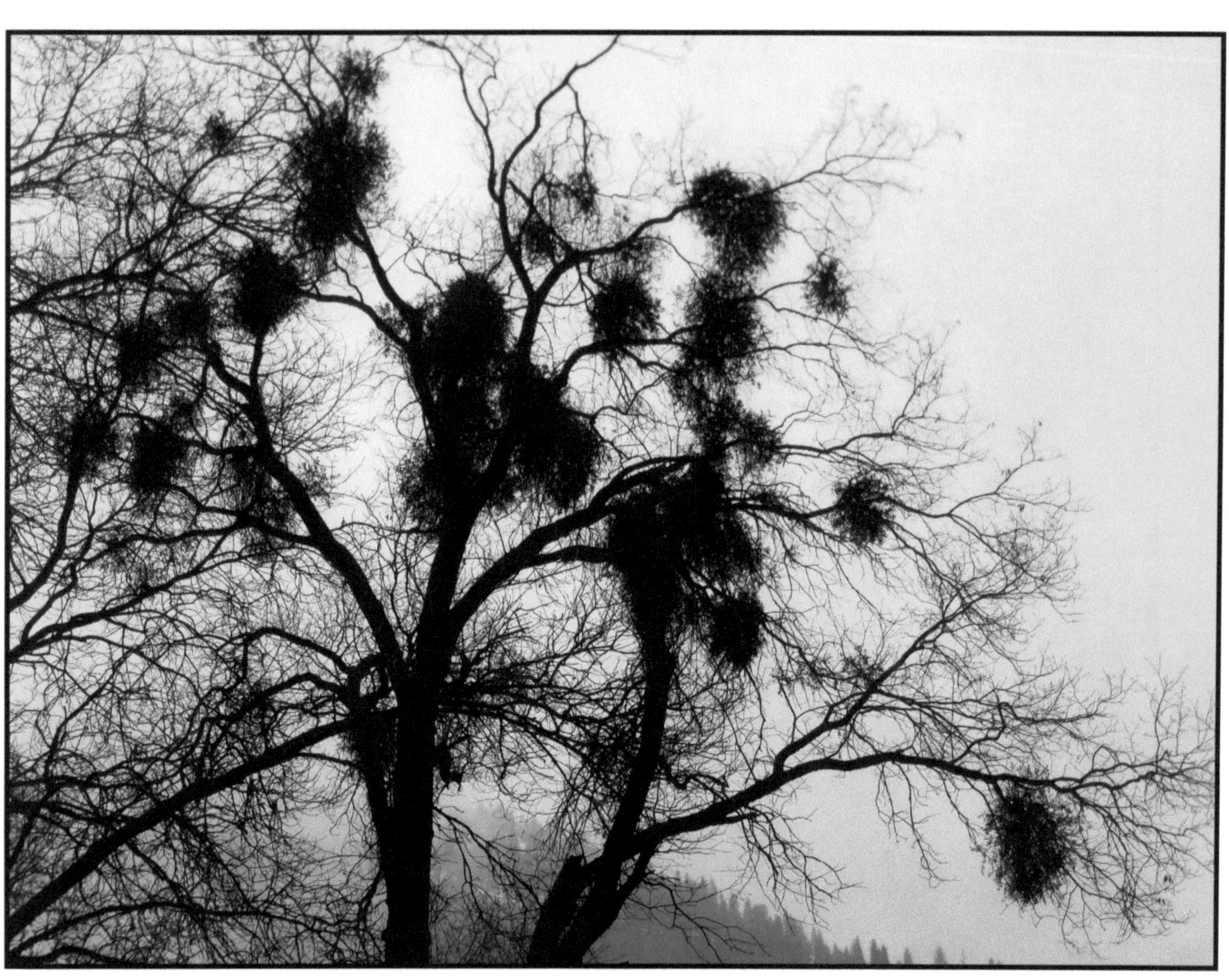

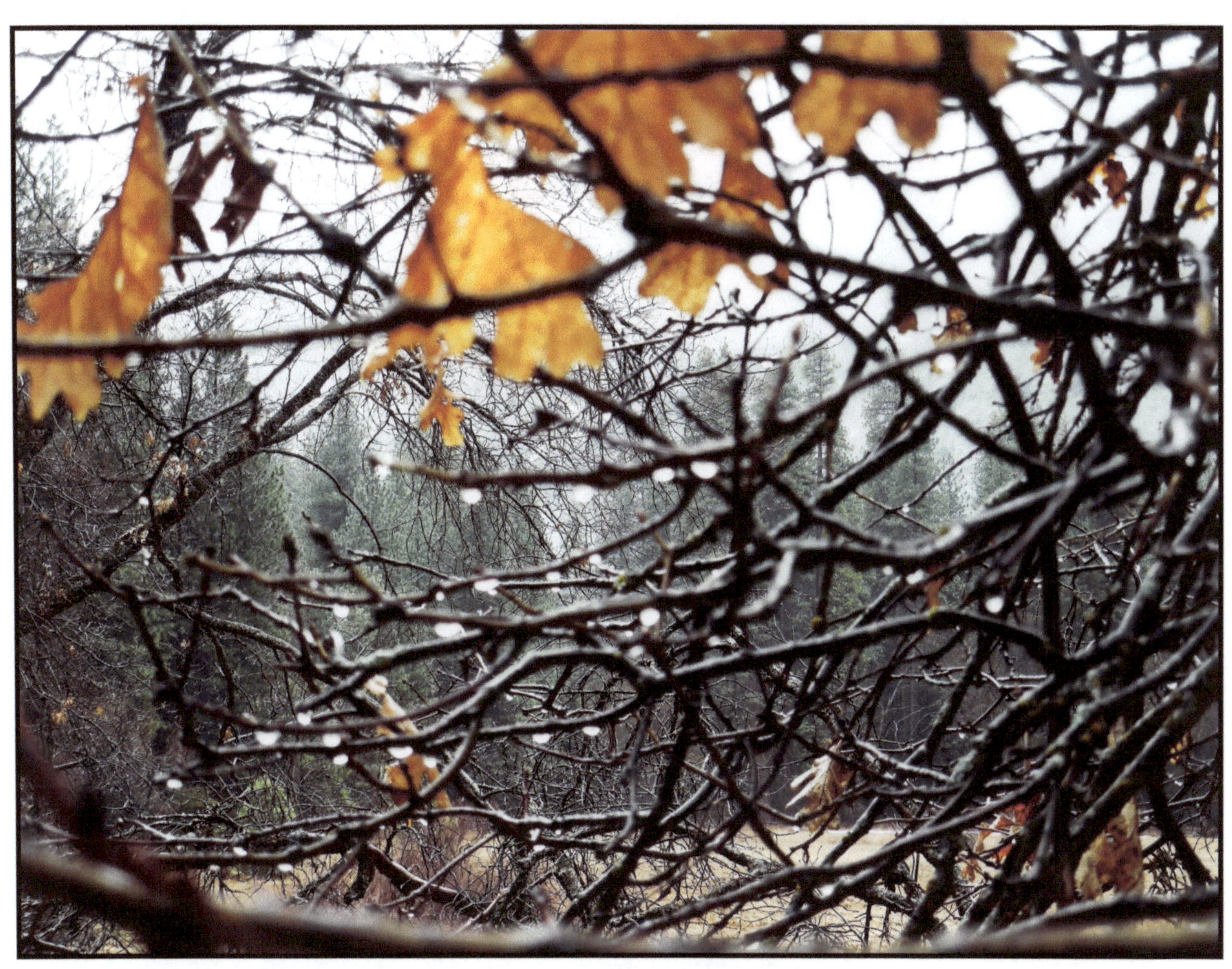

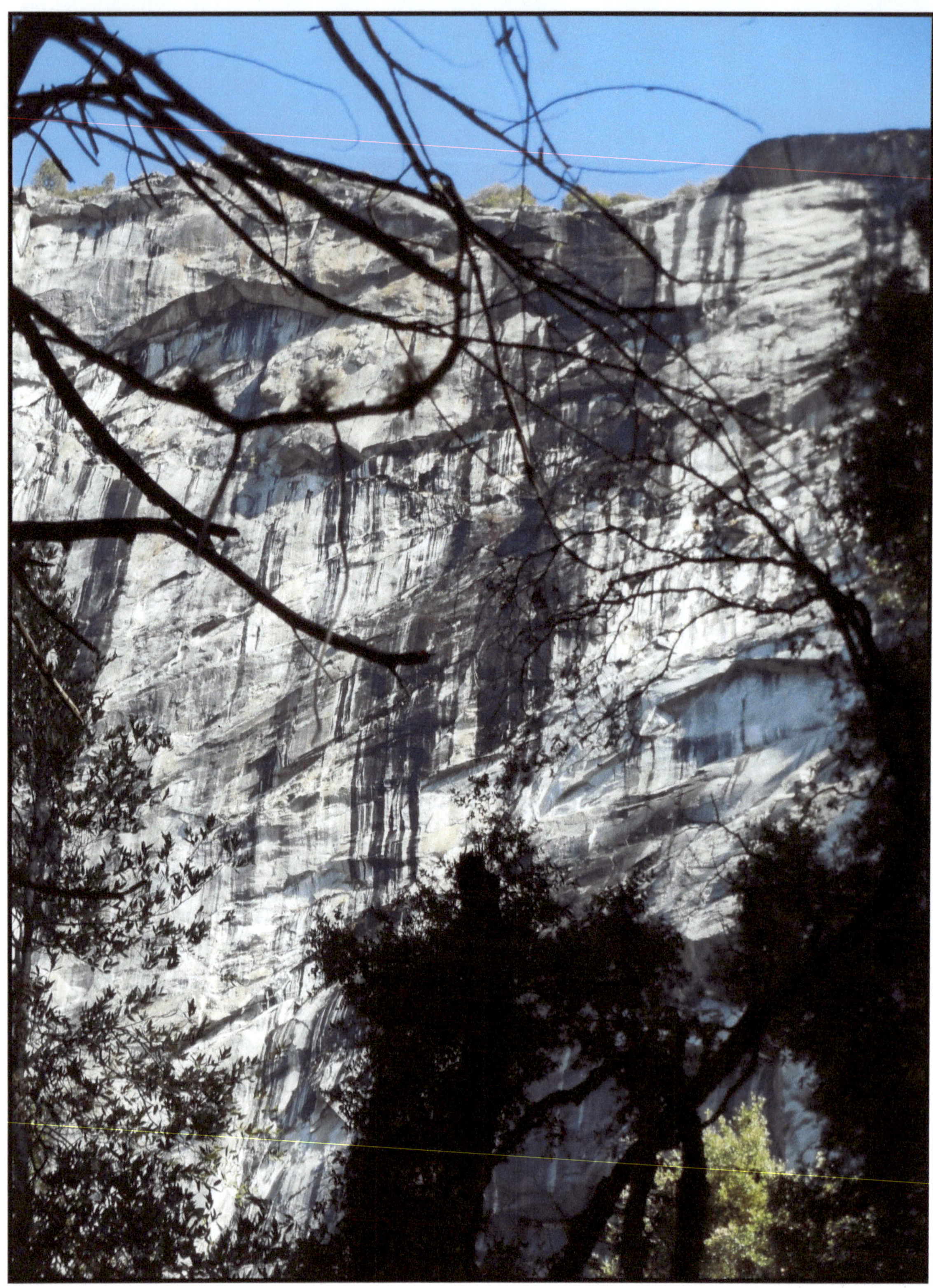

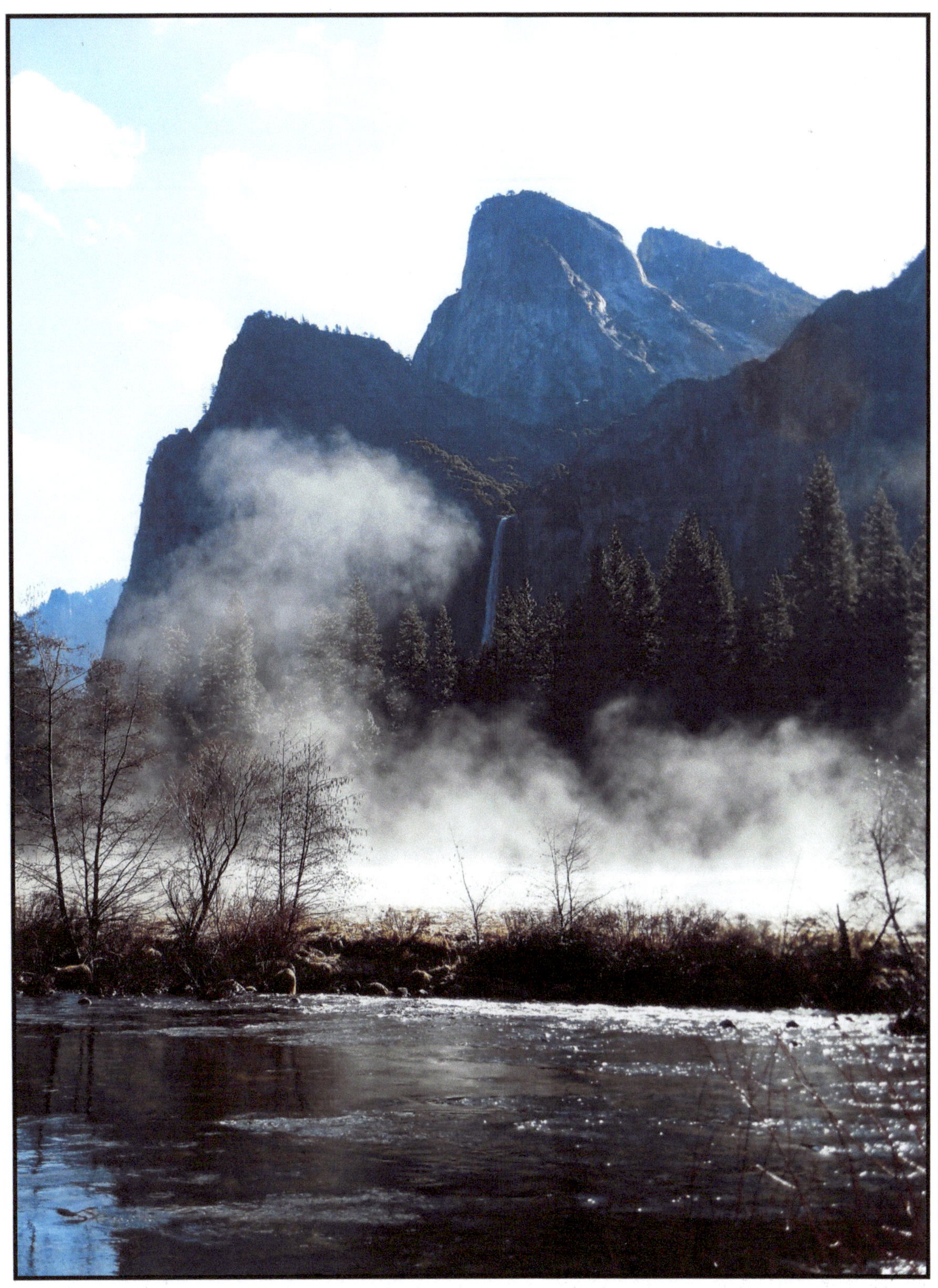

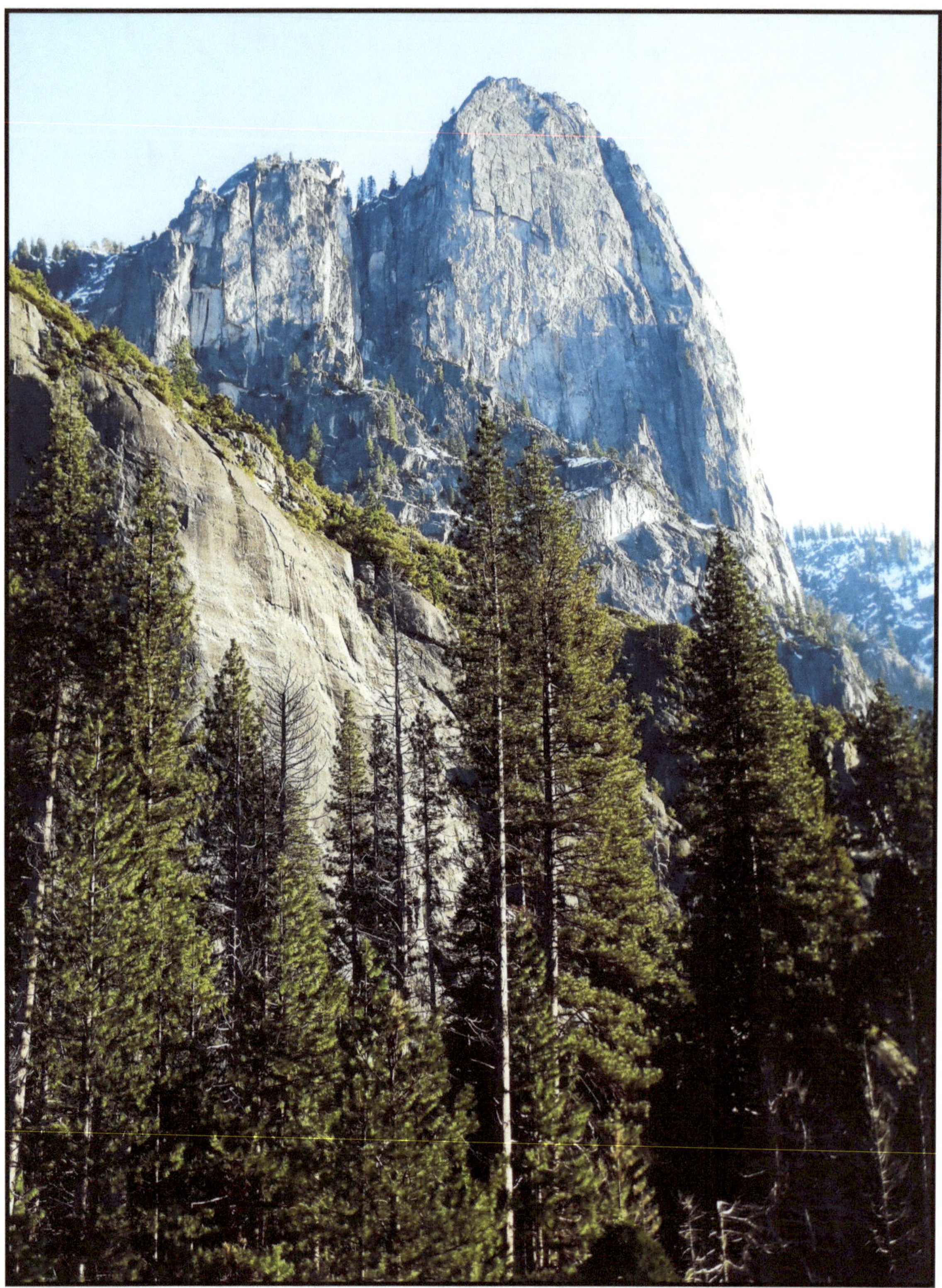

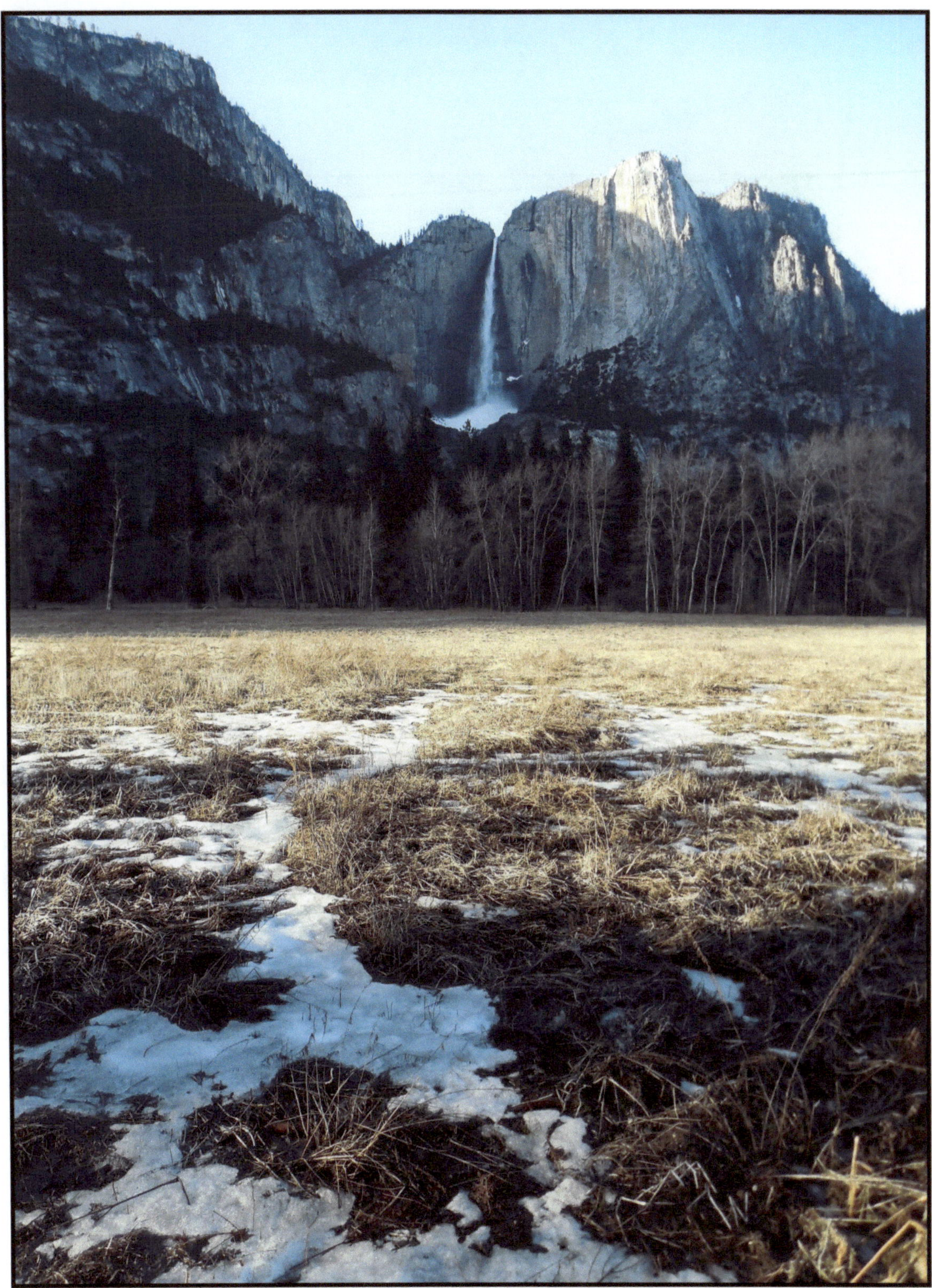

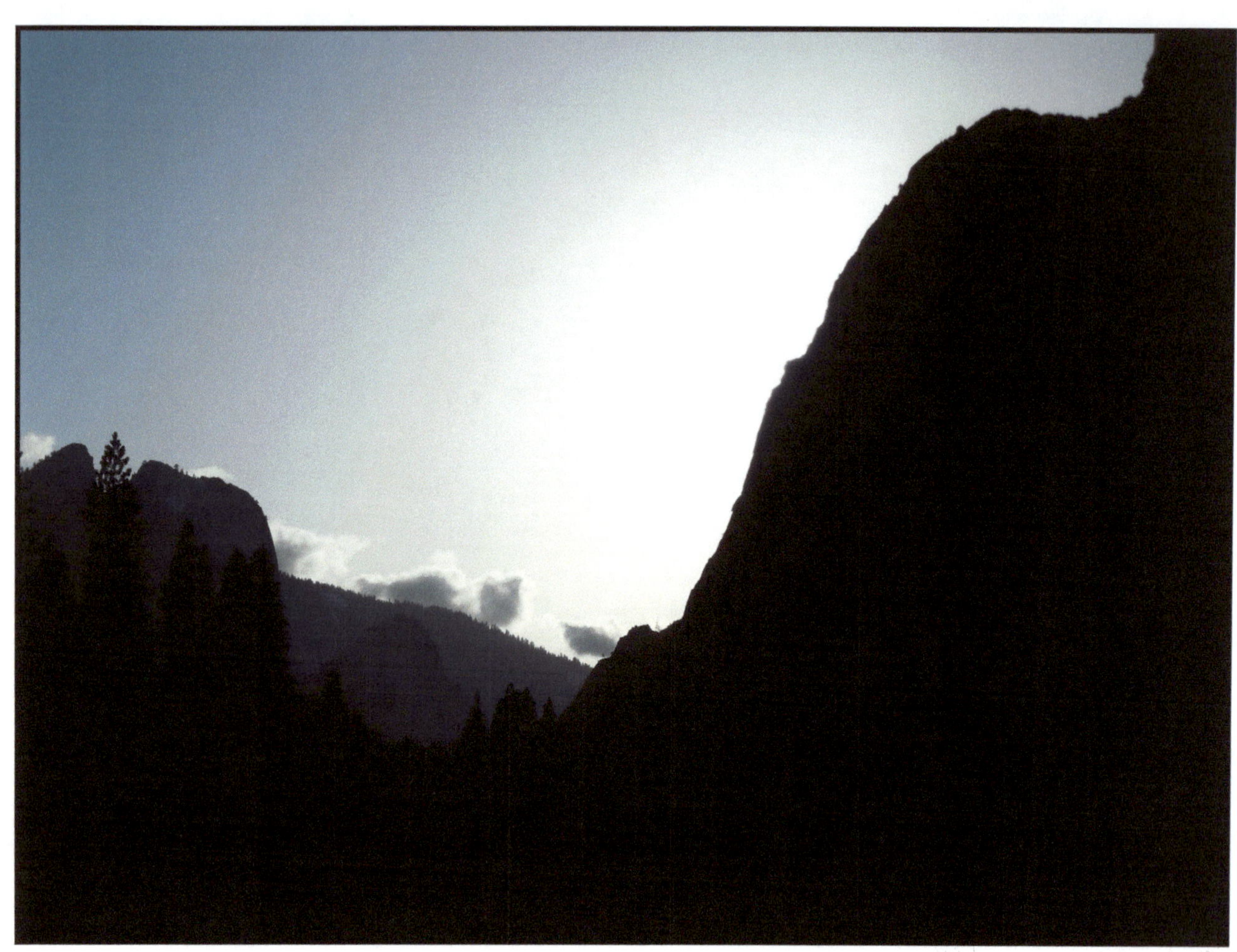

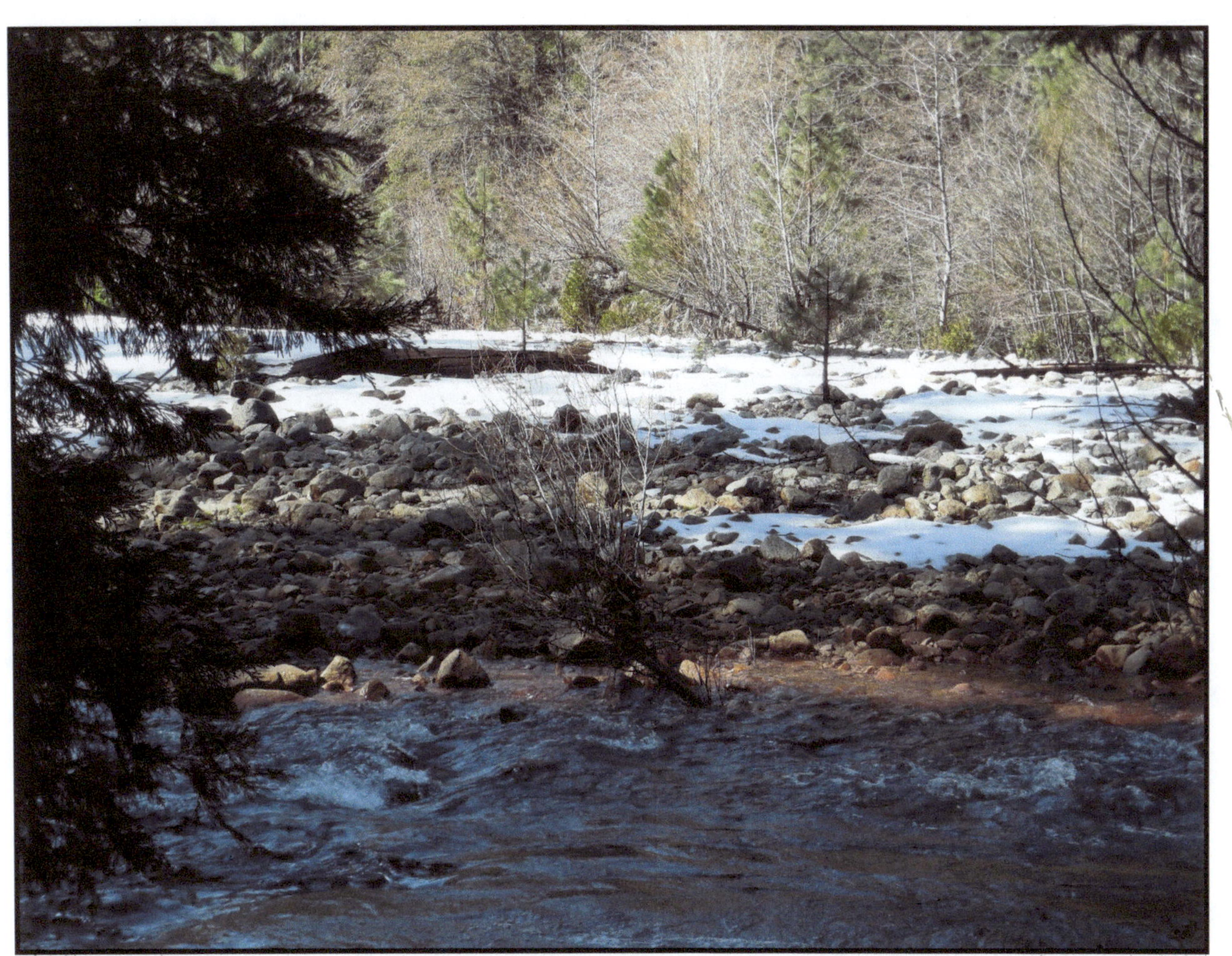

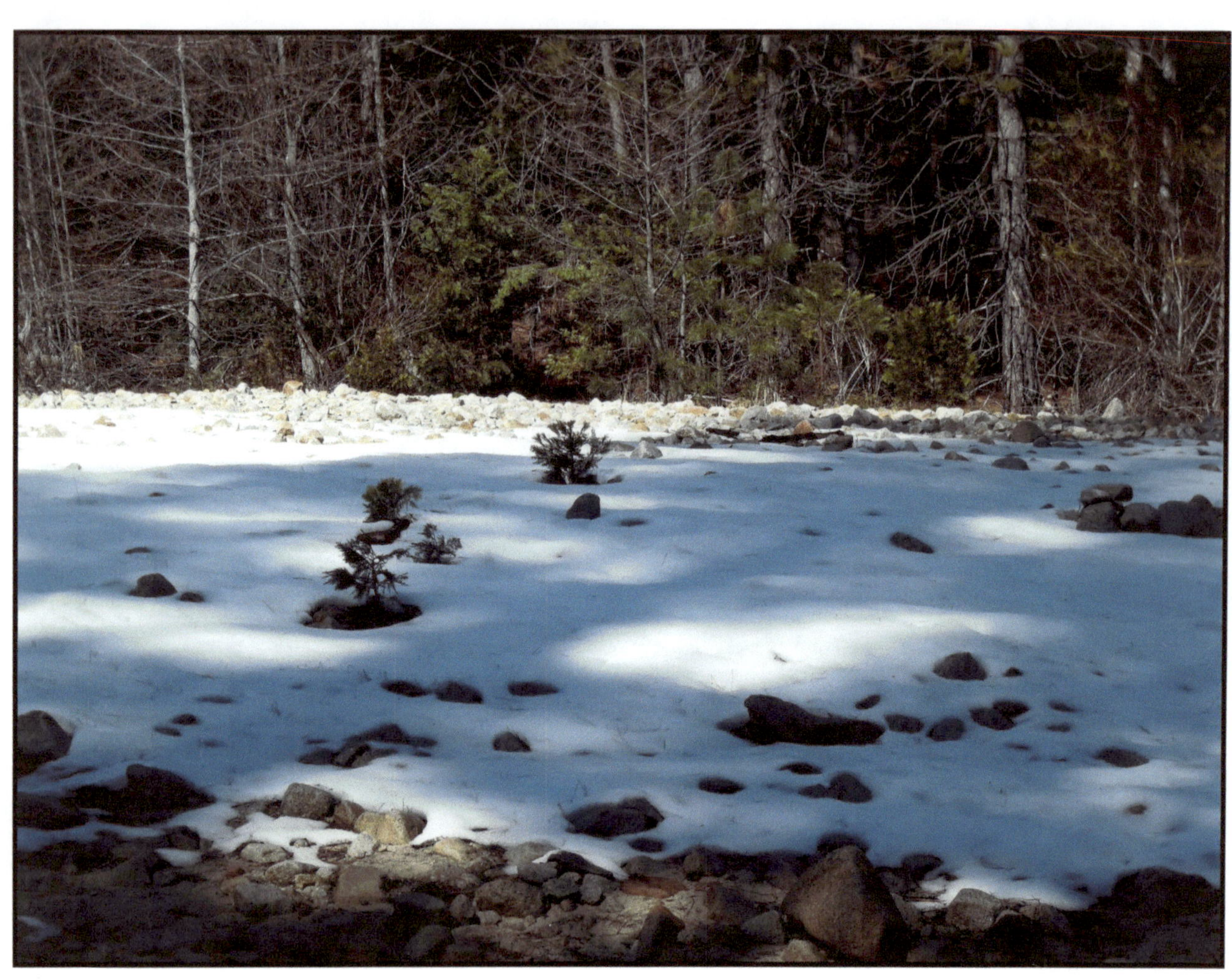

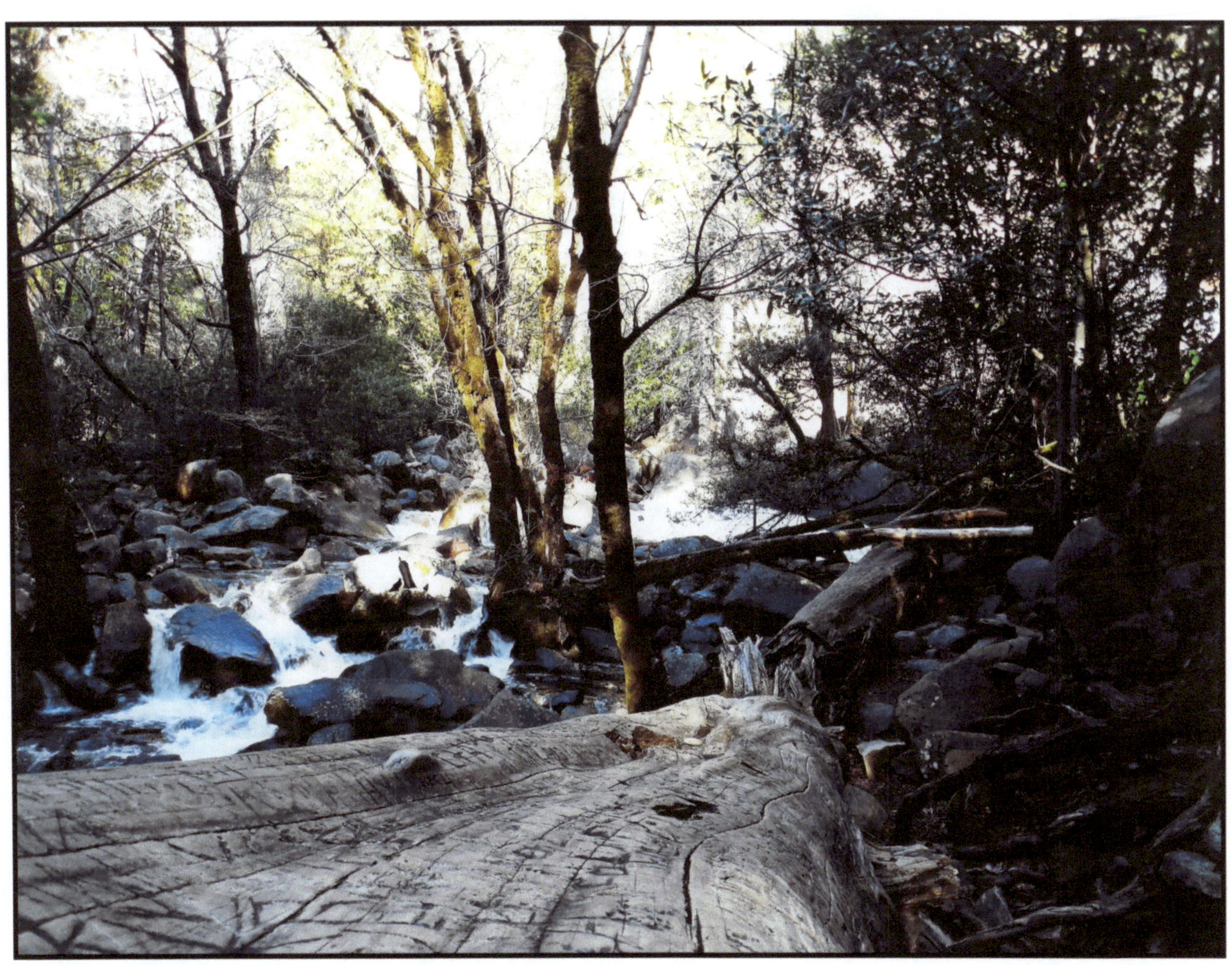

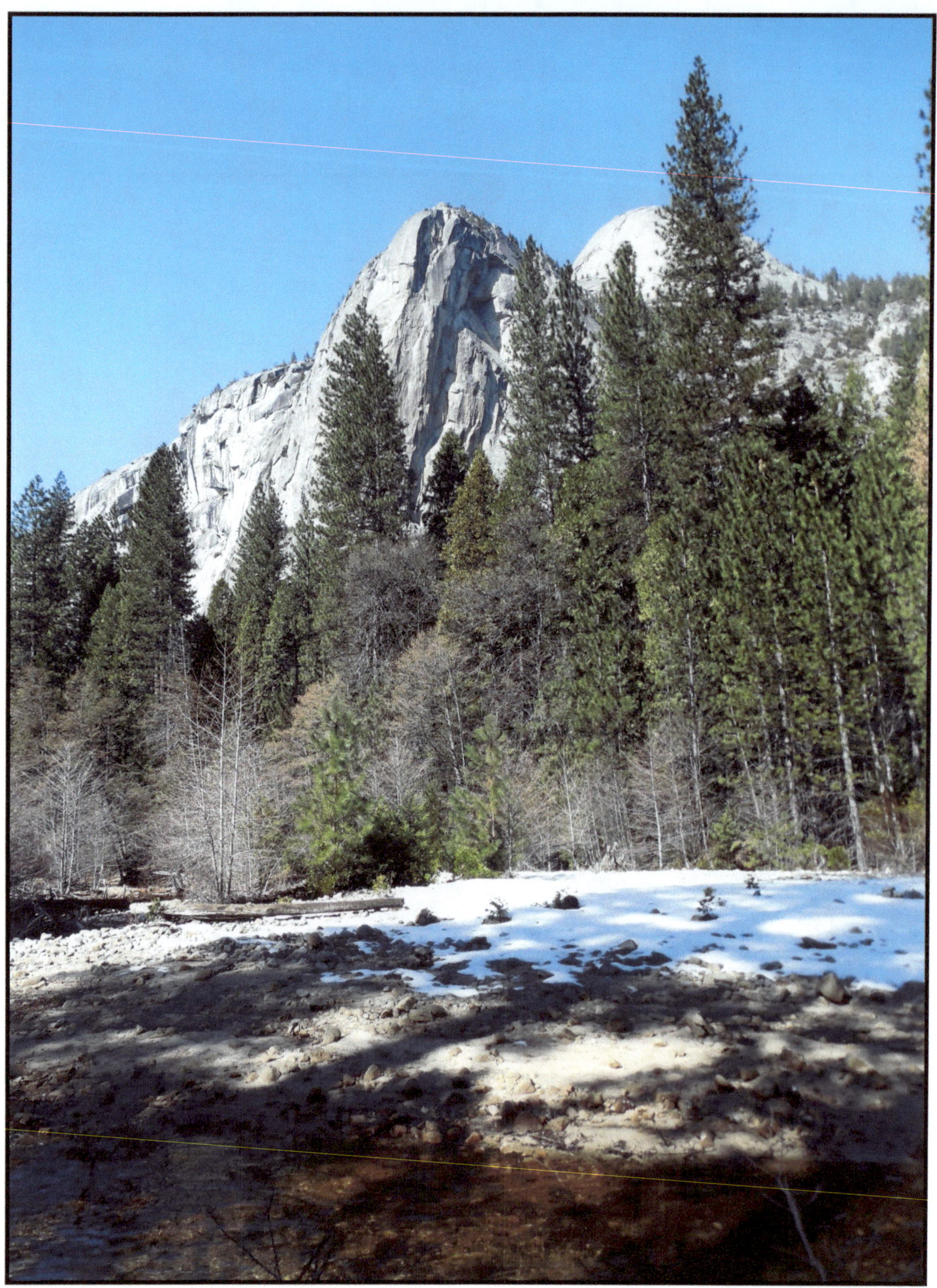

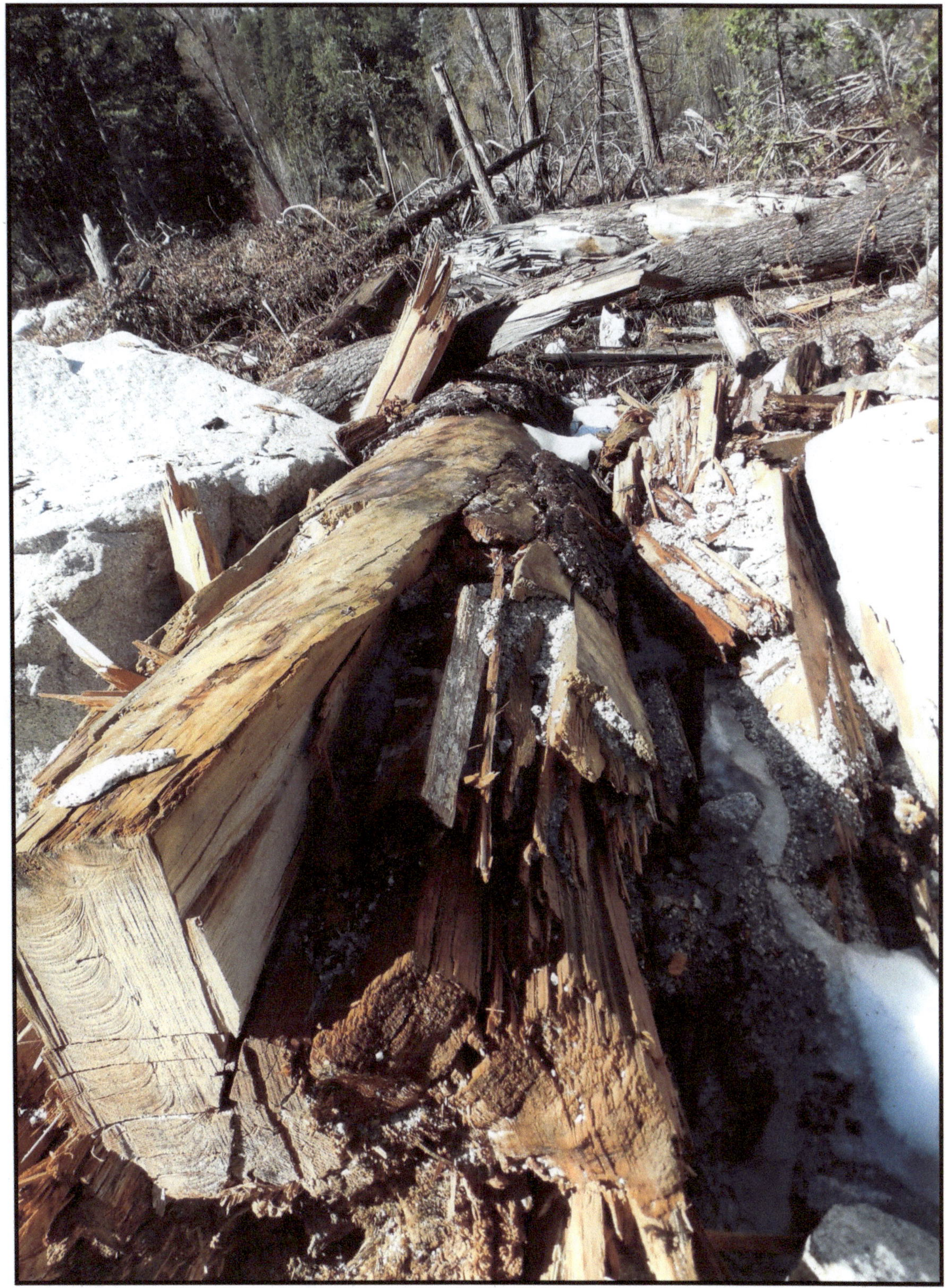

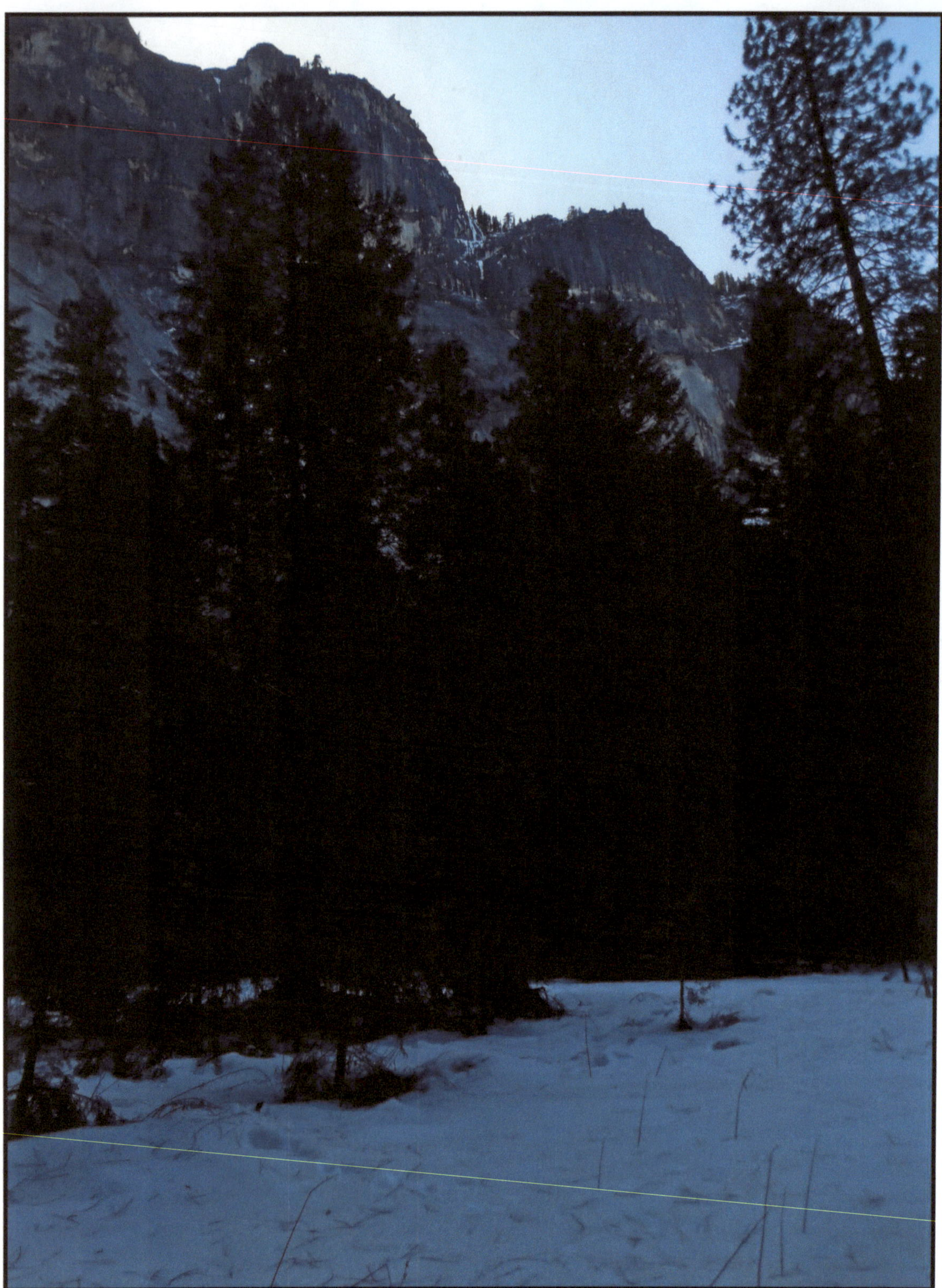

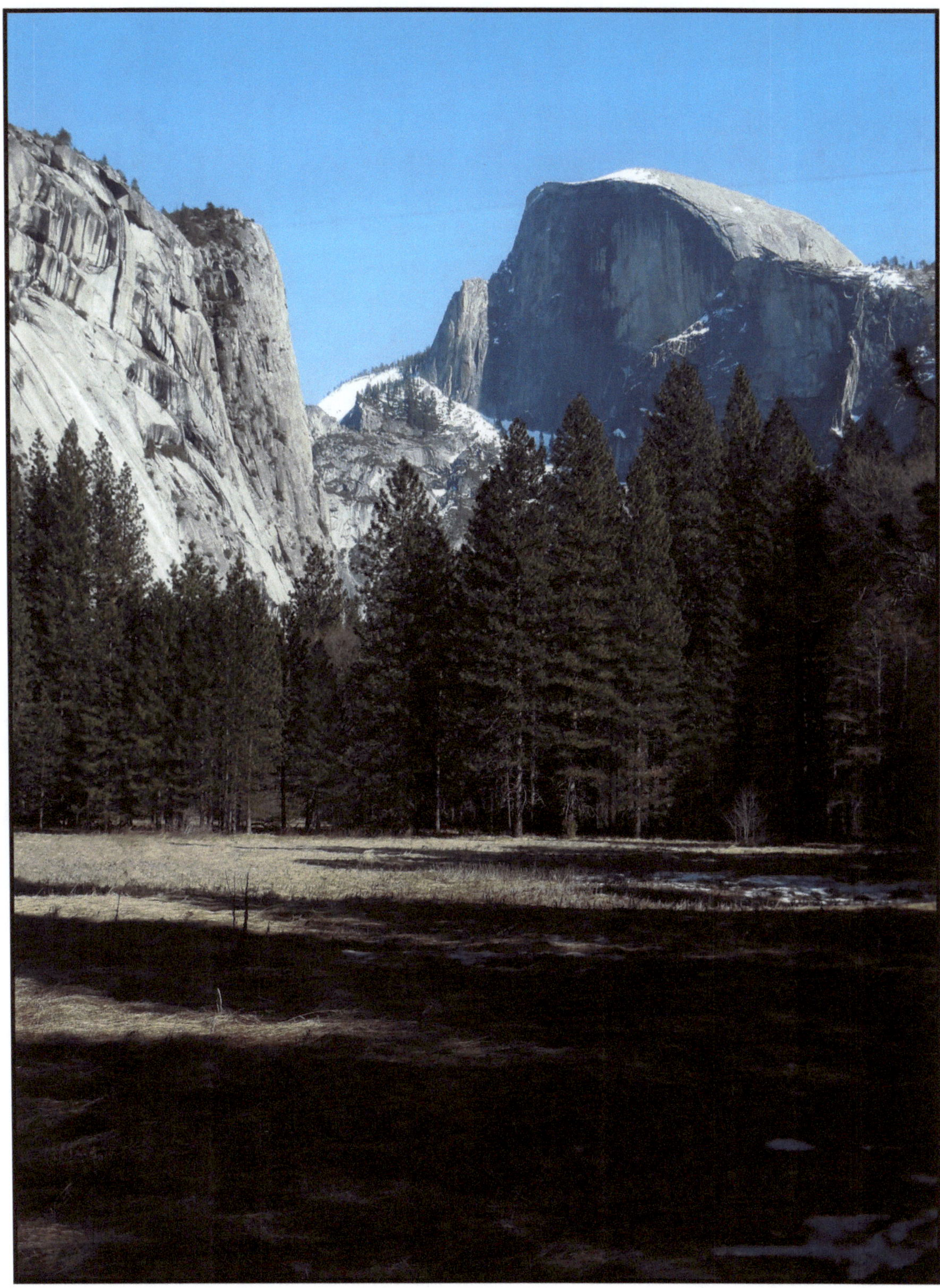

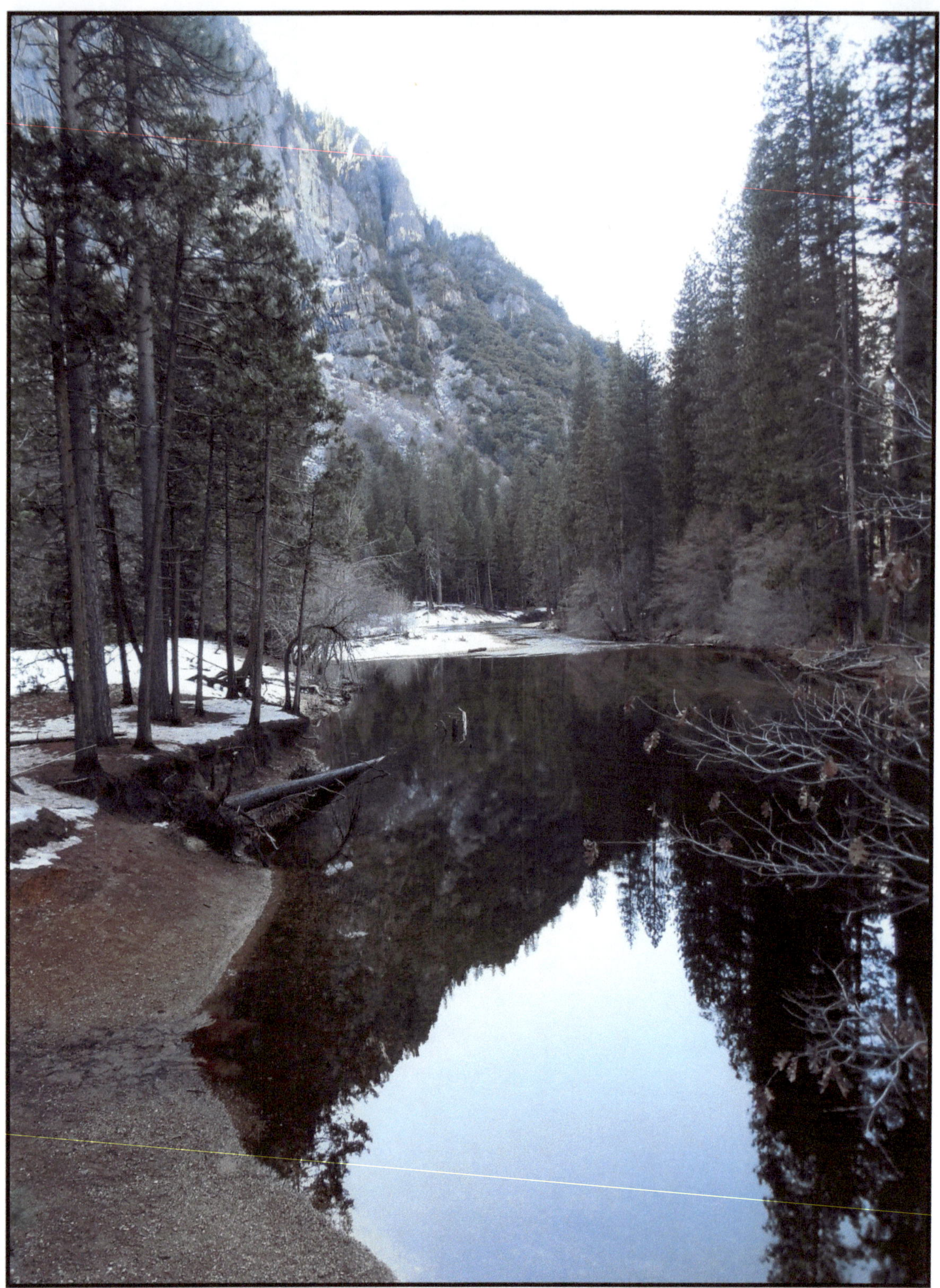

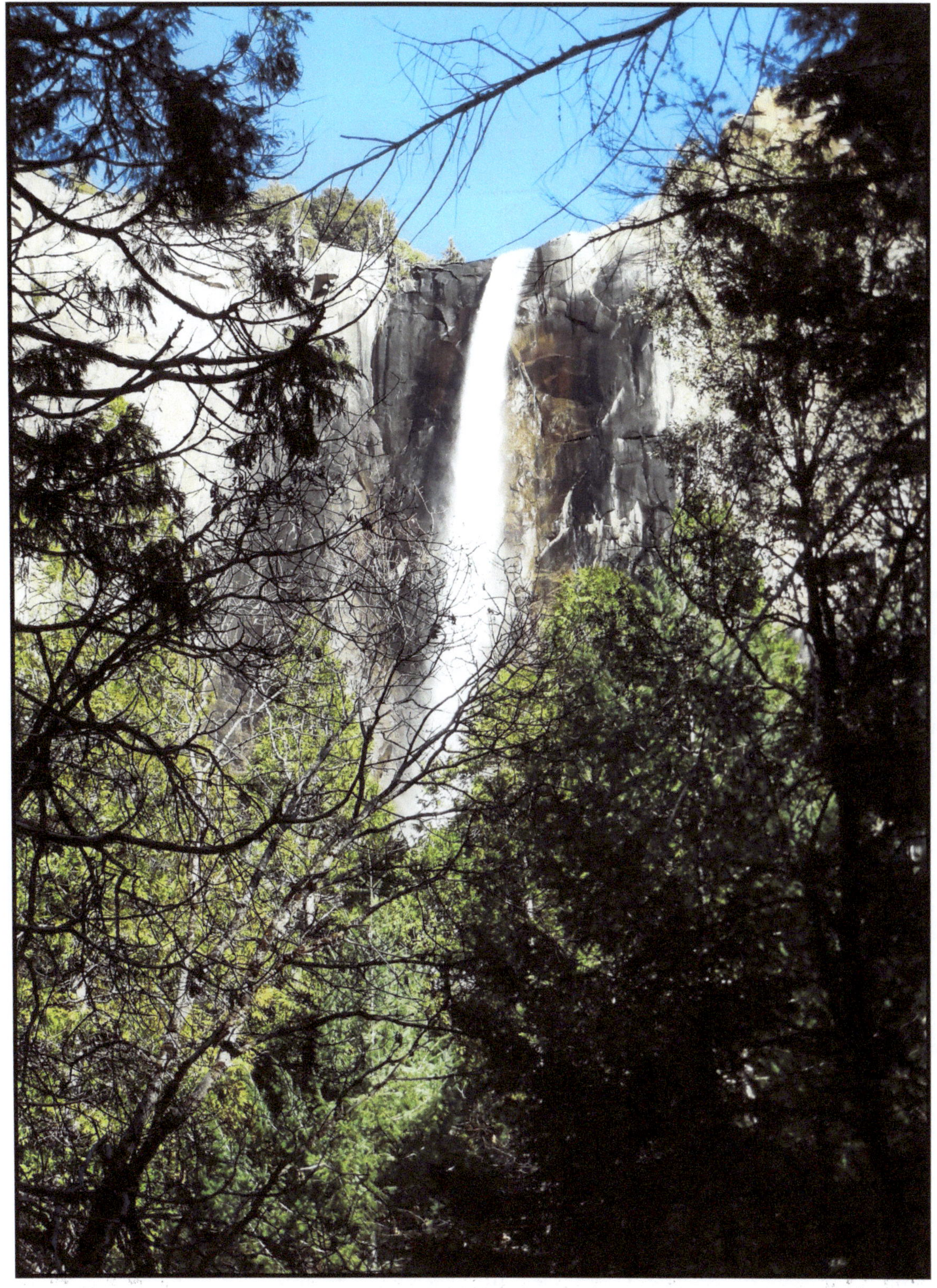

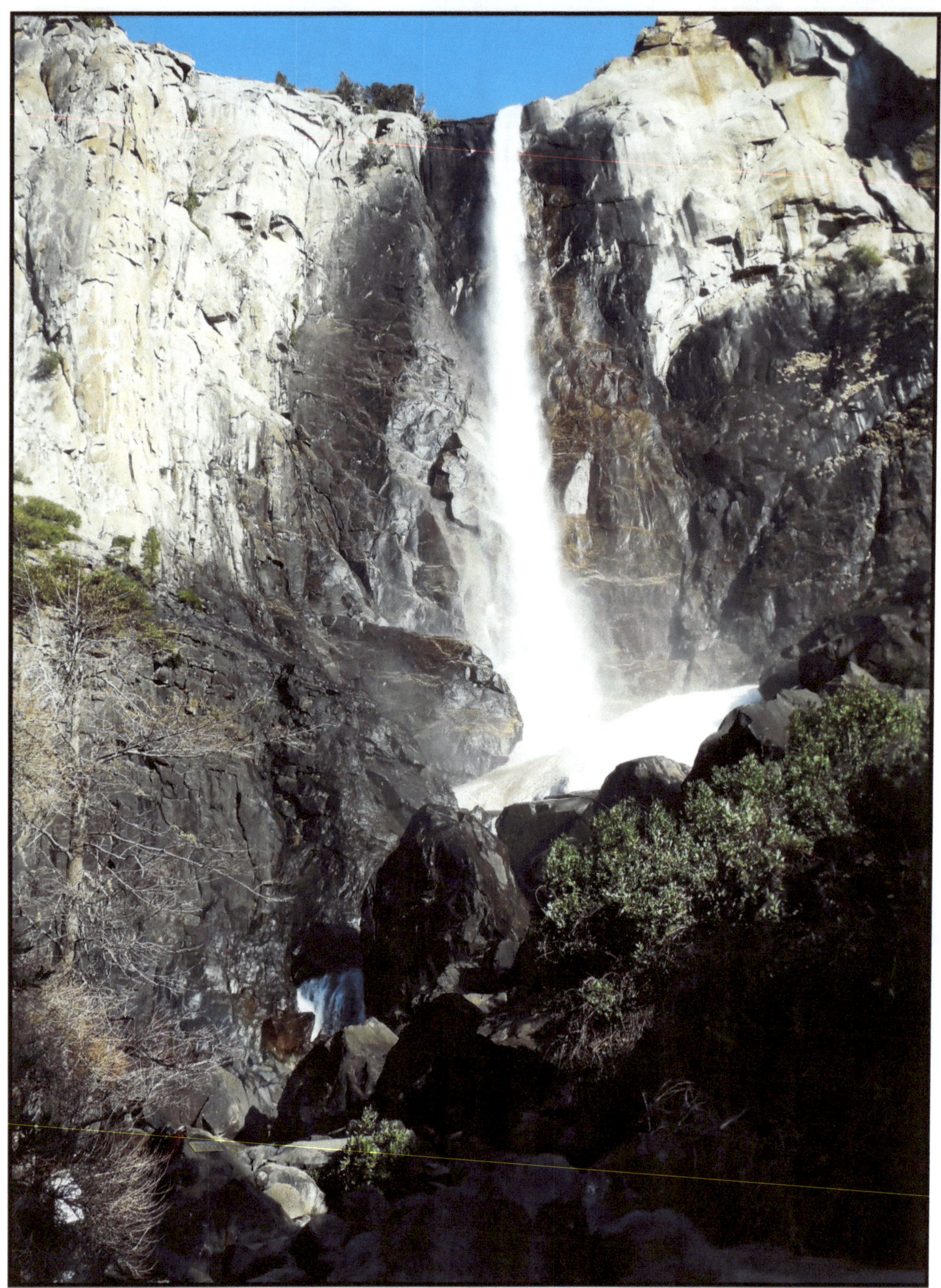

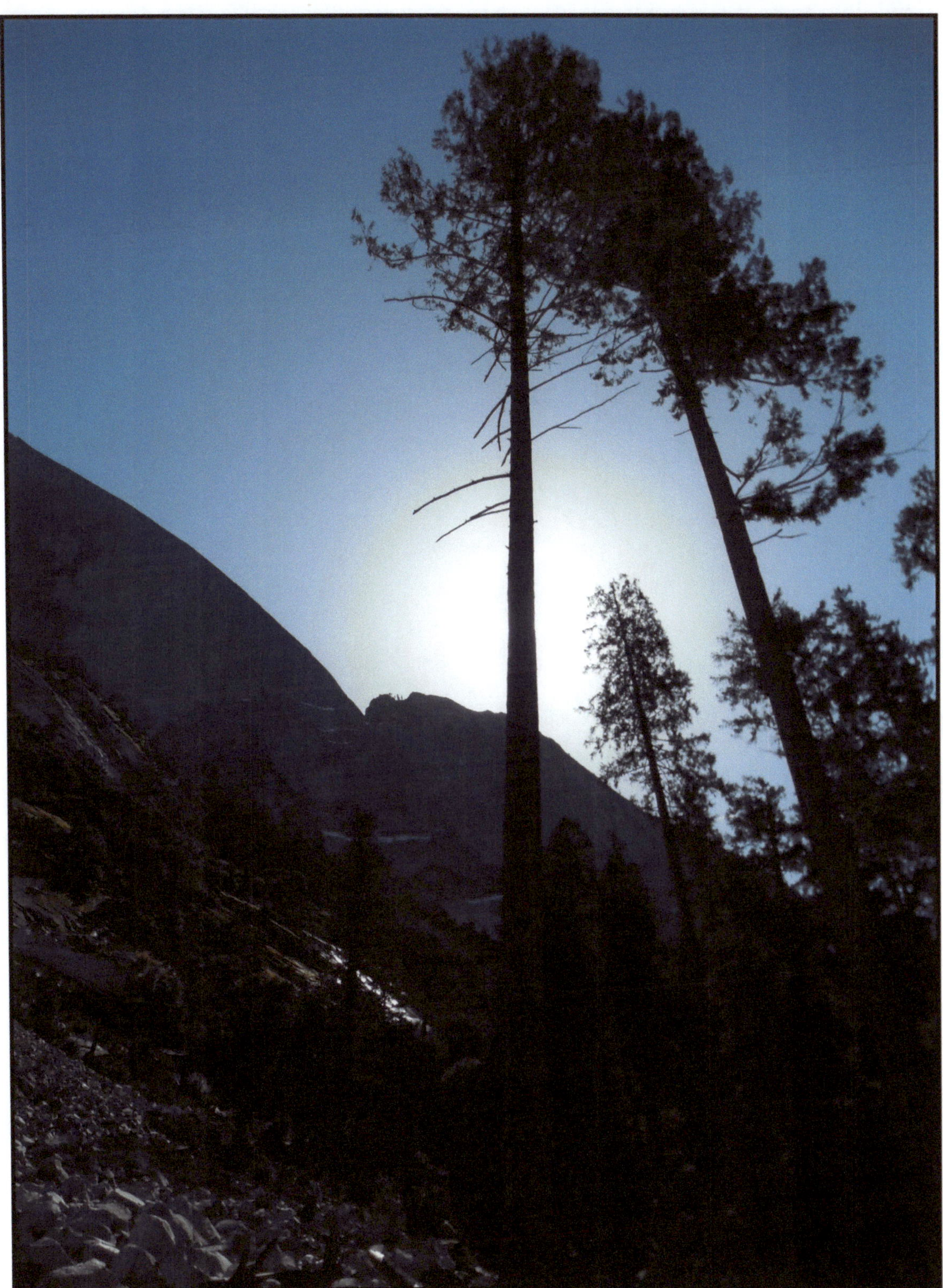

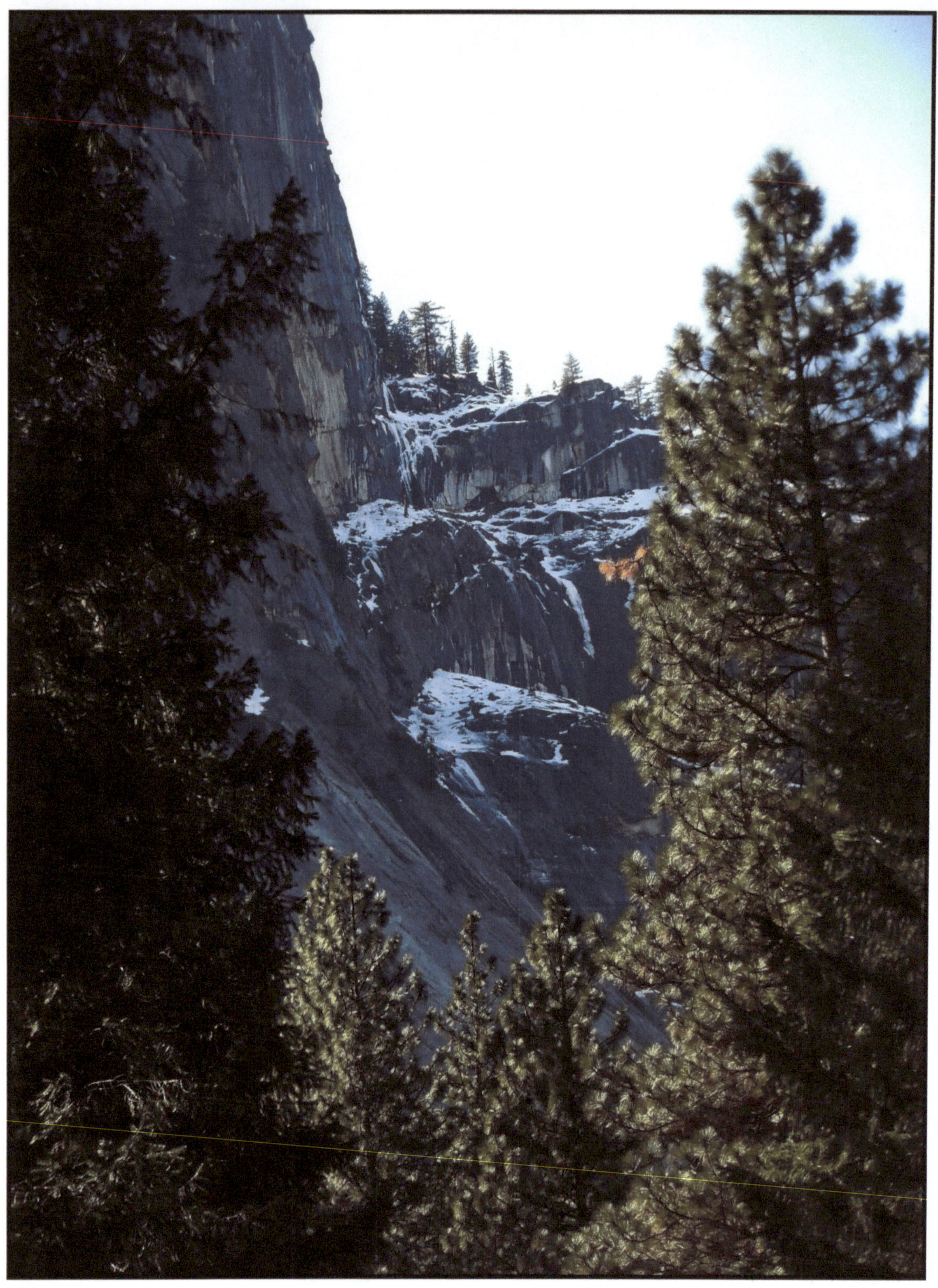

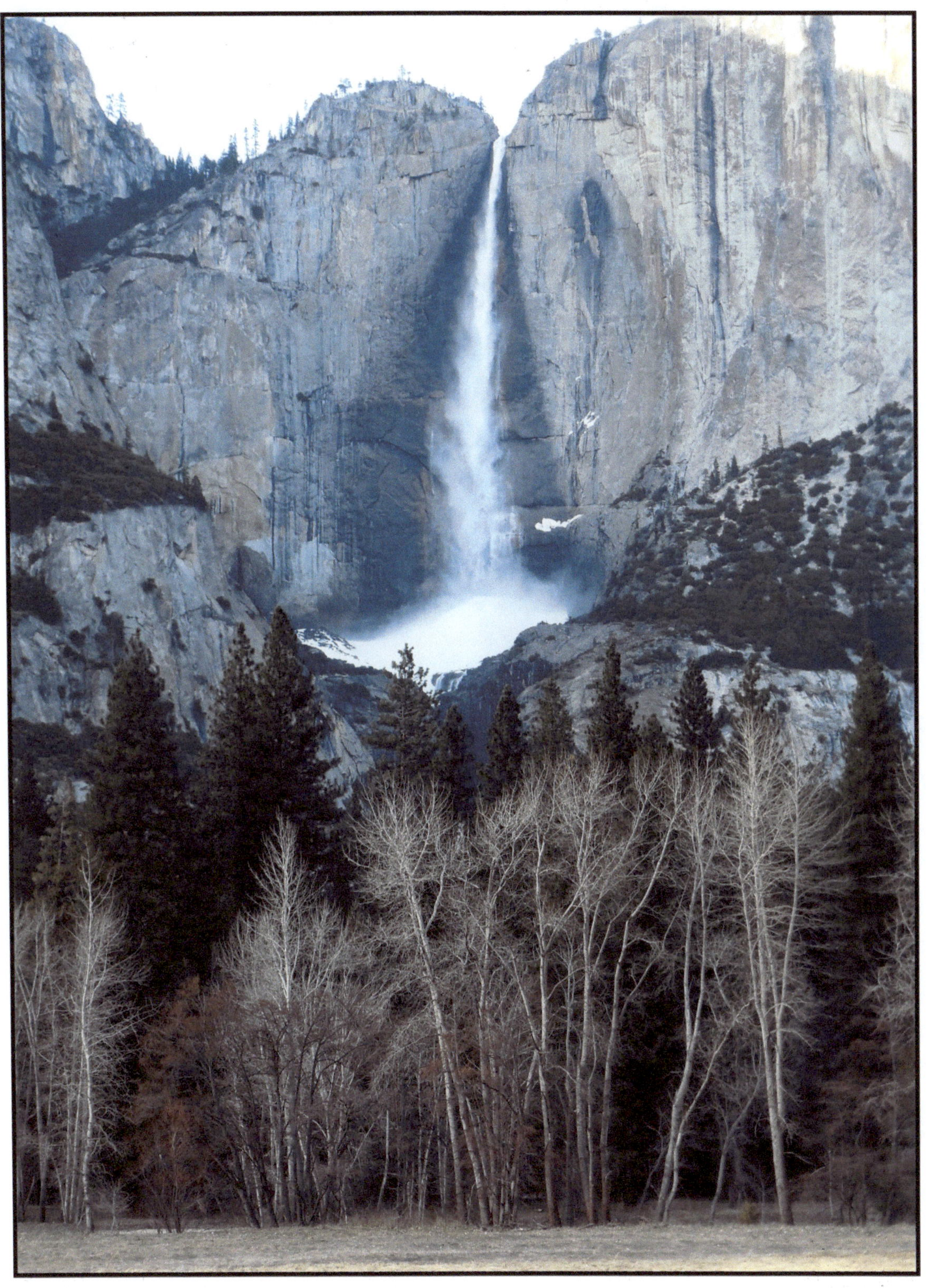

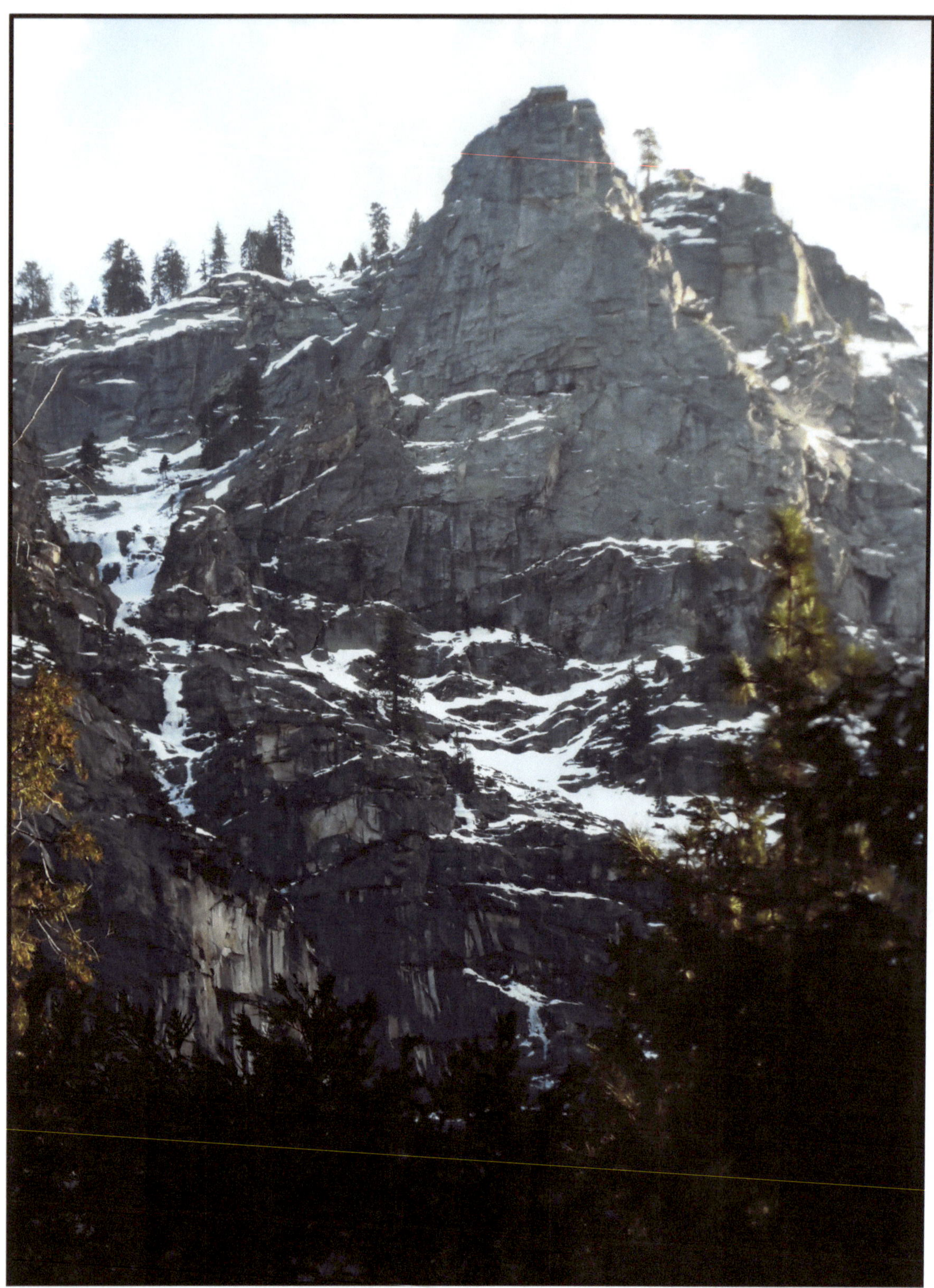

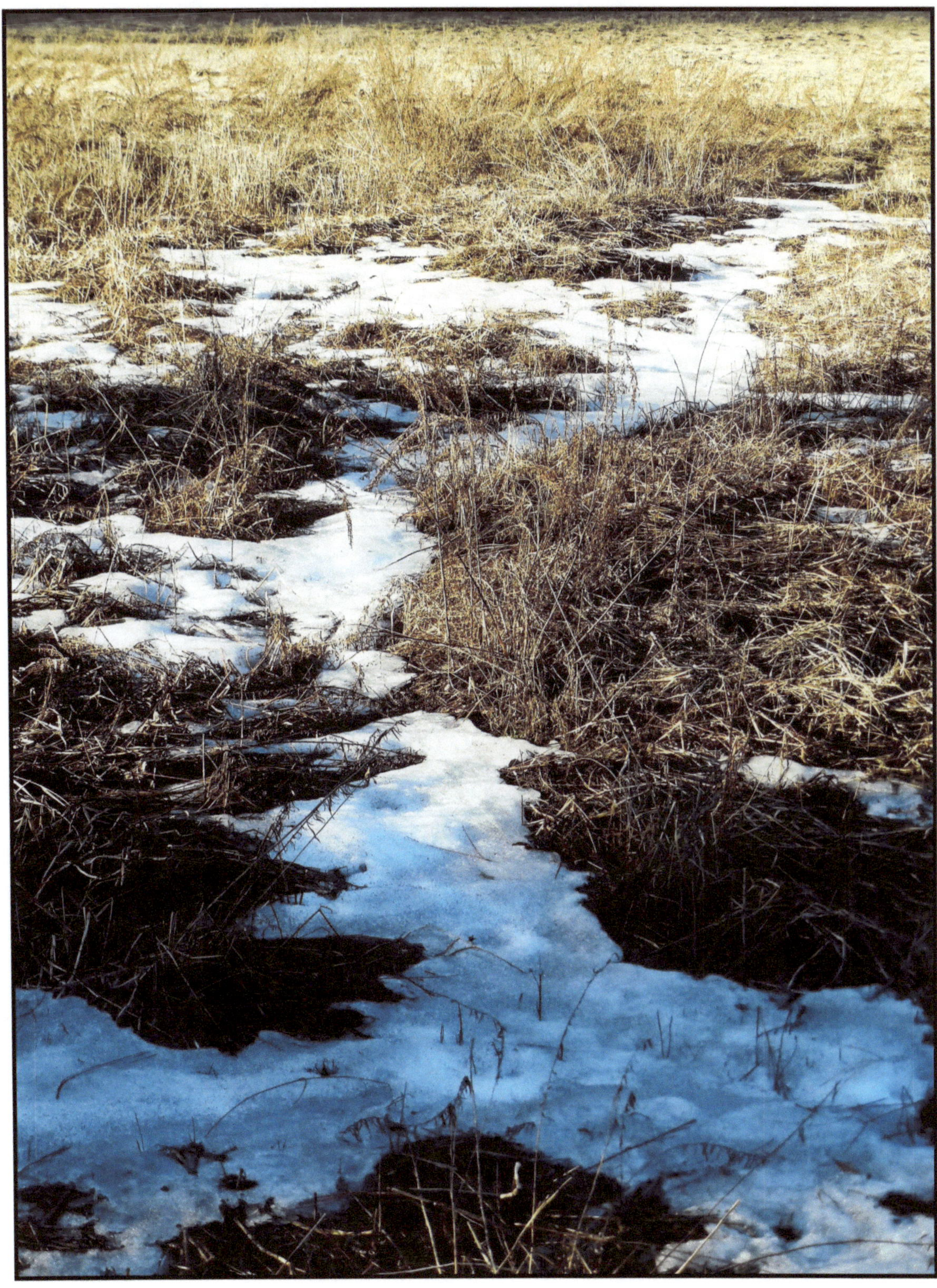

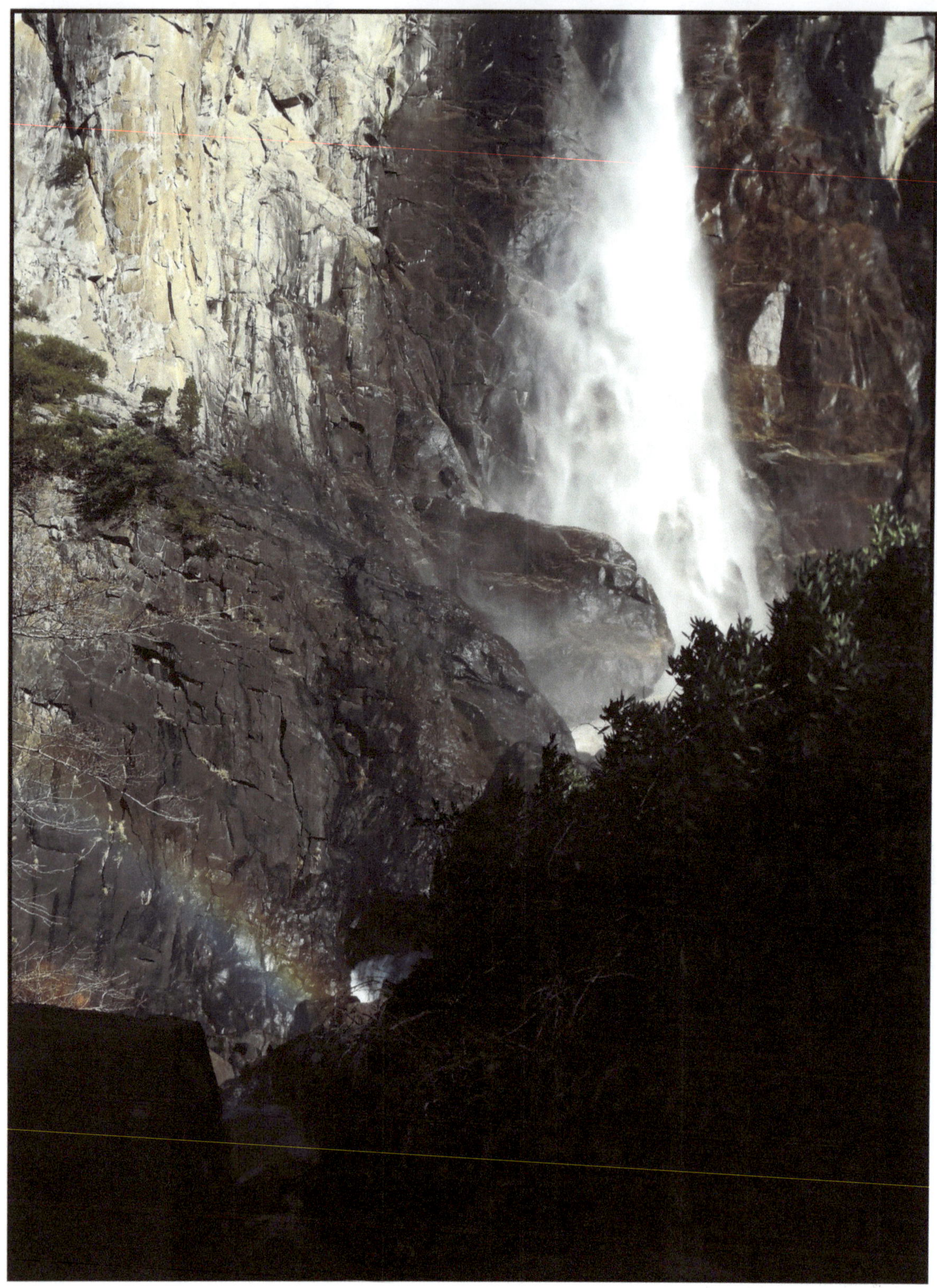

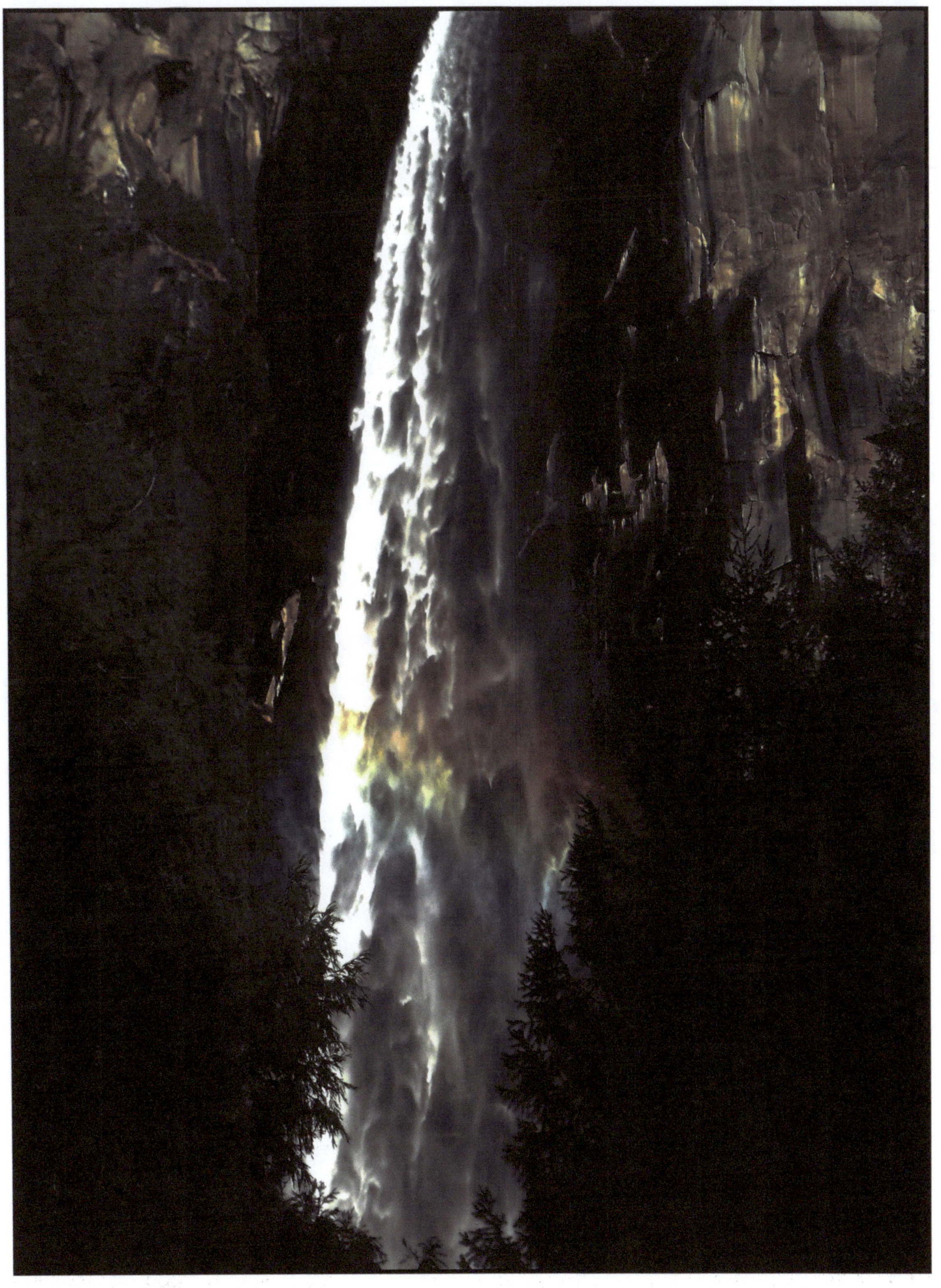

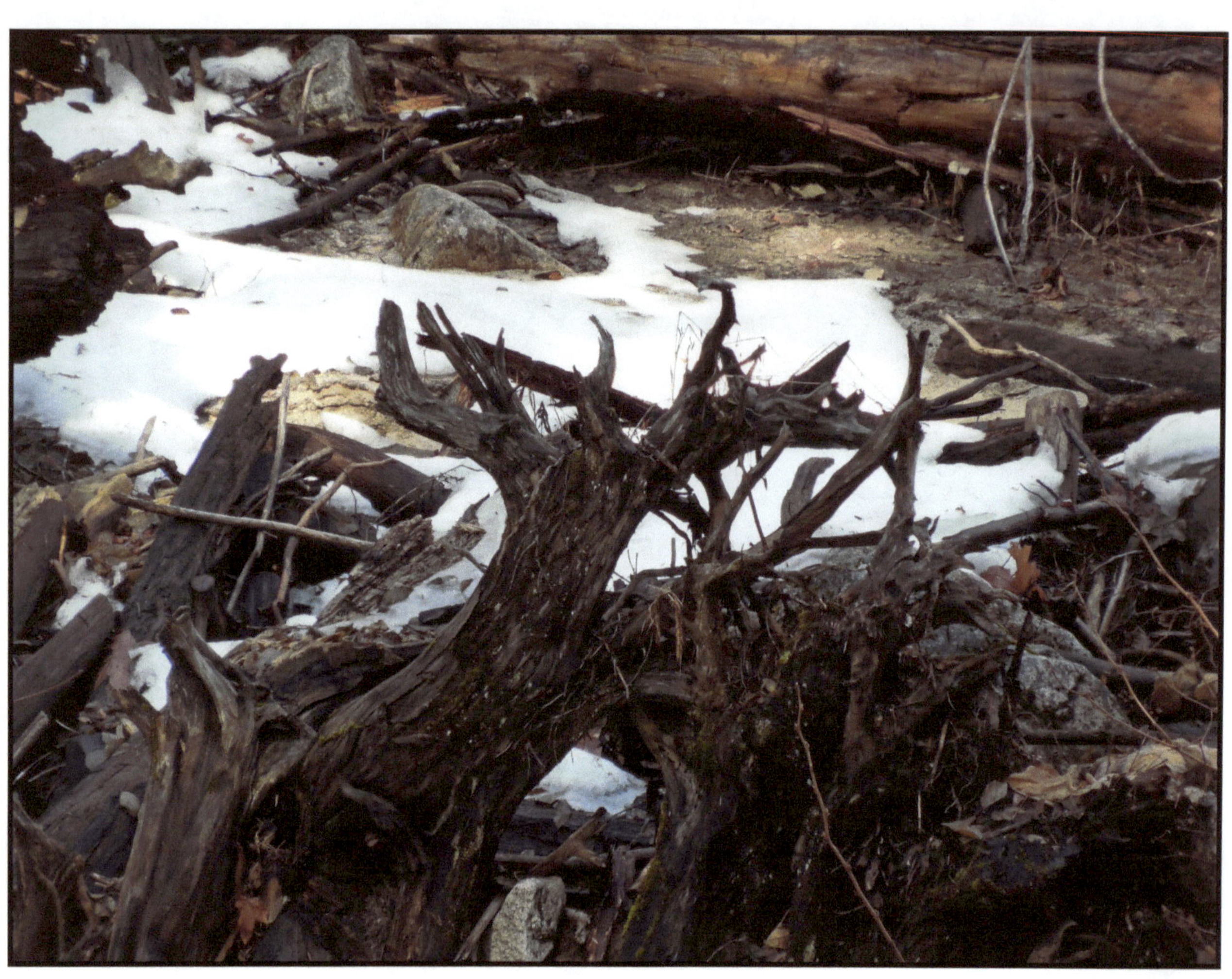

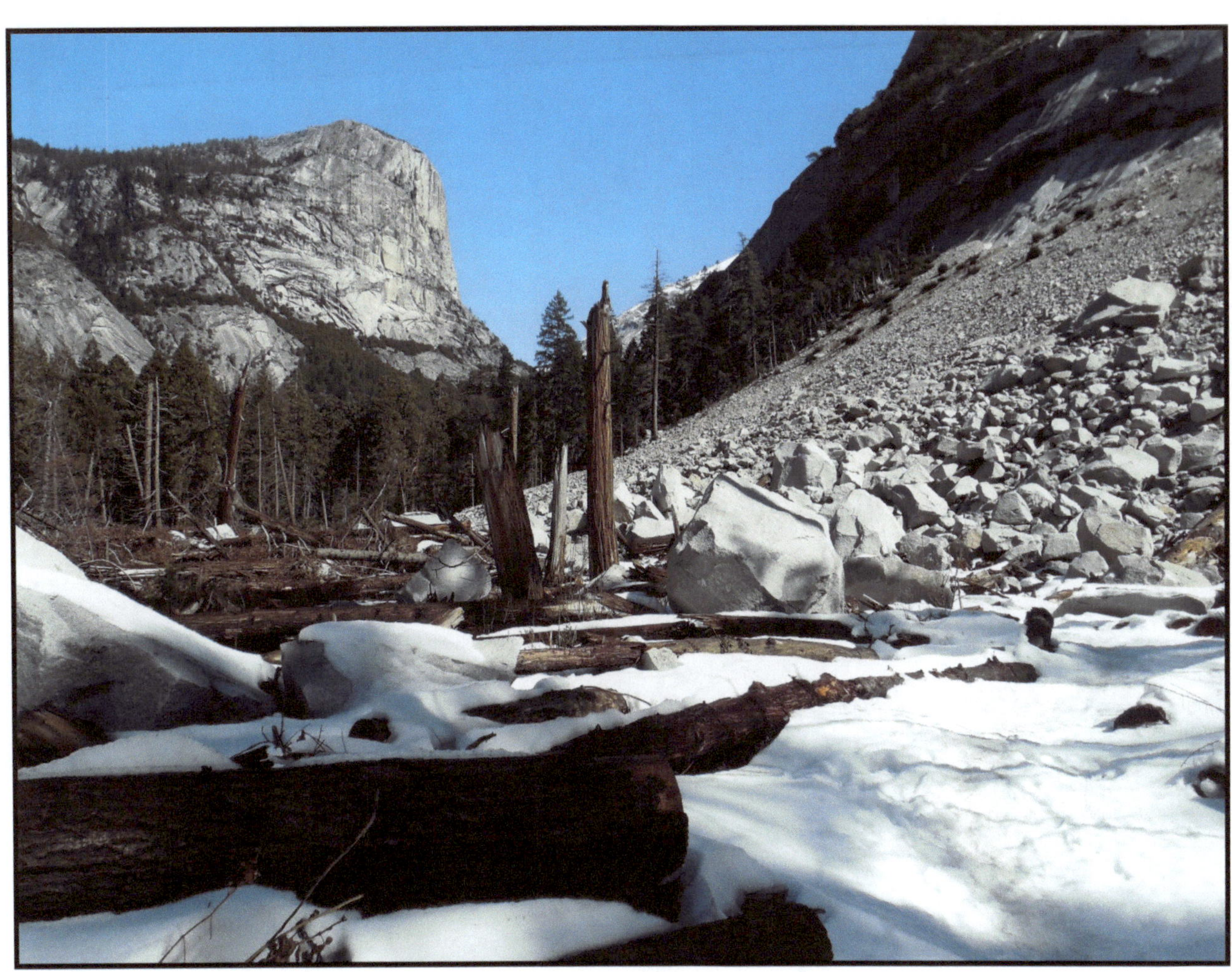

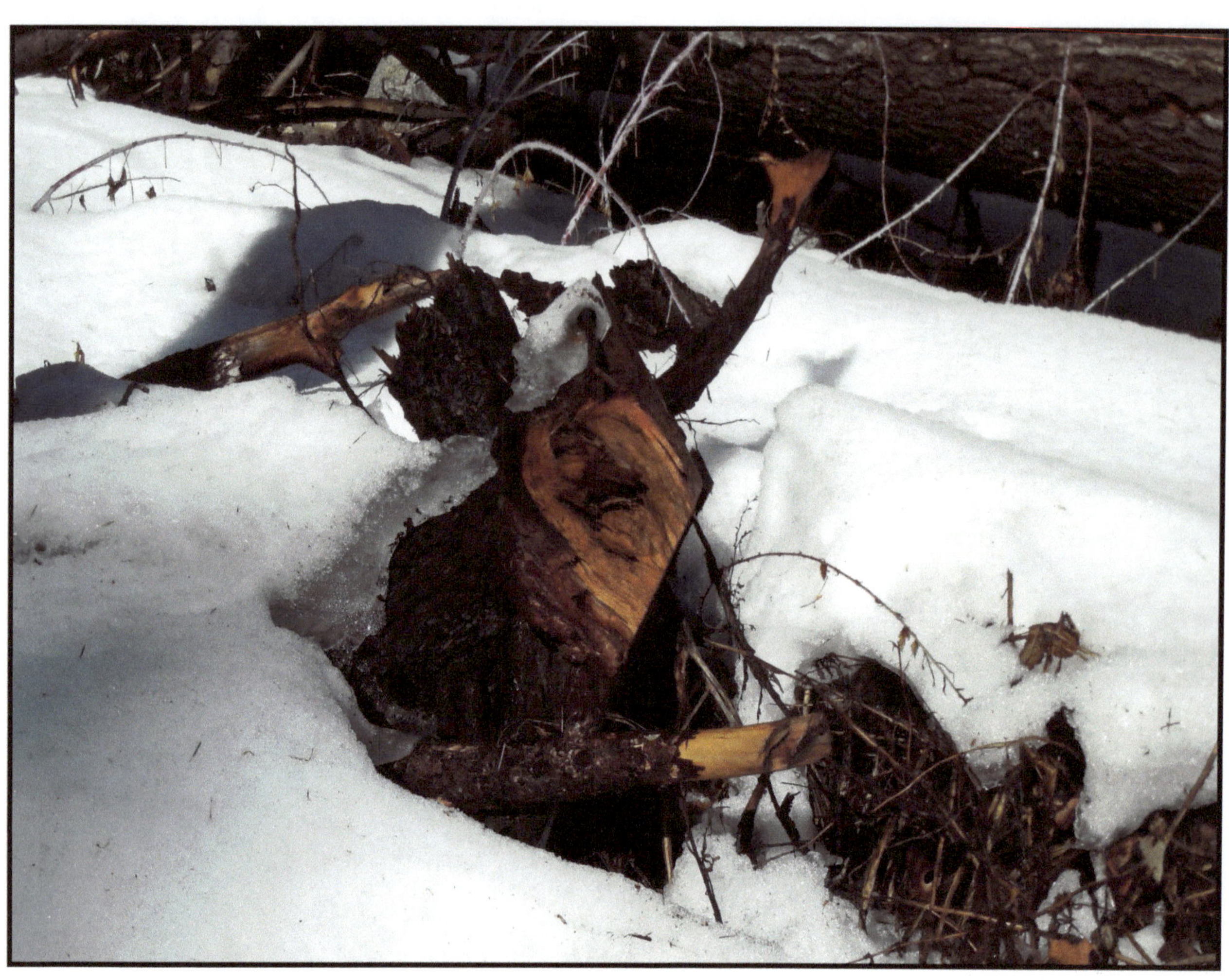

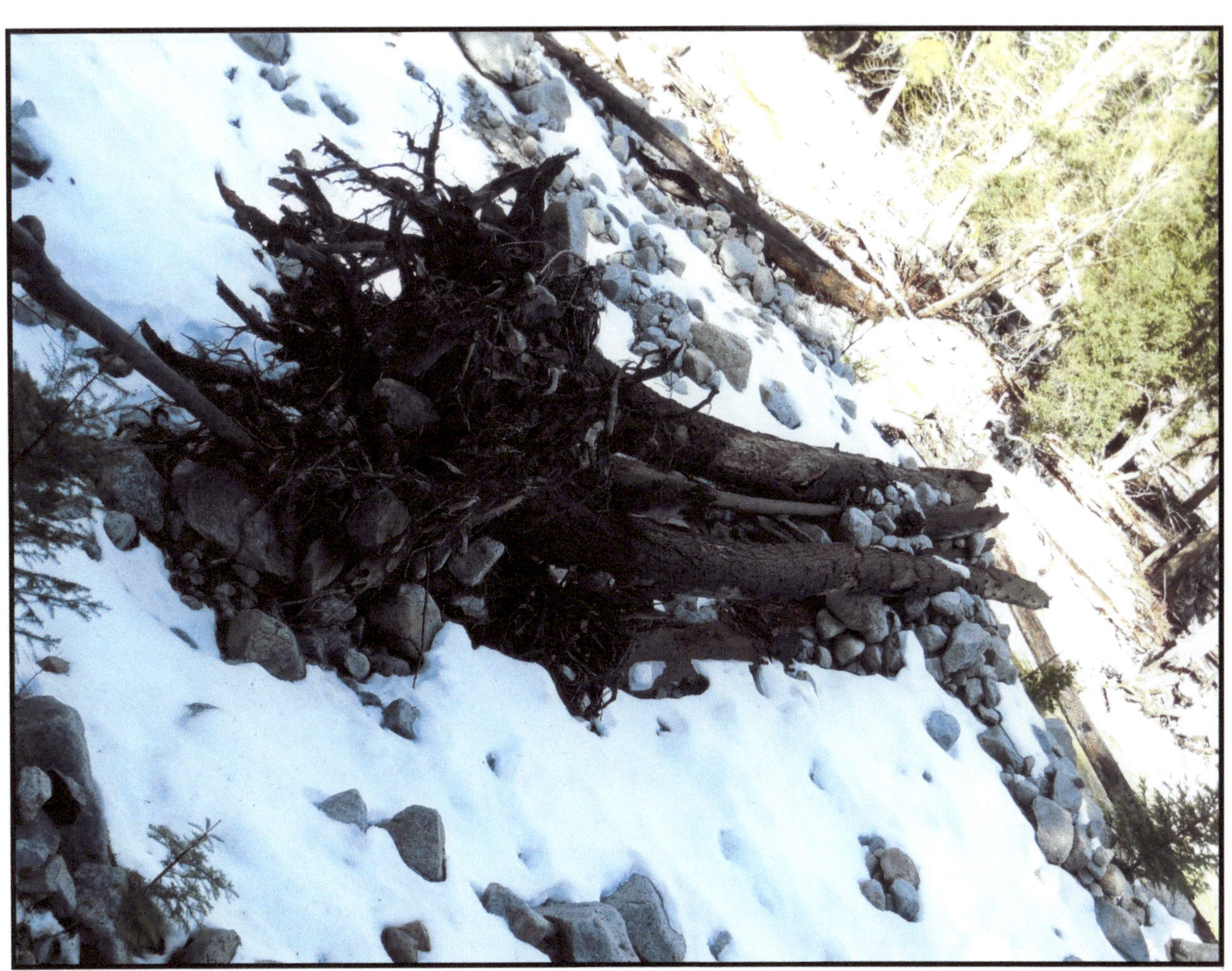

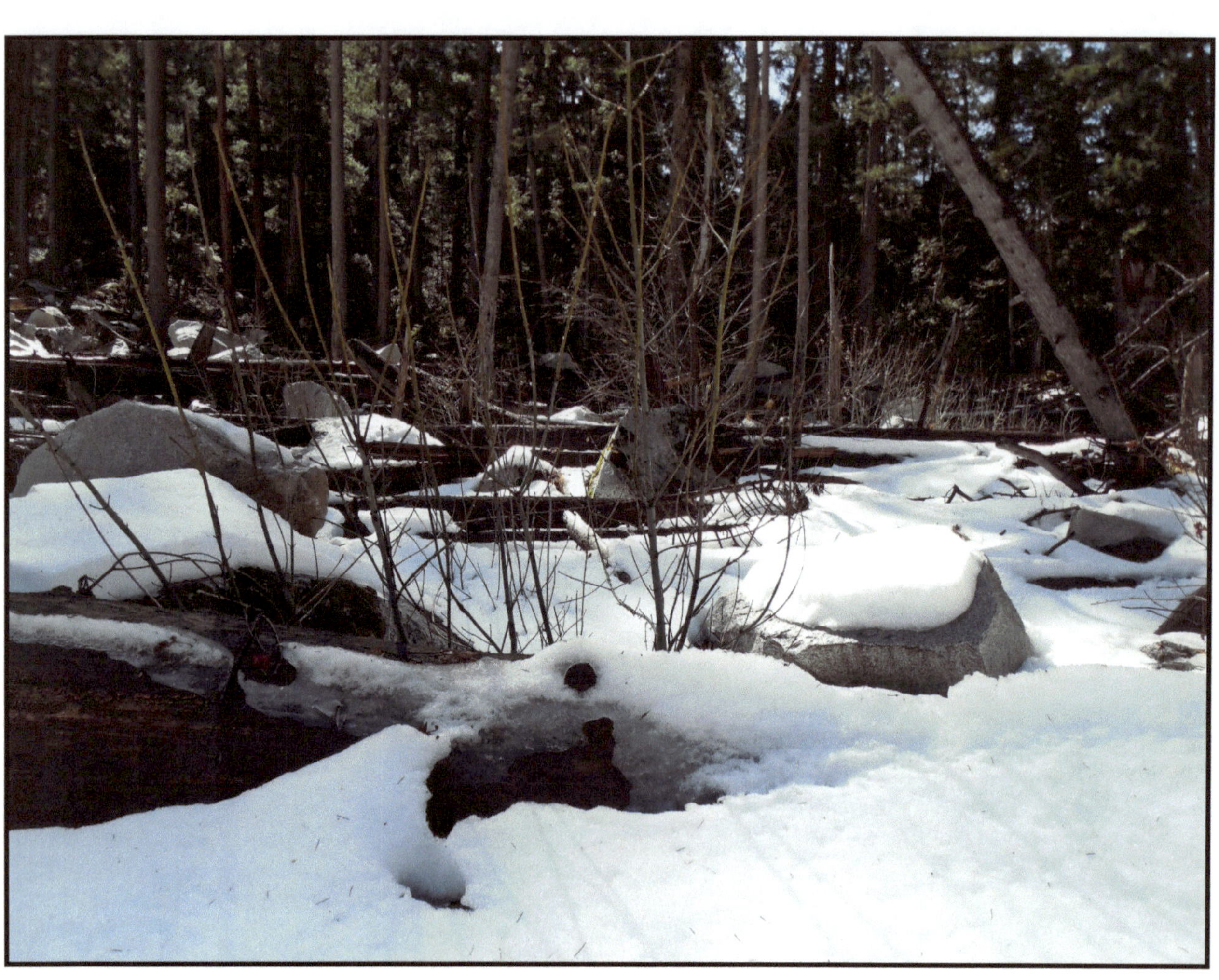

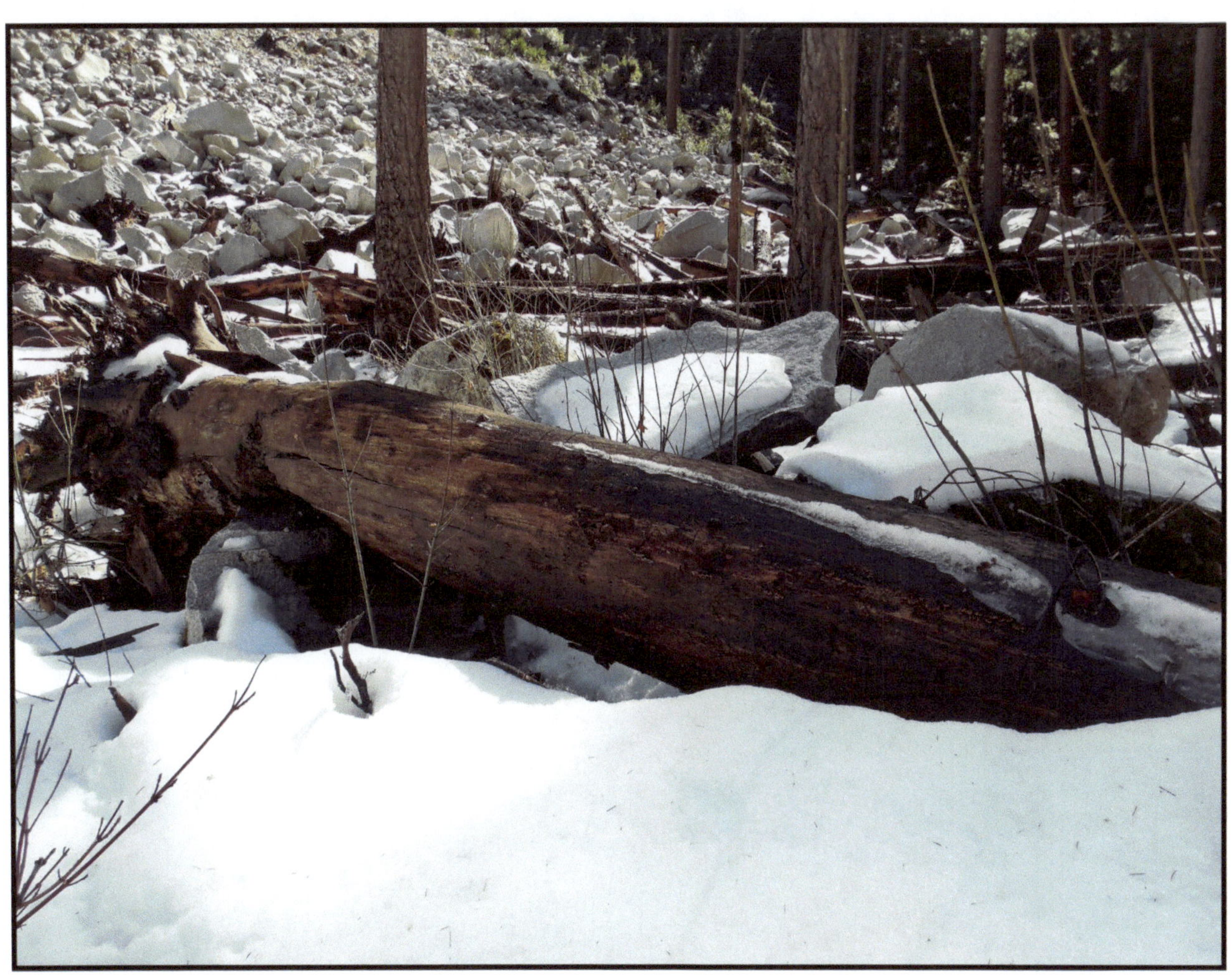

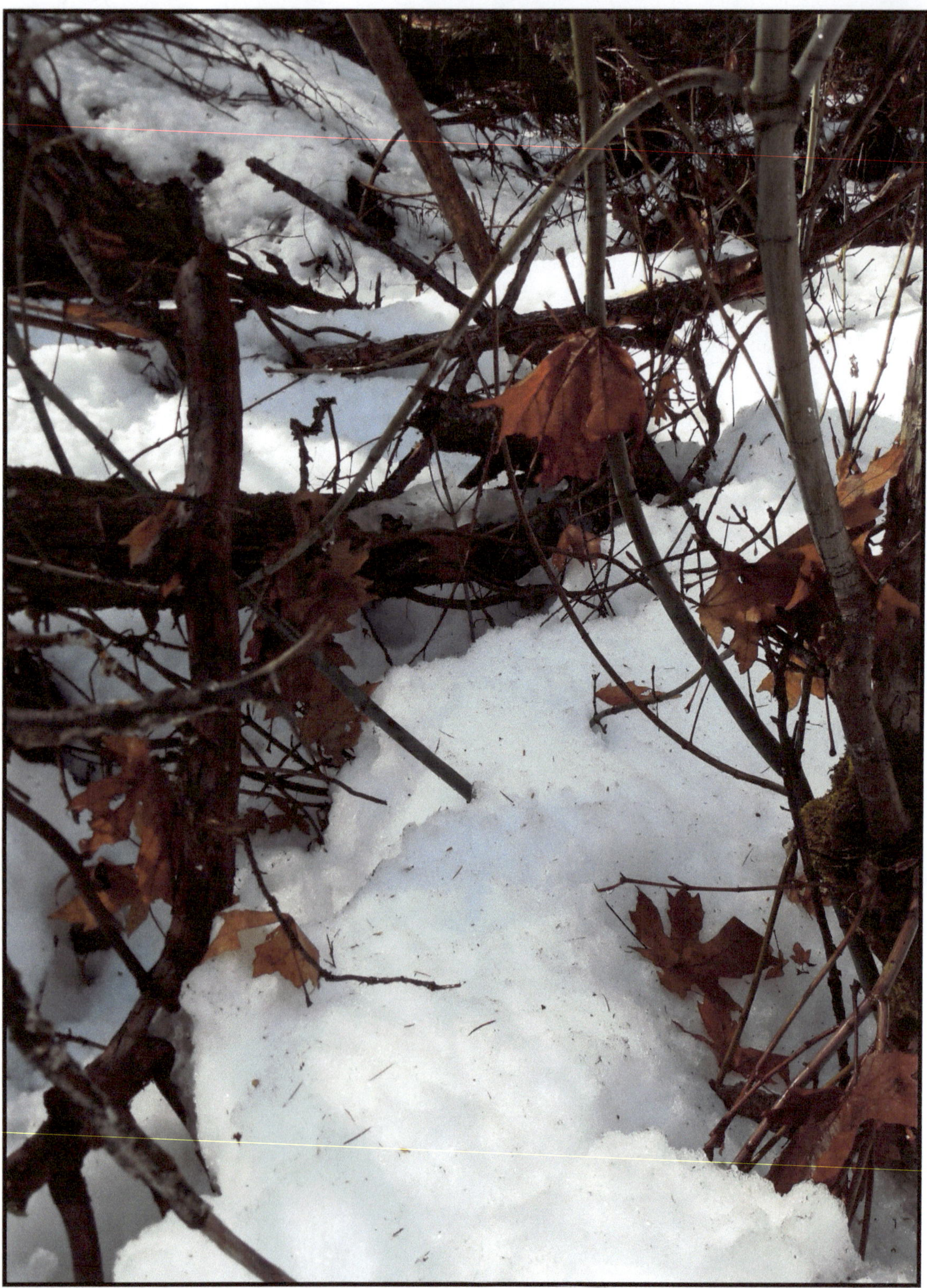

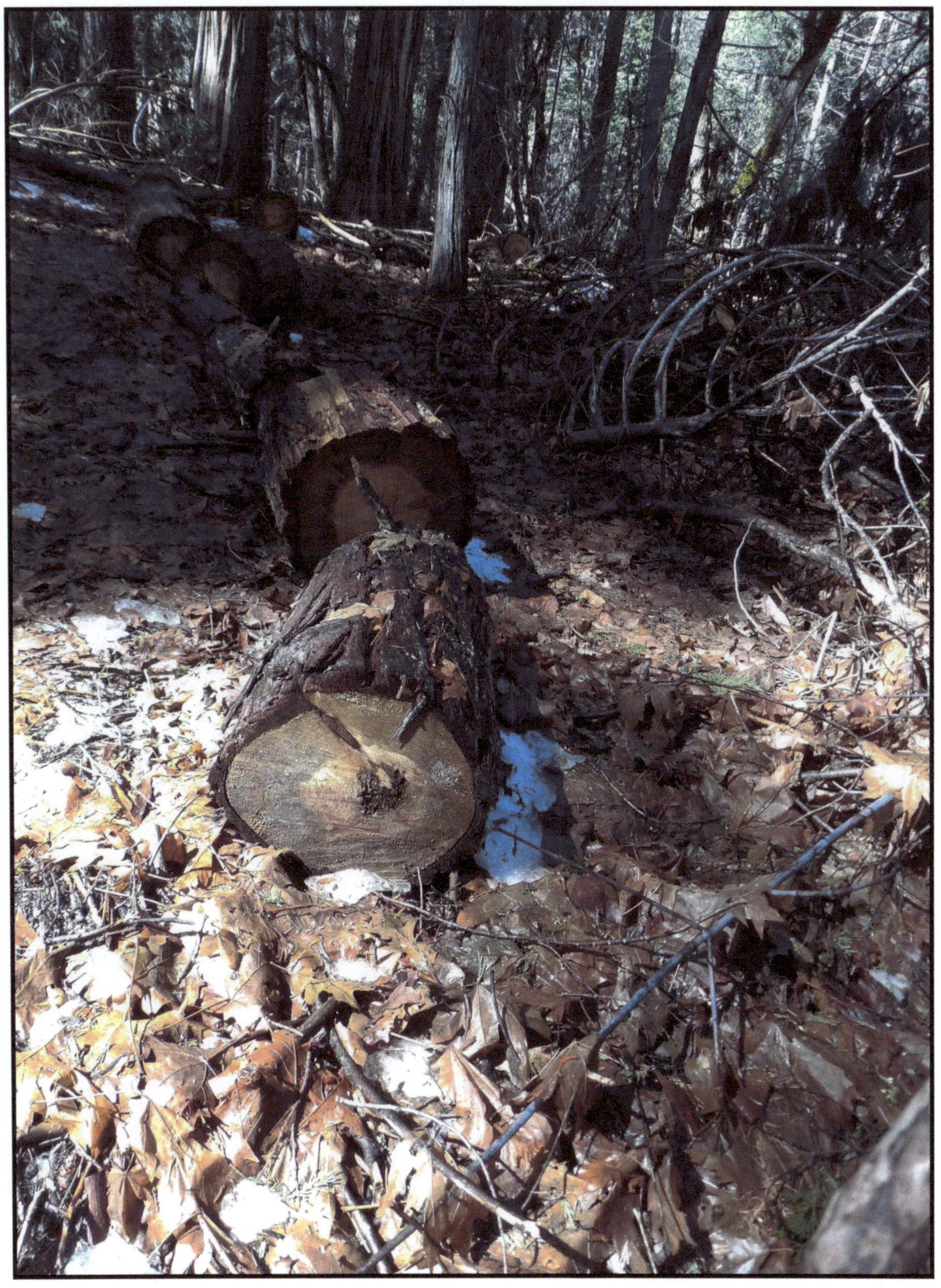

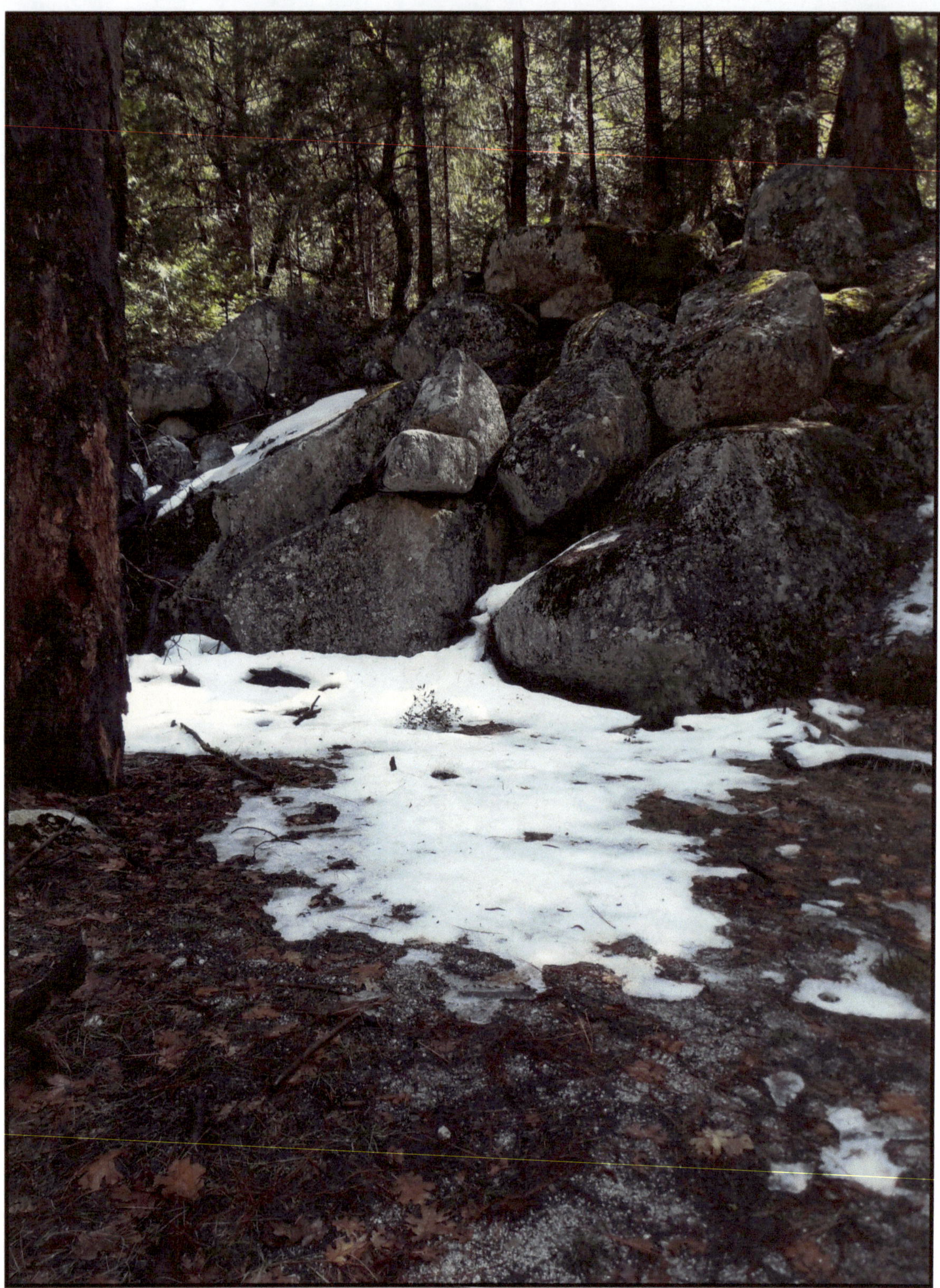

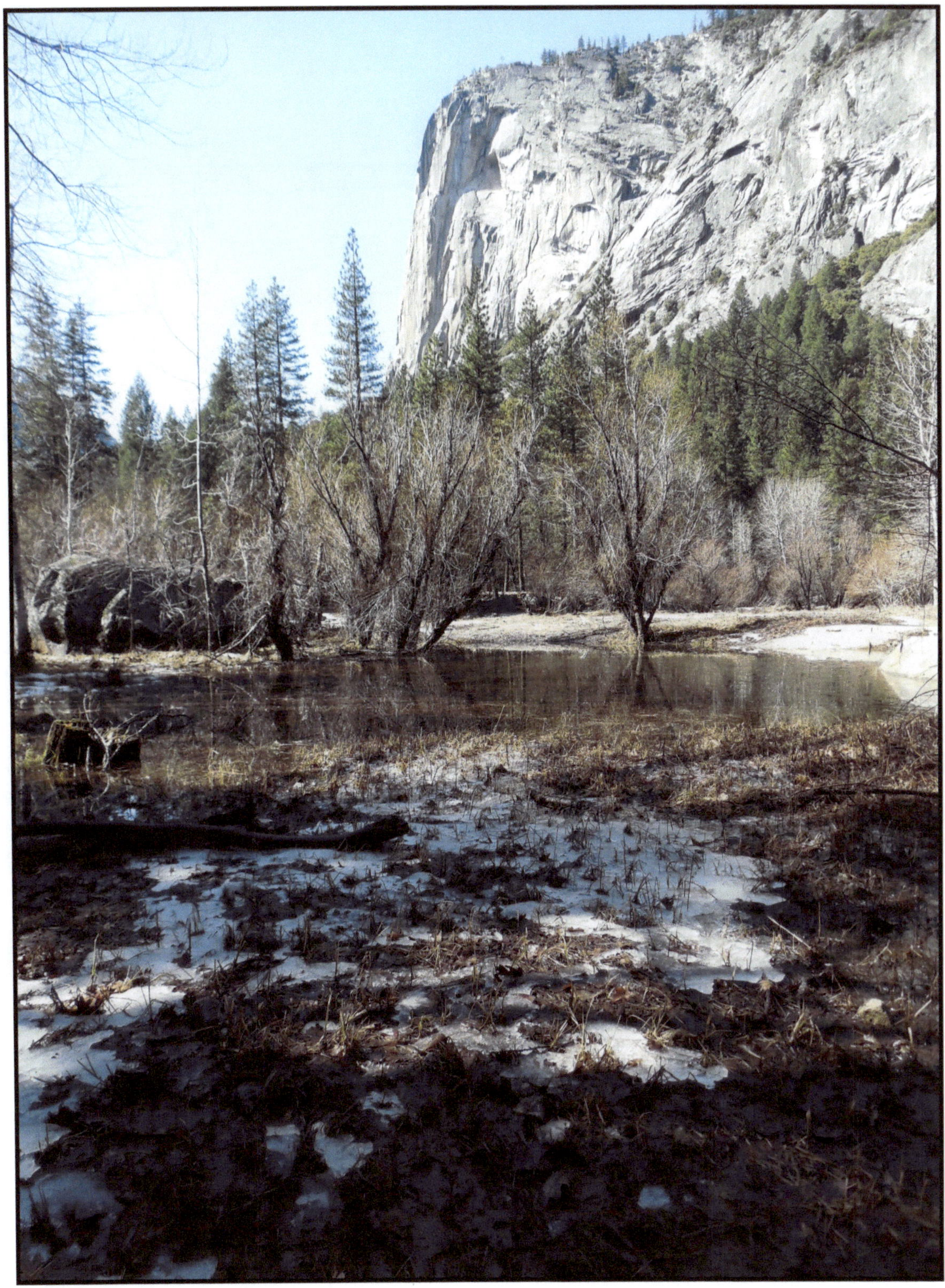

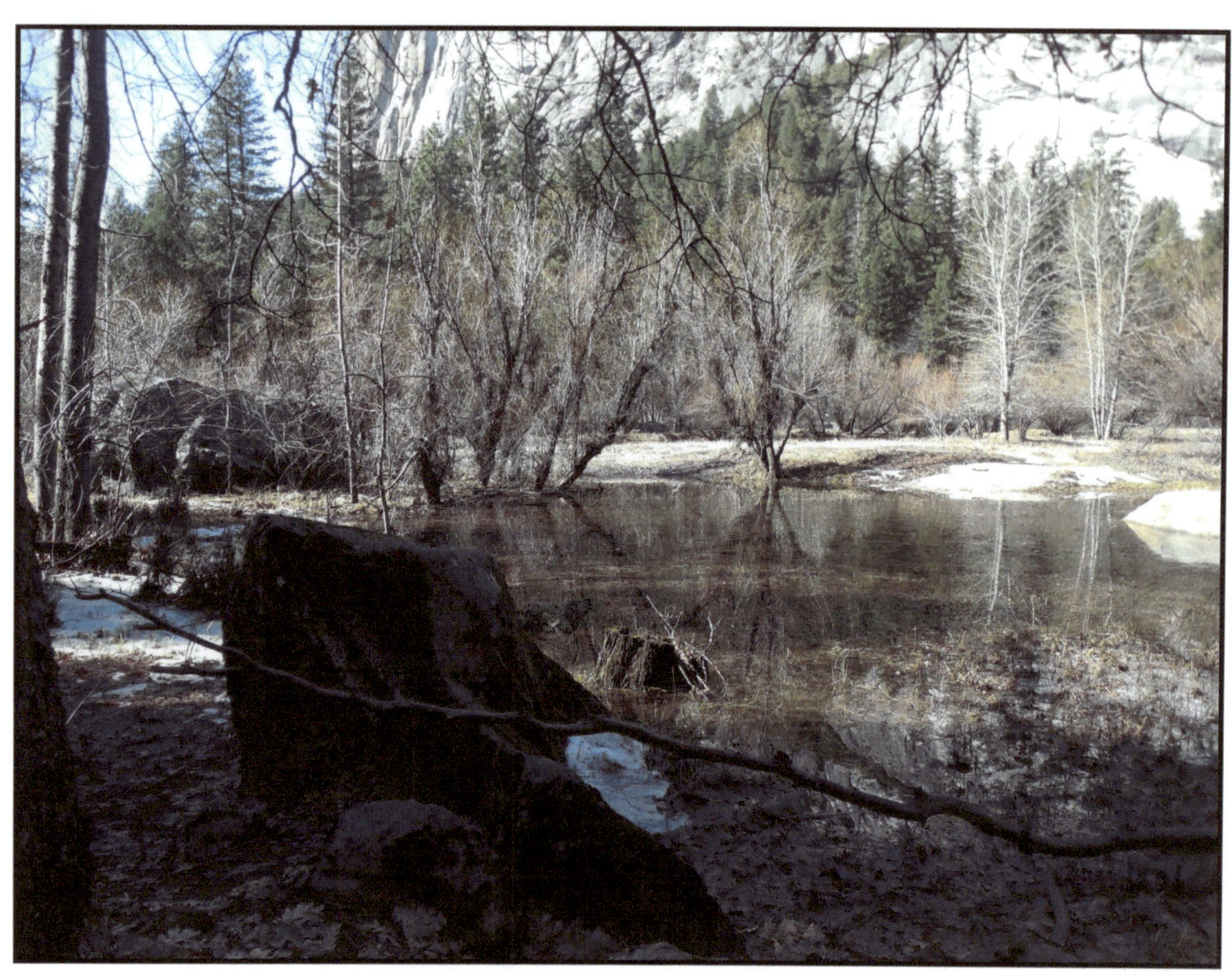

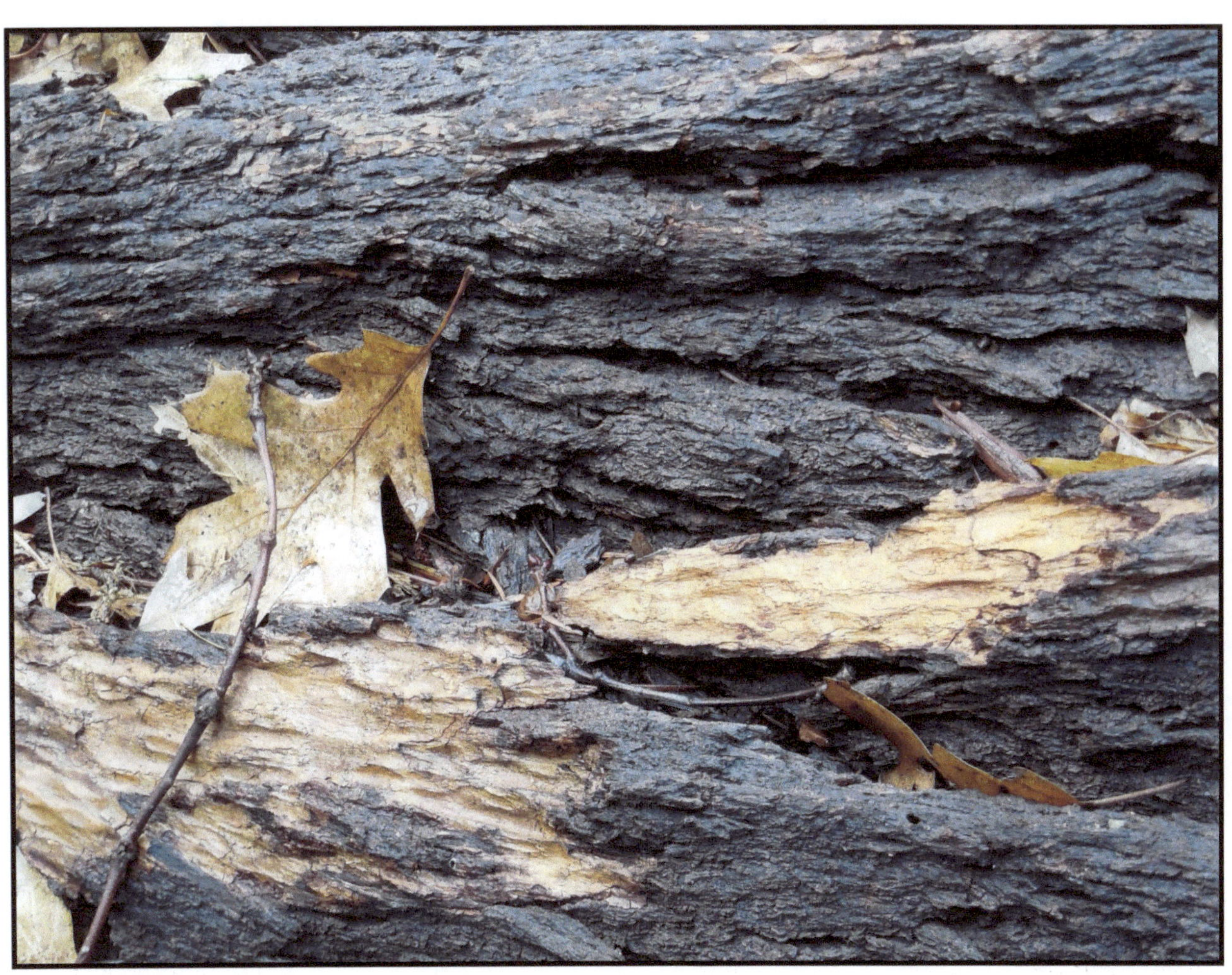

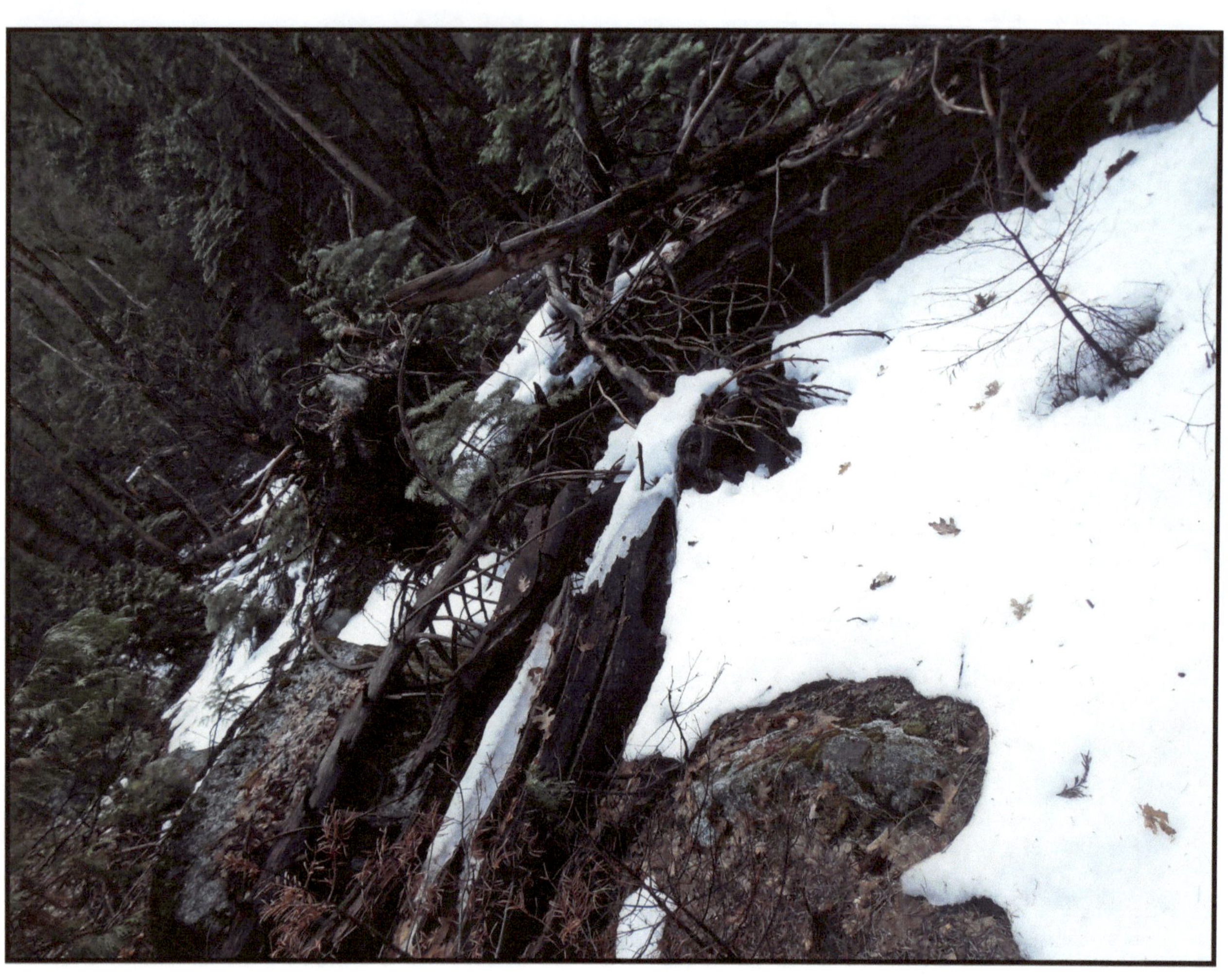

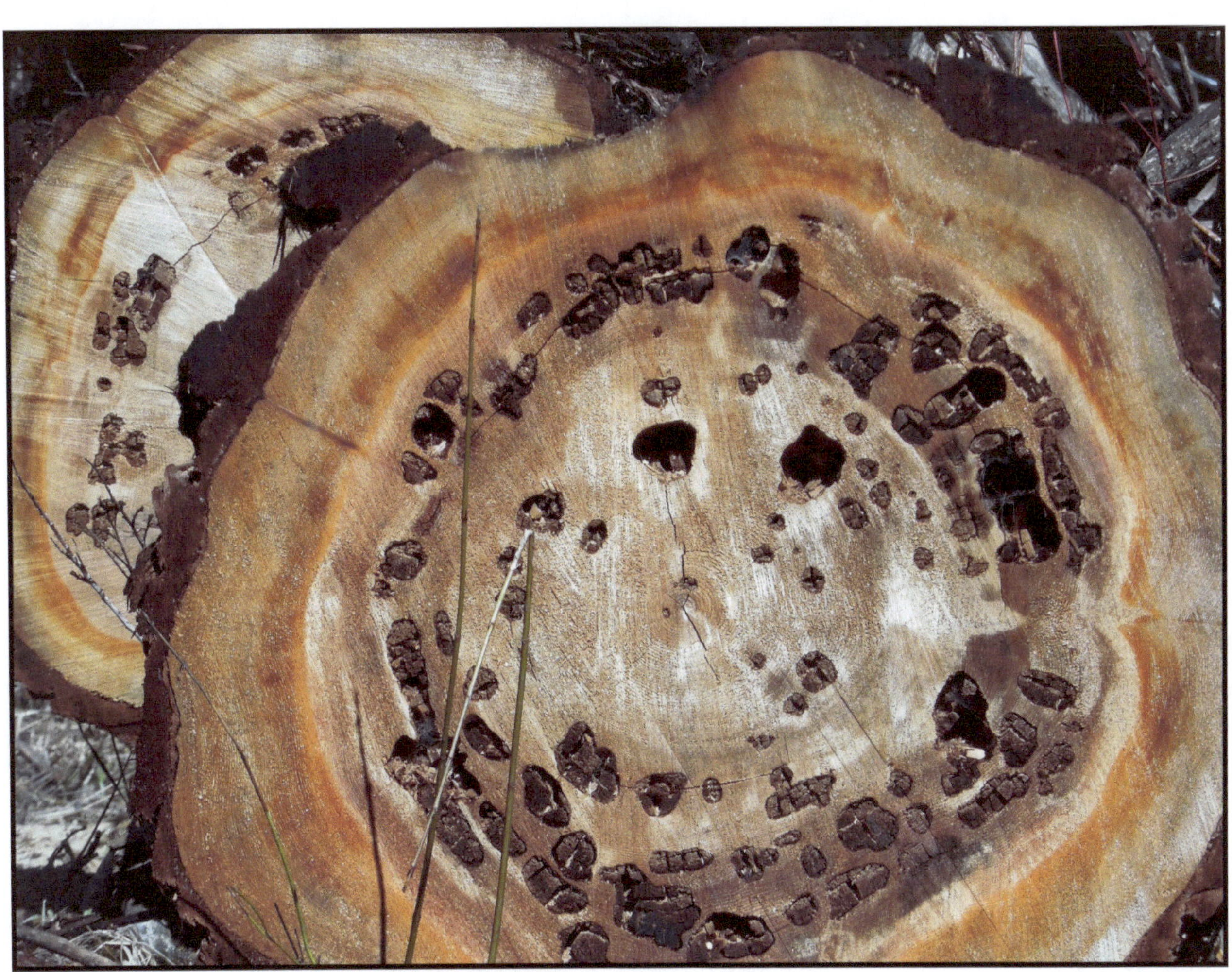

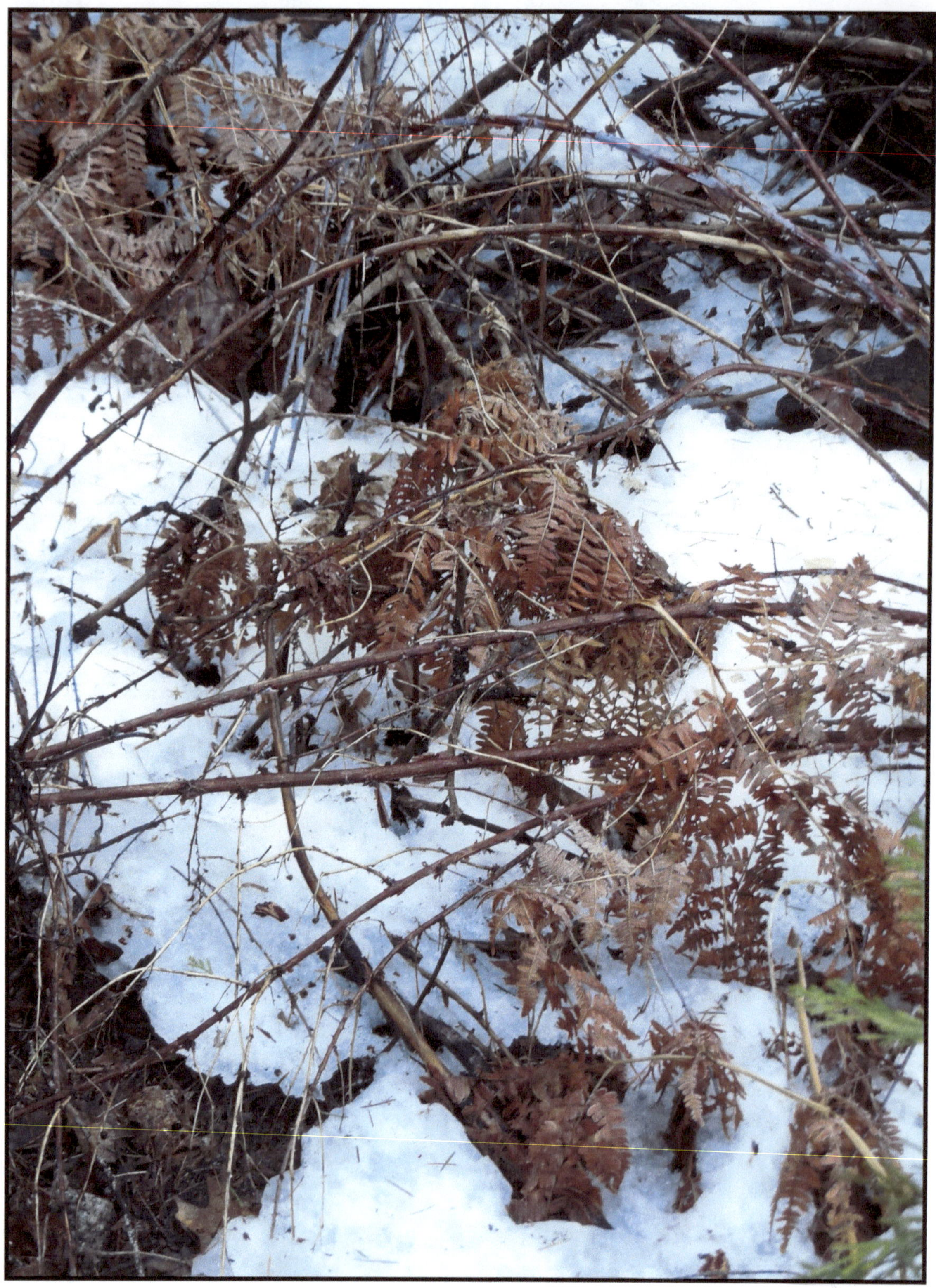

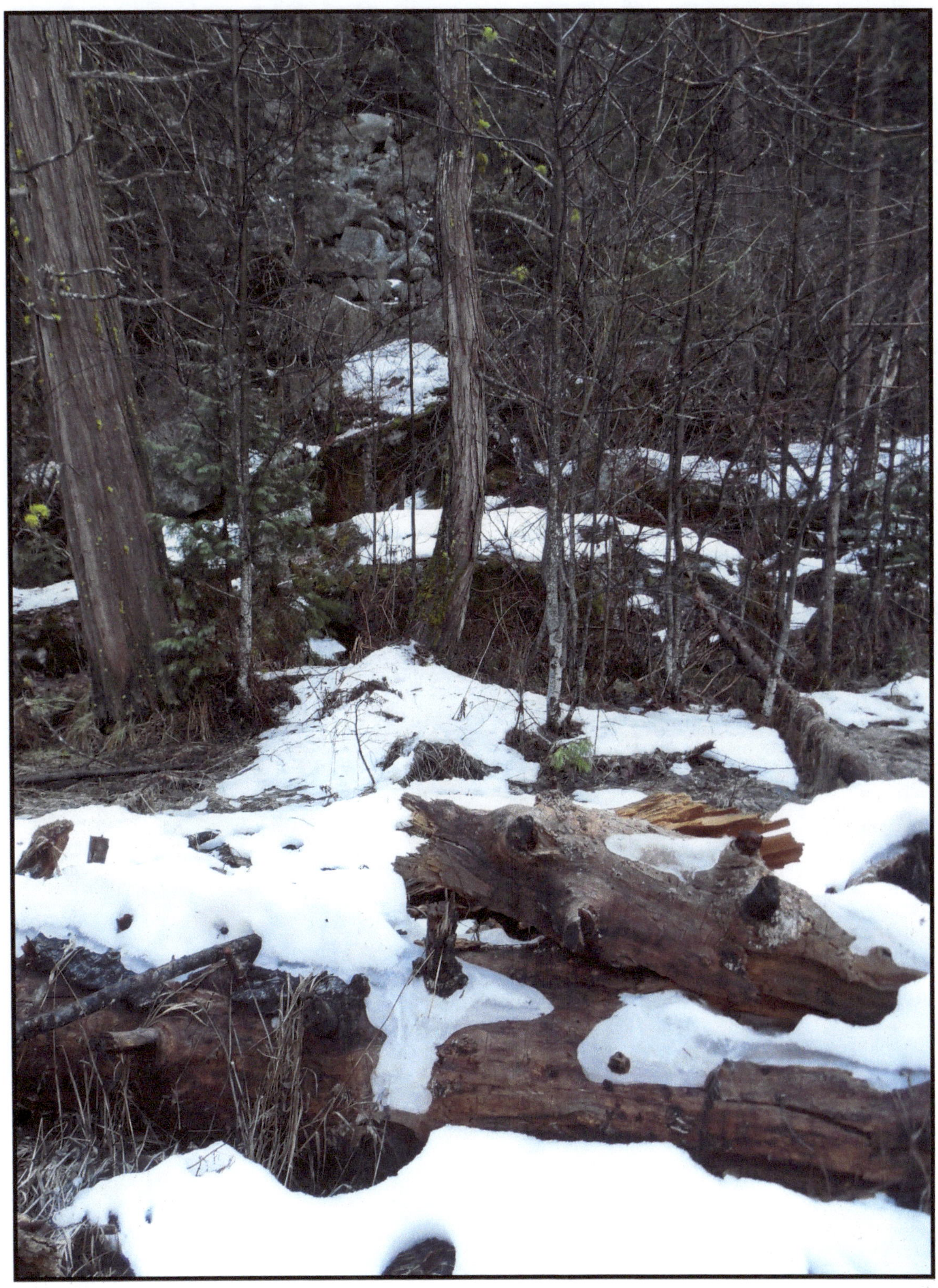

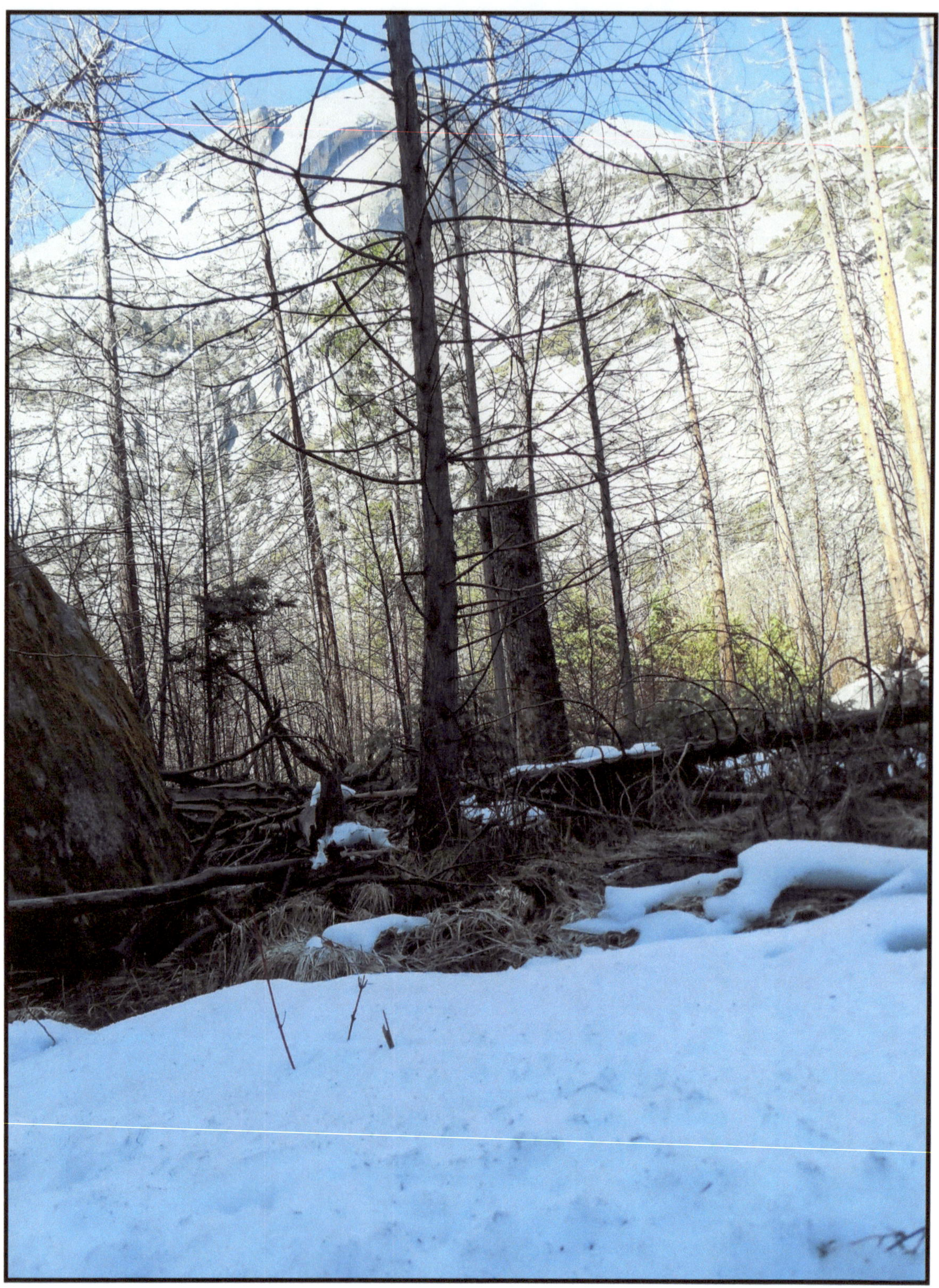

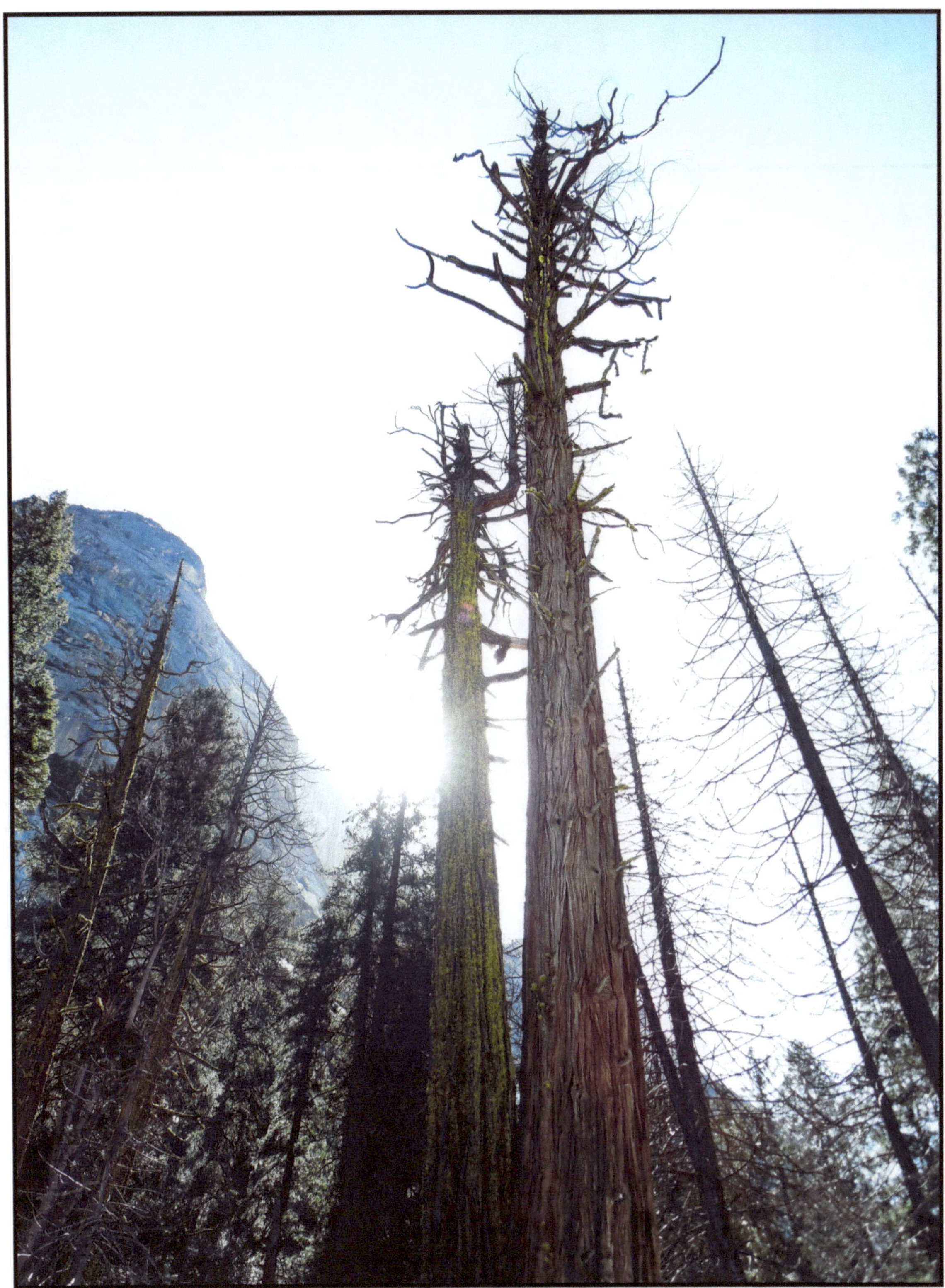

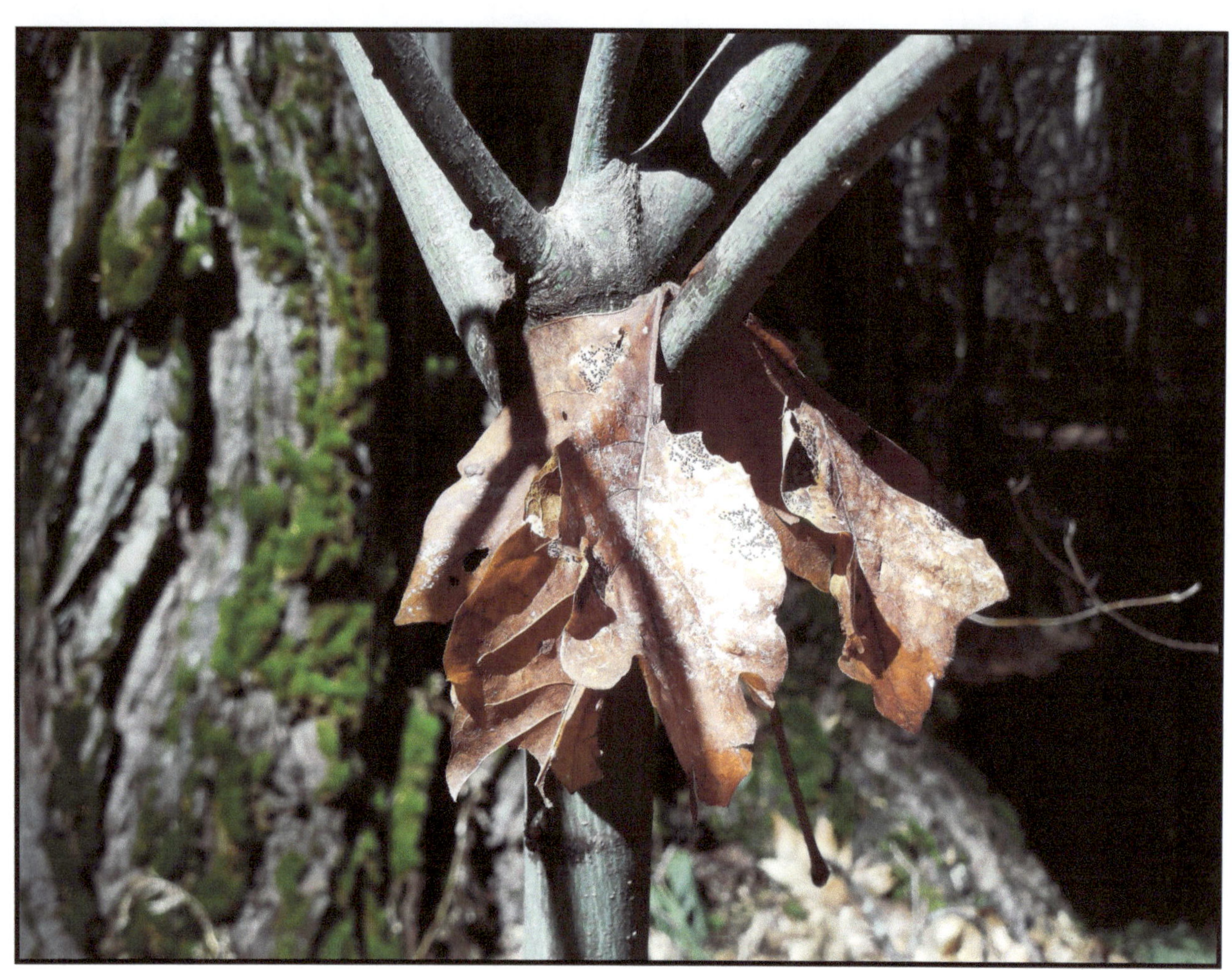

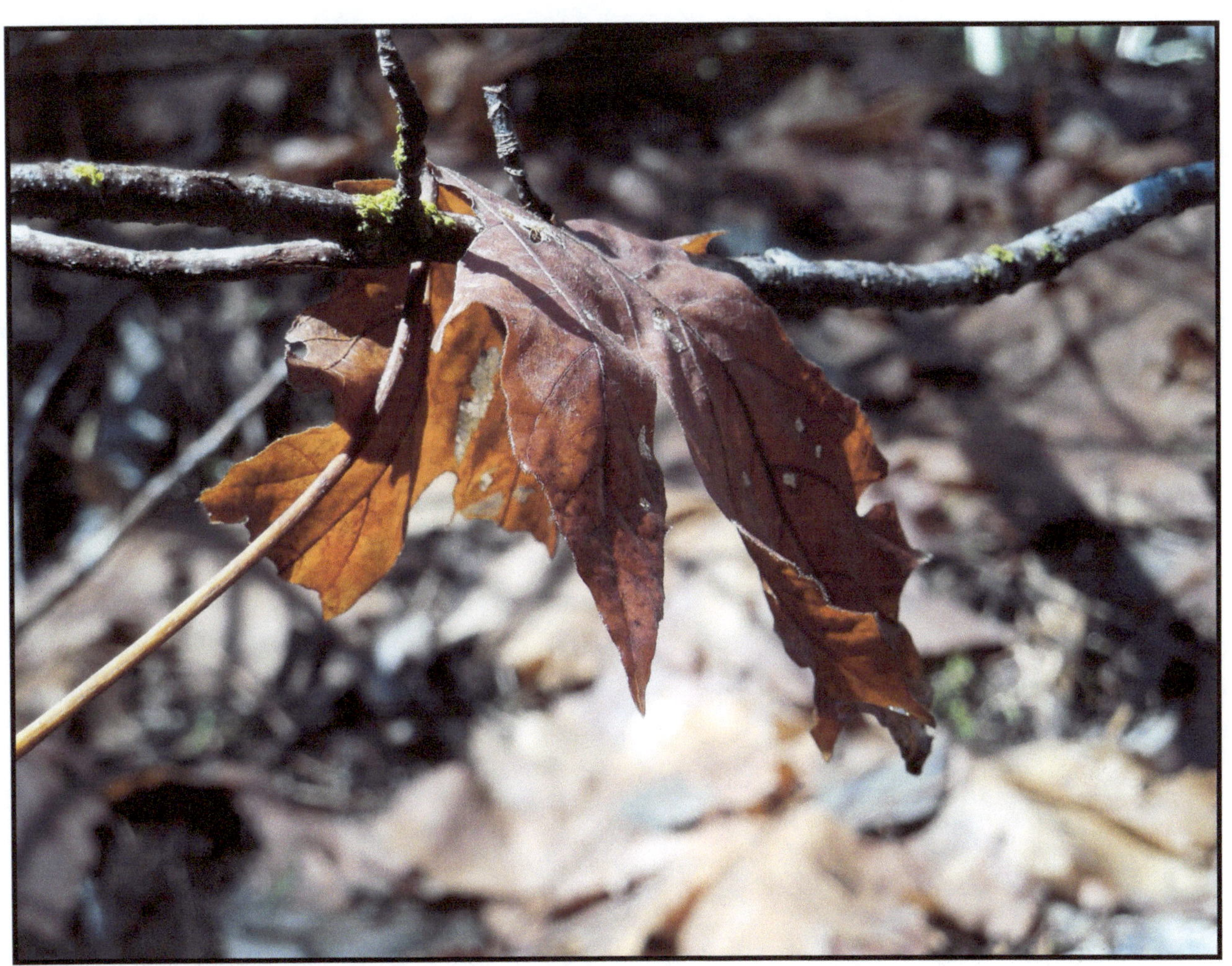

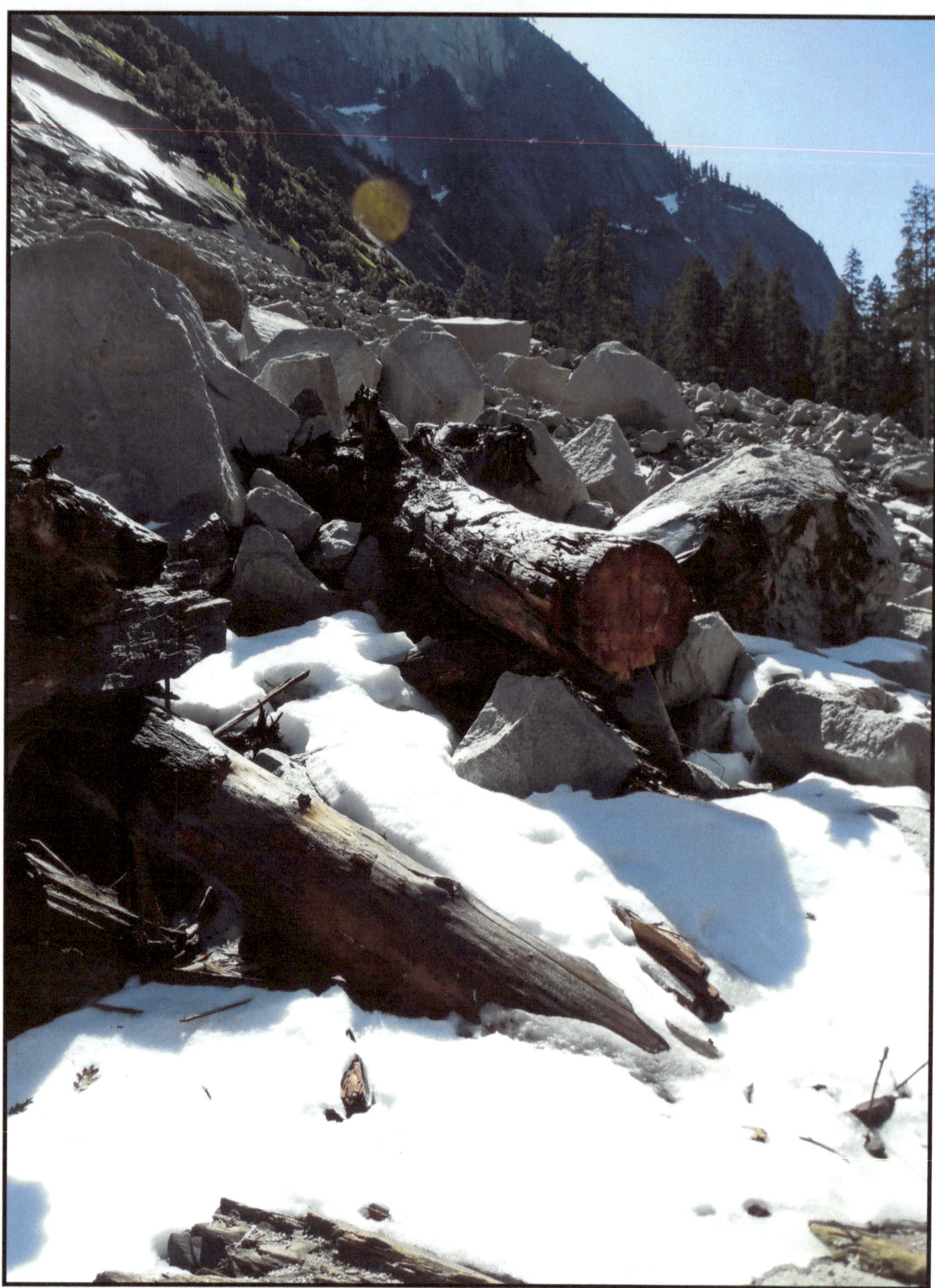

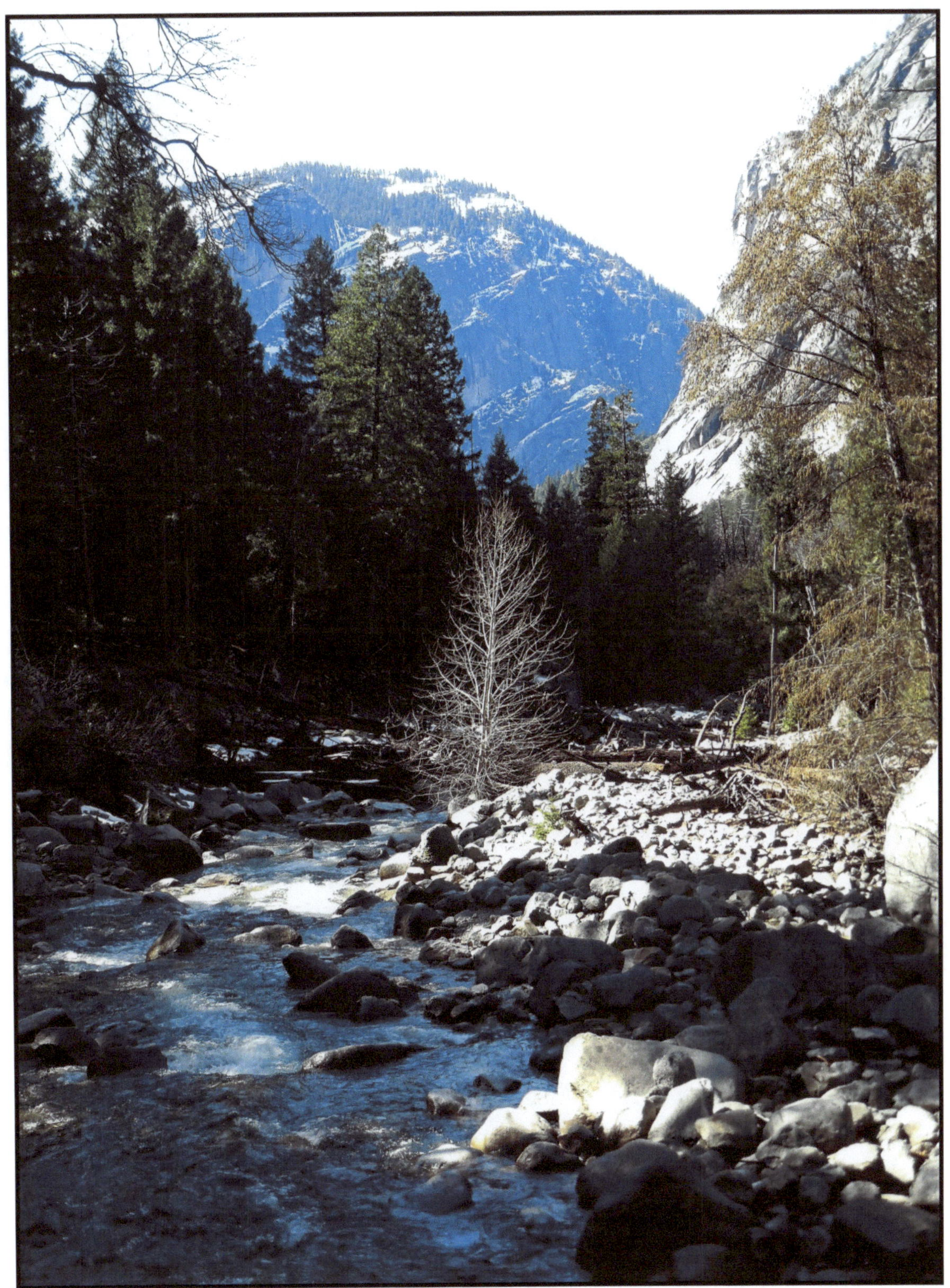

www.ingramcontent.com/pod-product-compliance
Lightning Source LLC
LaVergne TN
LVHW070121110826
845147LV00002B/167

9781877792700